Study Guide for use with

SIXTH CANADIAN EDITION
Macroeconomics

Rudiger Dornbusch
Massachusetts Institute of Technology

Stanley Fischer
International Monetary Fund/on leave from Massachusetts Institute of Technology

Richard Startz
University of Washington

Frank J. Atkins
University of Calgary

Gordon R. Sparks
Queen's University

PREPARED BY

Jessica Rutledge
University of Washington—Seattle

Lonnie Magee
McMaster University

**McGraw-Hill
Ryerson**

Toronto   Montréal   Boston   Burr Ridge, IL   Dubuque, IA   Madison, WI   New York   San Francisco   St. Louis   Bangkok
Bogotá   Caracas   Kuala Lumpur   Lisbon   London   Madrid   Mexico City   Milan   New Delhi   Santiago   Seoul
Singapore   Sydney   Taipei

McGraw-Hill
Ryerson Limited

A Subsidiary of The McGraw-Hill Companies

Study Guide for use with
Macroeconomics
Sixth Canadian Edition

ISBN: 0-07-089049-8

1 2 3 4 5 6 7 8 9 10 MP 0 9 8 7 6 5 4 3 2

Printed and bound in Canada.

Vice President, Editorial Director: Pat Ferrier
Senior Sponsoring Editor: Lynn Fisher
Economics Editor: Ron Doleman
Associate Sponsoring Editor: Jason Stanley
Developmental Editor: Daphne Scriabin
Supervising Editor: Alissa Messner
Marketing Manager: Kelly Smyth
Production Coordinator: Sue Penny
Printer: Maracle Press

TO THE STUDENT

This study guide is designed for use with Dornbusch, Fischer, Startz, Atkins, and Sparks' *Macroeconomics*, sixth Canadian edition.

FORMAT

Each of the twenty chapters in this study guide is comprised of the following sections:

Focus of the Chapter: A quick overview of the chapter's main conclusions.

Section Summaries: These briefly summarize each section of the text.

The Language of Economics: Presents a list of "key terms," which are new or important terms used in the chapter, followed by a brief definition and sometimes discussion of a piece of economic jargon.

Review of Technique: Presents a brief introduction to or review of a useful mathematical tool.

Fill-In Questions: Helps you review some of the terminology introduced in the chapter. Reviews important concepts.

True-False Questions: Encourage you to develop your intuition; reviews some of the chapter's basic conclusions.

Multiple-Choice Questions: Provide yet another way to review terminology and work out simple problems.

Conceptual Problems: Give you an opportunity to work through problems and ideas qualitatively rather than quantitatively, giving your intuition a bit more exercise.

Working with Data: Some of the chapters include this section, in which you plot data.

Application Questions: Allow you to work through numerical examples and mathematical problems.

At the back of the book you will find answers to the questions and problems in each chapter.

HOW TO STUDY MACROECONOMICS

Practice Macroeconomics

You can underline all of the points you want and spend hours upon hours trying to memorize facts and theories, but none of those will get you half as far as *practice*. Instead of looking at the graphs in the textbook, try to work through them. Instead of wasting valuable hours trying to memorize the material, spend a small amount of time trying to focus on its structure. Always ask, "why am I learning this?" "What question am I trying to answer?" Look for real–world applications of the material you're learning.

The questions in this study guide are not meant to serve as lists of points to remember. They are intended to illustrate basic principles, refine concepts, and give you a chance to develop your economic intuition. Try to answer the questions without consulting the answers at the back of the book. Often, struggling through a problem helps you to catch a glitch in your understanding. Many of the problems are quite easy. Some are more time consuming. If it becomes necessary for you to choose whether to reread the text or work through some problems, do the problems.

The Language of Economics

Economics, like many disciplines, is filled with jargon. Many words, when we use them, do not mean the same thing they do on the street. The language reviews nested in each chapter highlight the way a particular word or phrase is used in the discipline of macroeconomics. You may find that you know many of them, but they're worth reading through anyway. Understanding the language through which a model is presented can often be the key to a fuller understanding of the model itself.

Review of Technique

The Review of Technique found in each chapter presents a quick introduction to or review of a mathematical tool. Many are simply "tricks," facts that help you to simplify problems. You may find that you already are familiar with many of the techniques presented. Some you may not have seen in quite some time. Most of the reviews are at least somewhat connected to the material covered by the chapters in which they appear. A few are not, but seemed nonetheless worthy of inclusion. When you have time, browse through the reviews to find those most useful to you.

To the Student

1 INTRODUCTION

FOCUS OF THE CHAPTER

In this chapter we look at how economists use models, and how price in a market plays an important role in ensuring market equilibrium.

Price movements in some markets are slow, or prices may even be fixed. This is reflected in price flexibility assumptions in macroeconomic models.

Three time frames are used: the very long run, the long run, and the short run. They are related to the assumptions about price flexibility and ones concerning factors of production.

SECTION SUMMARIES

1. How Economists Think: Markets, Models, and Time Frames

Contradictory statements by economists often can be understood by recognizing that they are using different assumptions about how the economy works, and different time frames. The mechanism that drives a market back to equilibrium is price movement. If price moves slowly (e.g., real wages, the price of labour) then it may take a long time to reach equilibrium (e.g., for a period of high unemployment to end).

In the classical or market clearing paradigm, prices are assumed to be flexible. This makes sense for analyzing the economy over long periods of time. In the Keynesian or non-market clearing paradigm, at least some prices are assumed to move slowly or be fixed. This is reasonable for analyzing the economy over short periods of time.

In macroeconomics there are three time frames for analysis. First, there is the very long run, where growth theory is used. Short run fluctuations such as recessions are ignored, and all that matters is how quickly the economy grows on average. Second, there is the long run, in which there still are flexible prices and markets in equilibrium, but, unlike the very long run, the productive capacity of the economy is not changing. On an aggregate demand-aggregate supply diagram, in the long run the aggregate supply curve is fixed and vertical, while in the very long run it is vertical and shifting over time.

The third time frame is the short run. Prices are assumed fixed, making the aggregate supply curve horizontal. (See Figure 1-2.) In the short run, changes in aggregate demand will affect output, whereas in the long run, they affect the price level. Usually we do not have specific lengths of time in mind, but for concreteness you might think of the short run as being less than a year, the very long run as say a 20 year period, and the long run as something in between.

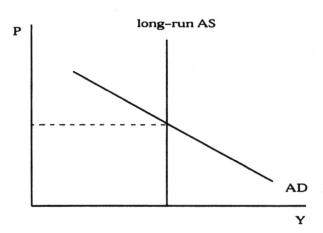

Aggregate Supply is _vertical_ in the long run, when output must equal potential output.

Figure 1-1

AS-AD IN THE LONG RUN

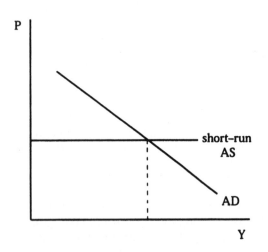

Aggregate Supply is _horizontal_ in the short run, when prices are fixed.

Figure 1-2

AS-AD IN THE SHORT RUN

2. The Data Our Models are Trying to Explain

The growth rate of the economy is the rate at which output is increasing. The very long run growth model would be used to study the annual growth rate averaged over a long period. The year-to-year fluctuations in real GDP characterize the business cycle, which is examined with the short run model.

The transition from the short run to the long run involves price adjustment (e.g., inflation), the speed of which can be summarized by the Phillips curve. The inflation rate often is calculated as the rate of increase in the Consumer Price Index (CPI), which measures the average cost faced by consumers when purchasing goods and services.

Another important macroeconomic variable is the unemployment rate, which measures the percentage of those in the labour force who do not have a job.

Canada is an open economy, that is, it engages in a substantial amount of international trade relative to the size of its economy. Important data in this area include the balance of trade, which is the difference between exports and imports. Another one is the foreign exchange rate, which can be expressed either as the price that foreign citizens must pay for one Canadian dollar, or as the price that Canadians must pay for one unit of foreign currency.

3. What's Next

After this introductory section, the book has five more parts. Part 2 looks at the long run and very long run models. Part 3 examines the "transition" from the short run to long run time horizon. Part 4 focuses on the short run. Part 5 deals with some of the components of the models in more detail, and Part 6 applies these models to major macroeconomic events.

4. Working with Data

Data from Statistics Canada's CANSIM data base is used to construct a quarterly per capita income series for the 1979 to 1983 period.

THE LANGUAGE OF ECONOMICS

Key Terms

models	endogenous and exogenous variables
speed of adjustment	Classical, or market clearing, paradigm
Keynesian, or non-market clearing, paradigm	flexible prices
sticky prices	aggregate demand–aggregate supply model
very long run	long run
short run	Phillips Curve
business cycle	inflation rate
Consumer Price Index	open economy
unemployment rate	foreign exchange rate
balance of trade	

Models

An economic model consists of a set of assumptions, and of one or more equations. The equations describe how the model's variables—inputs or outputs whose value is not necessarily constant—relate to one another.

Assumptions are very, very important. As we have seen in the case of the aggregate supply–aggregate demand model, an assumption (like a vertical AS curve) may be valid in some cases (when markets fully clear, for example), but not others. We would never assume the aggregate supply curve to be vertical in a case for which we did not believe that markets fully cleared, for example. And we would never use growth theory to describe business cycle fluctuations (it just can't do it). The validity of a model's assumptions is a key consideration when we decide whether to use it to answer a question.

We must always exercise judgment when applying models. A good model simplifies the real world by choosing not to worry about the aspects of it that aren't relevant to whatever problem it is meant to explain. Because it does this, there will be problems to which it should not be applied—problems for which some omitted relationship is relevant.

REVIEW OF TECHNIQUE

Active Learning

There are two components of active learning: active reading and active review. Active reading is a particularly good skill to develop, as you use it while reading your textbooks, reading the newspaper, or reading the reports of your many advisors once you become president. The key to reading actively is reading with a pencil. That way, as you read, you can underline key ideas, write down the assumptions that lie behind argumentative statements (a weather person, for example, might say "tomorrow will be sunny" and mean "tomorrow will be sunny if there is no change in the prevailing wind, which should blow the storm system directly to the north right past us"), and translate statements into graphs (the statement "this year the price of corn has increased, and the quantity sold has decreased," for example, could be illustrated as a shift in the supply curve on a basic, microeconomic supply/demand graph).

To review actively, look back through everything you've underlined. Work through as many problems as possible. Make flash cards for key terms, to make sure you are able to define them. If you have trouble defining key terms, consult the glossary at the back of the text. Make a list of key assumptions for each model, and think about when these assumptions are and are not valid. This will help you to decide when and when not to apply a particular model to a problem. Keep a "forest" map, where you can mark the connections between the various models that you learn. Then, when you get lost, you can simply refer to your map.

FILL-IN QUESTIONS

1. The very long-run behaviour of the economy is the domain of _____.

2. The economy's behaviour over the short, long, and very long run, however, can be described within the _____ model.

3. The _____ curve describes the quantity of output that firms are willing to supply at each level.

4. The _____ curve describes the total demand for goods at each price level.

5. Along the _____ curve, both goods markets and money markets are simultaneously in equilibrium.

6. The speed at which an economy's prices adjust is summarized by its _____ curve.

7. Short run fluctuations in real GDP per person are a rough characterization of a _____.

8. The _____ measures the cost of a typical urban consumer's purchases.

9. The difference between exports and imports is the _____.

TRUE-FALSE QUESTIONS

T F 1. In the long run, the aggregate supply curve is vertical.

T F 2. As a result, output in the long run is determined entirely by the aggregate demand curve.

T F 3. It turns out that prices adjust pretty slowly, so that over a one-year horizon, the aggregate supply curve is relatively flat.

T F 4. Very little you will learn about macroeconomics can be fit into a growth theory/aggregate supply/aggregate demand framework.

WORKING WITH DATA

The easiest way to see whether an economy is doing well is to chart its real GDP. When real GDP is increasing by more than usual, the economy is doing well—and vice versa. This Graph It asks you to plot the annual rate of change in Canadian real GDP for the years 1981 through 1998, and to compare it to the trend rate of growth. We assume the trend rate of growth to be 3 percent—a rough estimate of the economy's average growth rate since 1960. Can you identify the up-swings and down-swings of the business cycle?

In order to fill out the chart, you must first calculate the rates of change of GDP and then plot them. For example, real GDP was $431.8 billion in 1980, and $445.7 billion in 1981. The annual growth rate, therefore, was $100 \times \{(445.7 - 431.8) / 431.8\}$, or 3.2%. We've filled in the first few years for you on the chart, and on Table 1-1. You do the rest!

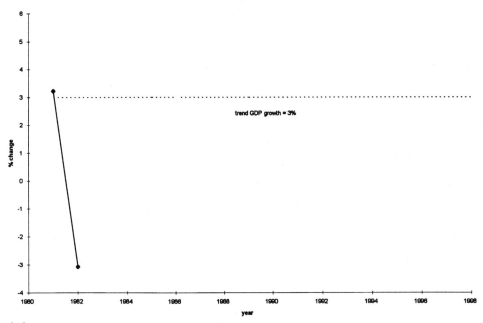

Chart 1-1

PERCENTAGE CHANGE IN GDP

TABLE 1-1

Year	Canadian GDP	Percent change from previous year
1980	431.8	
1981	445.7	3.2
1982	432.0	−3.1
1983	445.5	
1984	471.9	
1985	496.7	
1986	511.8	
1987	532.8	
1988	558.7	
1989	572.9	
1990	574.4	
1991	563.6	
1992	568.8	
1993	581.8	
1994	609.3	
1995	625.3	
1996	632.8	
1997	656.9	
1998	676.5	

2 MEASURING THE PERFORMANCE OF THE CANADIAN ECONOMY

FOCUS OF THE CHAPTER

Under the heading "national income accounting," we consider the different ways in which the national economic pie can be sliced into its component parts.

This is more than just simple accounting. While we dissect GDP, we are actually learning how the many sources of aggregate demand can be added together to determine total national income, and why a nation's income and output must necessarily be the same.

National income accounting involves identities linking saving, investment, the government budget deficit, and net exports.

SECTION SUMMARIES

1. Measuring Gross Domestic Product

Gross Domestic Product (GDP) is the sum of the dollar value of all final goods and services produced over some specified period such as a year or a quarter, in the Canadian (or in some other) economy. If we think of goods produced by firms and not yet sold as having been bought by the firm itself, then GDP can be measured as the value of the total amount produced (supply) or of the total amount sold (demand).

The value of the total amount produced can be expressed as the sum of the total amount paid to the various inputs, or factors of production, such as labour (e.g., wages) and capital (e.g., interest payments) plus profits.

GDP also can be calculated as the total value added, where a firm's value added is the difference between the value of its total output and its total purchases of intermediate goods from other firms. This prevents double counting, in which the same product is counted as a part of the output of several firms.

When thought of as the total amount sold, GDP is the sum of consumption (purchases by households), investment (purchases of final goods and services by firms), government spending on goods and services, and net exports. This identity is a key component of our short run model of the economy.

There is one serious problem associated with the interpretation of GDP as the total output of the economy: some types of output—cooking, cleaning, and child care in the home, for example—are not traded on the open market, and therefore do not contribute to measured GDP. A misleadingly large increase GDP can be a result when some of these outputs move from the home into the commercial sector.

There are serious problems with using GDP as a measure of welfare as well: (1) some types of output, such as the maintenance of a police force, are intended only to contain "bads," like crime; (2) natural resources are valued at zero, so that nothing is added for environmental reclamation or subtracted for environmental degradation; and (3) it is hard to account for changes in quality.

2. Some Important Identities

The most important identity of all to remember is that *income* $\equiv$ *output*. Some other important ones are written below, and are absolutely worth memorizing. A warning, however: be sure that you understand these identities in terms of the economic relationships they describe. Do *not* just memorize the symbols!

$Y \equiv C + I + G + NX$	*fundamental national income accounting identity*
$YD \equiv C + S$	*uses of disposable income*
$YD \equiv Y + TR - TA$	*sources of disposable income*
$BD \equiv G + TR - TA$	*definition of the budget deficit*
$S - I \equiv (G + TR - TA) + NX$	*link between saving, investment, government budget, and trade*

Where Y = income (or output); C = consumption; I = investment; G = government purchases; NX = net exports; YD = disposable income; TR = transfers; TA = taxes; S = savings; and BD = the budget deficit. The symbol " $\equiv$ " means "identically, or always, equal to."

The first four identities can be combined to give the following identity:

$$C + I + G + NX \equiv Y \equiv YD + (TA - TR) \equiv C + S + (TA - TR)$$

This reduces to the fifth identity in the above table, which equates excess saving with the sum of the budget deficit and net exports:

$$S - I \equiv (G + TR - TA) + NX$$

3. Inflation and Price Indexes

Because prices change from year to year, we distinguish real GDP from nominal GDP. Real GDP is a measure of physical production. Nominal GDP is the value of that output in current dollars (i.e., at prevailing prices).

Inflation (π) is measured as the change in the price level, or as:

$$\pi \equiv \frac{P_t - P_{t-1}}{P_{t-1}}$$

You must multiply the number that you get from this equation by 100 to express it properly in percentage terms. An answer $\pi = 0.12$, for example, means an inflation rate of 12 percent.

The price level can be measured by the consumer price index (CPI), the GDP deflator, or the industrial product price index (IPPI). The CPI measures the cost of living for a "typical" urban family. The IPPI tracks the prices of a range of goods used in production. Both measure the cost of a particular, unchanging basket of goods from year to year. (In fact, these baskets are revised every few years.) The GDP deflator is defined as the ratio of nominal GDP to real GDP. Its basket of goods changes every year to reflect the actual composition of output. It does not consider the effect of import prices on the domestic price level, however.

4. Nominal and Real Interest Rates

Economists define the real interest rate as the nominal (unadjusted) interest rate minus the inflation rate. Whereas the nominal interest rate of an investment measures the percentage increase in the dollar value of what you invested, the real interest rate measures the percentage change in the purchasing power of what you invested. It takes into account the fact that the prices of goods and services changed during the period of the investment.

5. Working with Data

The student is asked to retrieve and examine data on nominal and real GDP, both unadjusted and seasonally adjusted at annual rates. The three data series should be consistent for 1992, the base year.

THE LANGUAGE OF ECONOMICS

Key Terms

gross domestic product (GDP)
national income and expenditure accounts
factors of production
factor payments
production function
final goods and services
intermediate goods
value added
net domestic product at factor cost
net domestic product at market prices
depreciation
gross domestic product
gross national product (GNP)
national income accounting identity
consumption spending

investment spending
human capital
gross investment
net investment
government purchases
transfer payments
government expenditure
net exports
constant dollars
current dollars
GDP deflator
Consumer Price Index (CPI)
industrial product price index (IPPI)
nominal interest rate
real interest rate

Exogenous, Endogenous, and Policy Variables

Some variables are taken as inputs to a model. These are called *exogenous variables*. There are three general types of exogenous variables: those that are given by nature (the weather, for example) or taken to be outside the scope of a particular model (perhaps investor psychology); those, like taxes and government spending, that can be set by policymakers (these are also called *policy variables*); and variables that may affect the reactions of economic agents, but are not of direct interest themselves (these are *parameters*). The marginal propensity to consume is an important parameter in many macroeconomic models. It is also exogenous—determined outside of these models.

Other variables are determined within a model. These are, basically, the model's output. We call them *endogenous variables*. Endogenous variables are determined by exogenous variables, just as the equilibrium price and quantity exchanged of an item are determined by consumers' preferences, mood, and income, by the prices of its substitutes and complements, and by the technologies and resources available to its producers. A variable may be *endogenous* in one model and *exogenous* in another. In the simple model of aggregate demand presented in Chapter 8, for example, income and consumption are both endogenous, while the more modern theories of consumption presented in Chapter 14 take income to be exogenous.

Two points are useful in thinking about economics models. The first is of fundamental importance; the second is a useful trick.

The relationship between exogenous and endogenous variables is one of cause and effect. A useful question to ask is "when an exogenous variable changes by one unit, how much does the endogenous variable change in response?" It is not sensible to ask about the effect of a change in an endogenous variable. A change in an endogenous variable is always the result of some more fundamental change in one or more exogenous variables.

You should have at least as many equations as endogenous variables in your model. If you have more, some of your equations must be combinations of the others; this isn't a problem. If you have less, however, something fundamental has been omitted. Look for another equation.

REVIEW OF TECHNIQUE

Moving from Levels to Rates of Change

We measure the *rate of change* (or *percentage change*) of a variable by looking at the difference in its level between two consecutive periods, and then dividing that difference by its level in the first of these periods. For ease of expression, we generally multiply this number by 100.

The rate of change of some variable x, then would be equal to

$$\left[\frac{x_t - x_{t-1}}{x_{t-1}} \right] \times 100$$

where x_{t-1} represents the level of this variable x in the initial period, and x_t represents the level of x in the subsequent period. An increase in x from 100 to 120, then, will produce a rate of change equal to 100 times [(120 – 100)/100], or 20 percent. Notice that if x *decreased* from 120 to 100, its percentage change would be 100 times [(100 – 120)/120], or approximately –17 percent. Can a 20 percent increase and a 17 percent decrease return our variable x to its initial level? The answer, of course, is an emphatic *yes*. The base used in these calculations makes a difference. For small changes in x, however, it makes *less* of a difference: a jump in x from 99 to 100 is a 1.01 percent increase, and a drop in x from 100 to 99 is a 1 percent decrease. The difference is negligible.

FILL-IN QUESTIONS

1. _____ is the value of all final goods and services produced within the country.

2. To calculate net domestic product, it is necessary to adjust GDP for _____.

3. Inputs such as capital and labour are called _____; the payments to them are called _____.

4. To avoid double-counting, _____ like welfare payments and social security benefits are not counted as part of GDP.

5. _____ is a measure of the increase in the domestic business sector's stock of capital, not accounting for depreciation.

6. Net exports are defined as _____ minus _____.

7. The difference between government expenditures and taxes is called the _____.

8. The increase in the value of the output produced at a given stage in production is called the _____.

9. _____ is a series which attempts to correct for the presence of economic "bads," like pollution, in standard measures of output, and for the absence of other, difficult-to-measure economic goods.

10. The ratio of nominal to real GDP is a useful price index, called the _____.

11. The product approach to measuring GDP avoids_____ by adding up the value added at each stage of the manufacturing process.

12. The real interest rate is defined as the _____ minus the _____.

TRUE-FALSE QUESTIONS

T F 1. Roughly 3/4 of all factor payments are payments to capital.

T F 2. The accumulation of inventories is a kind of investment, as that term is defined in national income accounting.

T F 3. In a model with no government and no foreign trade, private saving must equal investment.

T F 4. In a model with both government and foreign trade, when *saving is equal to investment*, it must be the case that the government's budget deficit (TA – G – TR) is equal to its trade deficit (NX).

T F 5. GDP includes the transfers of existing commodities, like old houses.

T F 6. The sum of the value added to each good, at each stage of processing in an economy is equal to that economy's GDP.

T F 7. GDP is a nearly perfect measure of output.

T F 8. The CPI, IPPI, and the GDP deflator all include the prices of imports.

T F 9. The GDP deflator measures the price of a much wider basket of goods than either the CPI or IPPI.

T F 10. The IPPI, because it measures the prices of goods at an early stage of production, is a good business cycle indicator.

T F 11. The real interest rate has never been negative in Canada.

MULTIPLE-CHOICE QUESTIONS

1. Which of the following is not a component of aggregate demand?

   a. government spending
   b. investment spending
   c. tax payments
   d. foreign demand (NX)

2. Social security payments are counted as part of

   a. government purchases
   b. transfers
   c. net exports
   d. consumption

3. Which of the following is not considered a part of national income?

   a. factor payments
   b. welfare payments
   c. salaries
   d. net interest

4. Which of the following is *not* a measure of total output?

   a. all factor payments + profit
   b. the sum of all values added
   c. C + I + G + NX
   d. adjusted GNP

5. All of the following are considered physical investment *except*

   a. inventory accumulation
   b. housing construction
   c. building a new machine
   d. purchasing a government bond

6. Suppose that investment and output are fixed. Which of the following four items is able to change without affecting any of the others?

   a. government budget surplus
   b. net exports
   c. saving
   d. taxes

7. In an economy with both foreign trade and a government sector, the excess of private saving over investment $(S - I)$ is equal to

   a. net exports
   b. the trade surplus
   c. the budget deficit
   d. (b) & (c)

8. Which of the following measures of output is likely to be most directly useful for measuring the change in the quantity of output from year to year?

   a. real GDP
   b. nominal GDP
   c. adjusted GNP
   d. the GDP deflator

9. Which of the following price indices is based on a fixed basket of goods (one which remains constant from year to year)?

   a. CPI
   b. IPPI
   c. GDP deflator
   d. (a) & (b)

10. Which of the following is most likely to overstate the inflation which might result from an increase in the world price of grain?

    a. CPI
    b. IPPI
    c. GDP deflator
    d. (a) & (b)

11. If the inflation rate is 7 percent and the real interest rate is 11%, then the nominal interest rate is

   a.   minus 4 percent   b.   4 percent
   c.   9 percent   d.   18 percent

CONCEPTUAL PROBLEMS

1. What would happen to GDP if a large number of parents entered the workplace, and hired others to cook, clean, and care for their children? Is this change reflective of an actual change in the physical output of the economy?

2. Find an example of a product whose quality has changed over time, but whose price (in real terms) has not.

3. If savings = investment in the private sector, what must be true of the budget and trade deficits? (*Note: we have a trade deficit when imports exceed exports, or NX is negative.*)

4. Now suppose that we want to decrease the government's budget deficit. How could we accomplish this?

WORKING WITH DATA

CPI- and GDP deflator-based measures of inflation are not always the same. This Graph It asks you to calculate and plot CPI-based inflation between the years 1980 and 1998, and to compare it to GDP deflator-based inflation. We have already graphed CPI-based inflation for you, so your job won't be difficult.

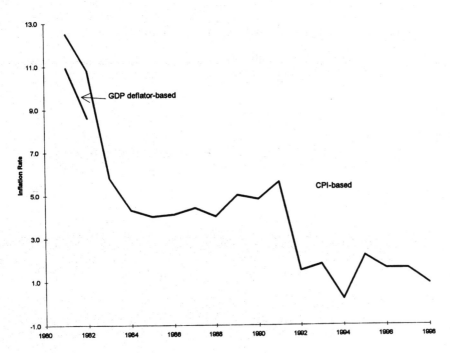

Chart 2-1
CPI- AND GDP DEFLATOR-BASED INFLATION

TABLE 2-1

Year	GDP deflator	Percent change from previous year	CPI-based inflation
1980	72.3		
1981	80.2	10.9	12.5
1982	87.1	8.6	10.8
1983	91.8		5.8
1984	94.8		4.3
1985	97.2		4.0
1986	100.0		4.1
1987	104.7		4.4
1988	109.4		4.0
1989	114.5		5.0
1990	117.9		4.8
1991	121.1		5.6
1992	122.7		1.5
1993	124.5		1.8
1994	125.9		0.2
1995	129.0		2.2
1996	130.9		1.6
1997	131.8		1.6
1998	131.3		0.9

Your first task is to convert the GDP deflator numbers into *rates of inflation*. We ask you to do this in Table 2-1. After you've done this, all you need to do is plot each year's rate of inflation and connect the dots. We've filled in the first few years for you on both the table and the chart. You do the rest.

APPLICATION QUESTIONS

1. This is a national income accounting problem. You are given the following facts about the economy: Consumption = $1,000; saving = $100; and government expenditures = $300. Net exports are zero. The government's budget is balanced. What is the value of GDP?

2. Suppose that saving = $200, the budget deficit = $50, and the trade deficit (the difference between imports and exports, or –NX) = $10. What must be the level of investment?

3. If GDP = $1,000, government expenditure = $250, consumption = $500, net exports = $100, and the budget deficit = $40, what is disposable income?

4. If GDP = $500, consumption = $350, transfers – taxes = $20, investment = $150, and the budget deficit = $120, what are net exports?

5. Calculate the rate of inflation that would result from an increase in the CPI from 1.75 to 2. The numbers are not intended to be realistic—don't worry if the rate of inflation seems too low or too high.

6. A dealer buys a rare stuffed tropical bird from South America for $500 and instructs an employee in Canada to sell it door-to-door. It is finally sold for $550. The dealer pays the employee $100 for his effort. The employee also incurred $30 in gasoline expenses in making the sale. What is the value added to the Canadian economy from all of this?

7. If the government reduced its tax revenues while holding spending constant, and there was no change in net exports, then what, if anything, can be said about the change in savings and investment?

3 THE ECONOMY IN THE LONG RUN: THE CLASSICAL MARKET CLEARING MODEL

FOCUS OF THE CHAPTER

In this chapter we study the long run Classical model of real output determination, where technology and the capital stock are held constant and prices are flexible. Output is then determined by labour market equilibrium.

Equilibrium in the market for goods and services in a closed economy requires that saving (public plus private) equals investment, which can be shown from national income accounting identities.

In this long run model, the price level is determined by the level of the money supply and inflation is determined by the rate of growth of the money supply.

SECTION SUMMARIES

1. The Supply of Goods and Services: The Production Function and the Labour Market

A popular form of production function is the Cobb-Douglas production function, written as

$$Y = AK^{\theta}N^{1-\theta}$$

where K is the level of capital input, N is the level of labour input, Y is output, A accounts for the level of productivity, and θ can be thought of as capital's share of income, which for Canada is approximately 0.3. We can approximate Canada's production function as

$$Y = AK^{0.3}N^{0.7}$$

Since Statistics Canada measures Y, K, and L, we can solve for A. Changes over time in A tell us about changes in Canada's "total factor productivity."

In the long run (as opposed to the very long run) we assume that productivity and the capital stock do not change. Output Y then changes only as a result of changes in labour input N. For this production function, as N (and Y) increase, there is a decrease in the amount that output increases for each additional unit increase in labour input. This is called diminishing marginal product of labour (MPN).

The amount of N will be determined by equilibrium in the labour market. Thinking of the economy as a big firm, the demand for labour is determined by a profit-maximizing assumption. N will be increased by one unit as long as the resulting increase in revenue (which is P, the price of a unit of output, times MPN) is greater than the increase in cost, which is the wage W. Once W equals P * MPN, this would stop. So W = P * MPN, or (W/P) = MPN, where W/P is the real wage. Since MPN is a decreasing function of N, this condition gives a downward-sloping labour demand curve, where W/P is a decreasing function of N.

From the workers' point of view (labour supply), the marginal benefit of providing an extra unit of labour is the extra purchasing power, which is W/P. If workers are willing to provide more labour at a higher real wage, the resulting labour supply curve is an upward-sloping relation between labour supply N and the real wage W/P.

The intersection of these labour supply and demand curves is the labour market equilibrium. In this long run equilibrium, the real wage has enough time to adjust to reach this equilibrium. There is no excess supply of labour, hence there is no unemployment.

Denoting this equilibrium level of labour as N^* and the fixed level of capital as $\overline{K}$, the resulting "full employment level of output" is $Y^* = F(\overline{K}, N^*)$. The classical aggregate supply curve is a vertical line in P-Y space, located at Y^*. In the long run, the nominal wage W will adjust to whatever level P is at to reach this output level Y^*.

2.   The Demand for Goods and Services

Recall the four components of the demand for goods and services from Chapter 2. In this section we will treat government spending G as exogenous. That is, the model will not try to explain G. The same will be done for net exports NX, which moreover will be set to zero. We then focus on consumption C and investment I.

Consumers will save more and consume less of a given amount of income when the real rate of interest is higher. This decision also depends on consumers' rate of time preference, which refers to how much consumers worry and plan ahead. Investment spending by firms also will be lower when the real interest rate is high.

With net exports equal to zero, we can show that when the demand equals the supply for goods and services, saving (private plus government) equals investment. Start with the national income accounting identity with $NX = 0$:

$$Y = C + I + G$$

Use the definition of disposable income (YD), $YD = Y + TR - TA$ to replace Y and rearrange terms to get

$$(YD - C) + (TA - TR - G) = I$$

The two left-hand side terms are private saving and government saving respectively.

3.   The Money Stock, the Price Level, and the Inflation Rate

The quantity equation:

$$MV = PY$$

Summarizes the relation between the price level (P), real output (Y) and the money supply (M). V is the velocity of money. Noting that $V = PY/M$, we see that V is nominal output divided by the nominal money supply. Roughly speaking then it is the average number of times a unit of money gets spent in a year.

The quantity theory of money is a long run proposition that assumes that V and Y remain constant in the above equation, implying that the proportional change in the money supply equals the proportional change in the price level, which is the inflation rate:

$$\Delta M/M = \Delta P/P$$

Another long run proposition, called the Fisher effect, is that inflation does not affect the real interest rate. Changes in the nominal interest rate, which is the sum of the real interest rate and the inflation rate, are matched by changes in the inflation rate while the real interest rate should vary as a result of other factors.

4.   Working with Data

Students are asked to retrieve data from CANSIM and reproduce Table 3-1.

THE LANGUAGE OF ECONOMICS

Key Terms

production function

marginal product of labour (MPN)

real wage

full employment

real rate of interest

government savings

money stock (or money supply)

quantity theory of money

Cobb-Douglas production function

diminishing marginal product of labour

leisure

rate of time preference

private savings

quantity equation

velocity of money

Fisher effect

Real and Nominal Variables

Given a price index P and a nominal (that is, not adjusted for inflation) variable, such as a nominal wage W, the real variable is derived by dividing the nominal variable by the price index, such as the real wage $w = W/P$.

For example, suppose that P =100 in year 1 and 110 in year 2. If P is the CPI, then a typical basket of goods and services that would have cost $100 in year 1 costs $110 in year 2. Now if the nominal wage is W = 50 in year 1 and W = 53 in year 2, then the real wage in year 1 is W/P = 50/100 = .50 and in year 2 it is W/P = 53/110 = .48. In year 1 the nominal wage of 50 can buy .5 market baskets, while in year 2 the higher nominal wage of 53 can buy only .48 market baskets.

Note that Y refers to real output, so it does not have to be divided by P to make it a real variable. In fact, the term PY that appears in the quantity equation is nominal output. M, however, refers to the nominal money supply, so that M/P is the real money supply or "real balances," just like W/P is the real wage.

The interest rate is different because it refers to the percentage change in the value of a financial asset rather than the value itself. As a result, the real rate of interest is computed by subtracting the inflation rate from the nominal interest rate instead of dividing the nominal interest rate by a price index.

REVIEW OF TECHNIQUE

Deriving the Marginal Product of Labour

The formula for the marginal product of labour from the Cobb-Douglas production function can be derived using the general rule of differentiation: $dx^a/dx = ax^{a-1}$.

Given the production function: $Y = AK^{\theta}N^{1-\theta}$, the marginal product of labour, dY/dN, is be derived by taking all of the terms that multiply into the $N^{1-\theta}$ term as constant, so that

$$dY/dN = AK^{\theta}(dN^{1-\theta}/dN)$$

Apply the differentiation rule given above, $dN^{1-\theta}/dN = (1-\theta)N^{1-\theta-1} = (1-\theta)N^{-\theta}$, which results in the MPN formula $dY/dN = A(1-\theta)K^{\theta}N^{-\theta}$

Similarly, the marginal product of capital is derived as $dY/dK = A(dK^{\theta}/dK)N^{1-\theta} = A\theta K^{\theta-1}N^{1-\theta}$.

FILL-IN QUESTIONS

1. $Y = AK^{\theta}N^{1-\theta}$ is the _____ production function.

2. The increase in real output per unit increase in the labour input N is the _____.

3. A profit-maximizing firm will employ a quantity of labour such that the _____ equals the marginal product of labour.

4. Economists refer to the non-work activities of workers as _____.

5. At equilibrium in the labour market in the long-run Classical model, the economy is at the _____ level of real output.

6. In the long run, the Classical _____ curve is vertical.

7. At a given income level, the amount saved by consumers depends on their _____ and the _____.

8. In a closed economy at equilibrium in the goods and services market, _____ equals investment.

9. $MV = PY$ is known as the _____ equation.

10. V in the above equation is the _____ .

TRUE-FALSE QUESTIONS

T F   1. The weights θ and $(1 - \theta)$ in the production function $Y = AK^{\theta}N^{1-\theta}$ are capital's share of income and labour's share of income, respectively.

T F   2. It is relatively easy to construct a direct measure of total factor productivity.

T F   3. In the long run Classical model, it is assumed that there are no changes in productivity or in the capital stock.

T F   4. The diminishing marginal product of labour implies that as the quantity of labour input increases, less extra labour is necessary to produce one more unit of output.

T F   5. The demand-side profit maximizing condition in the labour market states that the real wage equals marginal product of labour.

T F   6. If an increase in the real wage makes it more attractive for workers to give up an extra hour of leisure to work, then the labour supply curve slopes upward.

T F   7. The full employment level of real output is a misleading term, because there are still workers who wish to work at that real wage but cannot find work.

T   F   8.   The supply of goods and services in the long run Classical model does not depend on the price level.

T   F   9.   The marginal benefit of saving is given by the nominal rate of interest.

T   F   10.   When there is equilibrium in the goods and services market of a closed economy, investment equals government saving.

MULTIPLE-CHOICE QUESTIONS

1.   Two variables that are assumed not to change in the long run Classical model are:

   a.   real output and labour input
   b.   capital input and labour input
   c.   productivity and labour input
   d.   productivity and capital input

2.   A profit-maximizing firm will hire labour until:

   a.   the nominal wage equals the marginal benefit or revenue of labour
   b.   the real wage equals the marginal product of labour
   c.   the marginal cost of labour equals the marginal benefit of labour
   d.   all of the above

3.   A government budget deficit causes a

   a.   lower real interest rate and lower total saving
   b.   lower real interest rate and higher total saving
   c.   higher real interest rate and lower total saving
   d.   higher real interest rate and higher total saving

4.   The quantity theory of money predicts that, if the money stock increases,

   a.   the price level will rise and real income will rise
   b.   the price level will rise and real income will remain constant
   c.   the price level will remain constant and real income will rise
   d.   both the price level and real income will remain constant

5.   The Fisher effect says that a long run increase in the inflation rate will

   a.   increase the nominal interest rate and the real interest rate
   b.   increase the nominal interest rate but not the real interest rate
   c.   increase the real interest rate but not the nominal interest rate
   d.   not increase the nominal interest rate nor the real interest rate

CONCEPTUAL PROBLEMS

1.   Explain the argument supporting the Fisher effect..

2.   Why would a central bank choose to announce a target rate of growth for the money supply?

APPLICATION QUESTIONS

1.   Given the production function $Y = 4K^5N^5$, derive the marginal product of labour function, MPN.

2.   Using the labour demand equilibrium condition MPN = W/P, derive the equilibrium levels of labour and real output Y when K = 9, W = 20, and P = 10.

3. As in Question 2, let MPN = W/P, with the same MPN function as before. But now assume that the labour supply function is given by $W/P = 1.5N^5$. Find the equilibrium levels of labour, real output, and the real wage.

4. If the government budget deficit is 20 and investment spending is 25, what is the level of private saving?

Chapter 3

4 THE ECONOMY IN THE VERY LONG RUN: THE ECONOMICS OF GROWTH

FOCUS OF THE CHAPTER

In this chapter we study how *potential output*—the output that *would* be produced if all factors were fully employed—grows over time.

To better accomplish this, we learn growth accounting and the fundamentals of neoclassical growth theory. Together, they tell us that output growth results both from improvements in technology and from increases in one or more of the inputs to the production process—capital and labour.

Next we examine two growth theories: the neoclassical model and endogenous growth. In the neoclassical model there are decreasing returns to capital per worker, resulting in a steady-state level of per capita output. In the endogenous growth model there is constant returns to capital per worker, which allows per capita output to grow steadily if conditions allow.

Finally we briefly consider reasons for variation in saving rates across countries.

SECTION SUMMARIES

1. Growth Accounting

Output grows because of increases in *factors of production* like capital and labour, and because of improvements in technology. The *production function* provides a link between the level of technology (A), the amount of capital (K), labour (N), and other inputs used, and the amount of output (Y) created. The generic formula for the production function is

$$Y = AF(K,N)$$

The *Cobb-Douglas production function*, a more specific formula, is frequently used as well, as it provides a good approximation of production in the actual economy. The formula for the Cobb-Douglas production function is

$$Y = AK^{\theta}N^{1-\theta}$$

θ, pronounced "theta," represents *capital's share of income*—total payments to capital, as a fraction of output, or $(iK)/Y$. $(1–\theta)$ is *labour's share of income*, given by $(wN)/Y$. To derive these results algebraically, you need one more fact: When the markets for capital and labour are in equilibrium (i.e., when the supply of capital equals the demand for capital, and the supply of labour equals the demand for labour), capital and labour are each paid their *marginal product*.

For the Cobb-Douglas function, the *marginal product of capital (MPK) is* $\theta A K^{\theta-1} N^{1-\theta}$.

The *marginal product of labor (MPL)* is $(1–\theta)A K^{\theta} N^{-\theta}$.

We can express our production function in terms of growth rates rather than levels:

$$\Delta Y/Y = [(1–\theta) \times \Delta N/N] + [\theta \times \Delta K/K] + \Delta A/A$$

The symbol Δ, pronounced "delta" means "change in." The term $\Delta Y/Y$, then, should be interpreted as the growth rate of output. The terms $\Delta N/N$ and $\Delta K/K$ should be interpreted as the growth rates of labour and capital, respectively. The last term, $\Delta A/A$, is the rate of improvement of technology, often called the growth rate of *total factor productivity (TFP)*. It is the amount that output increases as a result of technological progress alone (plug in $\Delta N/N = \Delta K/K = 0$, and you'll see why).

When this growth accounting method is applied to Canadian data, a dramatic slowdown in productivity growth can be noticed after 1973. This experience is common to most OECD countries. There is no single accepted explanation for this phenomenon, but alternative explanations include: a measurement problem, a result of oil price shocks, and a slowdown in the pace of innovation.

When it is applied to four very high-growth Asian countries, Hong Kong, Singapore, South Korea, and Taiwan, it is found that most of their growth is explained by higher input levels, not by higher productivity, especially Singapore.

Because growth in *GDP per capita* (output per person) tells us more about increases in the standard of living, it is useful to subtract the rate of population growth ($\Delta N/N$) from both sides, and write the above equation in per capita terms:

$$\Delta y/y = (\theta \times \Delta k/k) + \Delta A/A$$

The terms y and k represent output and capital per person: $y = Y/N$, $k = K/N$. (There is an implicit assumption here that the fraction of the population in the labour force is constant. This is why we can get away with using the terms "population" and "labour supply" interchangeably.) The terms $(\Delta y/y)$ and $(\Delta k/k)$ are the growth rates of output and capital per person. $\Delta y/y = \Delta Y/Y – \Delta N/N$, and $\Delta k/k = \Delta K/K \Delta N/N$. The term $k = K/N$ is often called the *capital-labour ratio*.

2.   Growth Theory: The Neo-Classical Model

Neo-classical growth theory studies the way that growth in the capital stock per worker affects the long run level of *per capita potential output*. A key result is that, while the rate of saving has a significant impact on the *level* of per capita potential output in the long run, the rate of improvement in technology entirely determines its growth rate.

To build our model, we begin with a few *simplifying assumptions*: (1) the level of technology is fixed, so that there is no growth in total factor productivity; (2) the production function has *constant returns to scale* (see Review of Technique), so that increasing the amount every input used in production will increase output by the same amount.

A consequence of this second assumption is that all factors of production must have *diminishing marginal products*—as more of one input is added, and the others are held constant, each unit contributes less to output than did the previous one. (Buying more tractors for your construction company but not hiring any more workers eventually won't increase your output at all!)

We also need to write our variables in *per capita* form—as before, $y = Y/N$ and $k = K/N$. We write the per capita production function:

$$y = f(k)$$

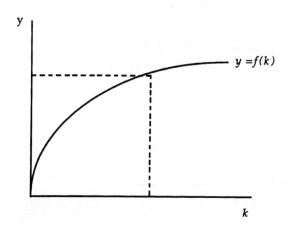

Figure 4-1

THE PER CAPITA PRODUCTION FUNCTION

We then consider the flows into and out of k—the stock of capital per worker.

Investment increases the total stock of capital (K), which increases k. It can be thought of as a flow *into* each worker's pool of capital.

Both depreciation and population growth decrease k—depreciation because it decreases the stock of total capital, and population growth because it increases the number of workers sharing this capital. Both depreciation and population growth can be visualized as flows *out of* each worker's pool of capital.

When the flow into this pool is greater than the flows out, k grows. When the flows out of this pool are greater than the flow in, k shrinks. And when the flows in and out exactly balance, the level of capital per worker will remain fixed.

We call this last case the *steady state*, because it is the point at which the level of capital in each worker's pool remains steady, or stable. It is the point of *equilibrium* in our model; we will find that the capital stock per worker grows or shrinks toward this point, and that once it gets there it stays…at least until some shock forces it to move.

It is not difficult to express the dynamics described above as an equation. We know that saving must equal investment. If we assume that people save a constant fraction (s) of their incomes, we can write the flow into k as ($s \times y$), or, using our per capita production function, as ($s \times f(k)$). The standard assumption about depreciation is that a constant fraction (d) of the capital stock becomes obsolete each period. Using this assumption, we can express the flow out of each worker's pool of capital which results from depreciation as ($d \times k$). Similarly, when population grows at a constant rate (n), we can express the flow out of this pool resulting from population growth as ($n \times k$). Putting all of these terms together, we get the following equation:

$$\Delta k = sf(k) - (n + d)k$$

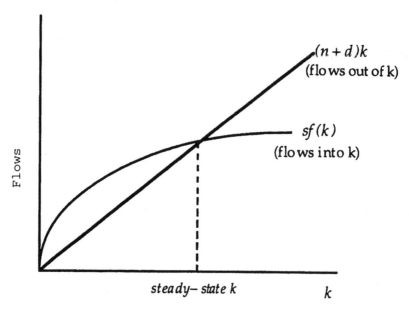

Figure 4-2

STEADY-STATE IN THE NEO-CLASSICAL MODEL

We find an expression for the **steady-state** by simply plugging in the requirement $\Delta k = 0$:

$$sf(k^*) = (n + d)k^*$$

k^* represents the steady-state value of k. The steady-state value of y *is* $y^* = f(k^*)$.

The growth process can be studied graphically as well. Figure 4-2 graphs the flows into and out of k against the **level** of k. The outflows are graphed as a straight line, with slope $(n + d)$. This is often called the **investment requirement line**, as it shows the amount that must be invested, if the capital stock is to remain constant. The slope of the line which represents the flow into k shrinks as k increases, because we have assumed it to have **diminishing marginal returns**. Where these two lines intersect, the flows into and out of k balance, and k is at its steady-state. Whether the savings line lies above the investment requirement line, so that k is increasing, or the investment requirement line lies above the savings line, so that k is decreasing, **k always moves toward the steady-state**.

Using this graph, it is particularly easy to see the consequences of changes in **s, n,** or **d**. An increase in the savings rate (s) will shift the savings line, **sf(k)**, upward, increasing the steady-state capital-labour ratio, and hence the steady-state level of per capita potential output. It will also, temporarily, increase the **growth rate** of both y and k (remember, the growth rate of k is zero at the steady-state, and without improvements in technology per capita output has no other reason to grow). Figure 4-3 shows the opposite case, where the savings rate falls from s_0 to s_1. An increase in either the rate of depreciation or the rate of population growth will increase the slope of the investment requirement line, **decreasing** the steady-state levels of k and y, and causing both to "grow," temporarily, at a negative rate.

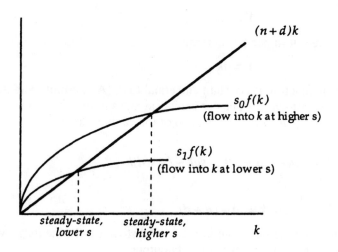

Figure 4-3

A DECREASE IN THE SAVINGS RATE DECREASES
THE STEADY-STATE CAPITAL-LABOUR RATIO

Endogenous growth theory does something fairly radical—it uses a production function which has *increasing returns to scale*. It is able to do this by assuming that there are *external benefits* associated with private investment, so that an individual firm does not reap all of the benefits from its own investment. New knowledge, inventions, and discoveries are a by-product of some kinds of investment, and all of these benefit society as well. Thus it turns out that capital can have a *diminishing marginal product* in the eyes of individual producers, but, because of these external benefits, a *constant marginal product* in the eyes of society.

This tiny modification makes a world of difference. It was capital's diminishing marginal product that gave us a savings curve with a declining slope, and it was this savings curve with the declining slope that guaranteed that the investment requirement line and the savings line would eventually intersect, so that there would be a steady-state. (See Figure 4-2.)

When we allow capital to have a constant marginal product, the saving curve becomes a straight line. There is no steady-state.

When the saving curve is everywhere above the investment requirement line, as in Figure 4-4, we get ongoing growth. When it is everywhere below the investment requirement line (not shown), output and the capital stock eventually fall to zero, as depreciation and population growth erode each worker's stock of capital more quickly than it can be replaced.

Interestingly, if the savings and investment requirement lines happen to coincide (if one is right on top of the other), whatever level of capital per worker (and, thus, of per capita output) exists will be in a steady-state. The growth rate of per capita output will be zero.

The simplest production function that will produce endogenous growth is:

$$Y = aK$$

Dividing both sides by N, we can express it in per capita terms:

$$y = ak$$

The marginal product of capital in this function is constant and equal to a. (A one-unit increase in the capital stock will increase output by an amount a.) The per capita savings curve is just equal to sak, giving the savings line a constant slope equal to sa. The growth of the capital-labour ratio, $\Delta k/k$, is determined by the following equation:

$$\Delta k = sf(k) - (n + d)k = sak - (n + d)k$$

so that

$$\Delta k/k = sa - (n + d)$$

The difference between the flows into and the flows out of the capital stock determine its growth rate, and, as a result, the growth rates of technology and of per capita output.

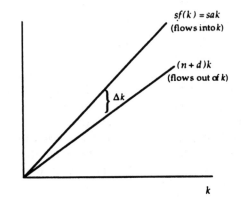

In endogenous growth theory, there is no steady-state.

The growth rate of per capita potential output depends on the rate of saving.

Figure 4-4

THE ENDOGENOUS GROWTH MODEL

Neoclassical and endogenous growth theories have different predictions regarding **convergence**—the theory that growth rates and, under certain conditions, standards of living (measured as levels of per capita output) should become equal across countries.

Neoclassical theory predicts that countries will **absolutely converge**—will reach the same level of steady-state income, and that their steady-state income will grow at the same rate—when they have the same rate of saving, the same rate of population growth, and have access to the same technologies. When population growth or saving rates differ, it predicts that they will **conditionally converge**, or that while their steady-state incomes will differ, the growth rate of these incomes will be the same. Endogenous growth theory does not predict any kind of convergence.

Many of the problems associated with reform in the formerly communist countries of Eastern Europe are associated with their lack of a market infrastructure (much of the legal framework required to run an organized market was simply absent at the beginning of reform in many places, as were institutions such as banks). Some of these countries have experienced substantial declines in output—some of them more severe than the decline that occurred during the Great Depression in Canada—during the early stages of reform.

The importance of natural resources, in particular energy, has not been accounted for in these models. The risk of resource-depletion disasters is mitigated somewhat by two factors: efficiencies resulting from technological progress, and price increases once the resources come into short supply. A strong argument can be made for governments to intervene on environmental issues, since they involve public goods.

3. Growth Policy

The theories from Section 2 suggest that government policies that affect the saving rate have important effects on long term growth. Differences between the saving rates of Canada, the U.S., and Japan have been attributed to differences in tax laws, public pensions, desired bequest levels, and land prices.

The rate of technological innovation in a country is influenced by tax laws that affect the costs and benefits of research and development (R&D). Canada's combination of relatively generous tax laws and low R&D poses an interesting problem.

Appendix

The appendix discusses the two assumptions needed to derive the fundamental growth equation $\Delta Y/Y = [(1-\theta) \times \Delta N/N] + [\theta \times \Delta K/K] + \Delta A/A$: the assumption that the production function has constant returns to scale, and the assumption that markets are perfectly competitive, so that capital and labour are paid their marginal products. Using these two assumptions, it explicitly derives the fundamental growth equation from the production function.

THE LANGUAGE OF ECONOMICS

Key Terms

growth accounting equation
total factor productivity
GDP per capita
capital-labour ratio
diminishing marginal returns
neo-classical growth theory

steady-state equilibrium
marginal product of capital (MPK)
endogenous growth
absolute convergence
conditional convergence

Stocks and Flows, or "About Your Bathtub"

It is always important to know whether a given variable is a *stock* or a *flow*. It is easiest to understand the difference between stocks and flows in the context of your bathtub. The *level* of the water in your bathtub is a *stock variable*—it rises and falls depending on the amount of water entering through the faucet, and, if the drain is unplugged, leaving through the drain. The amounts of water *flowing* into and out of the tub are, not surprisingly, *flow variables*.

Let's think through some examples of stock and flow variables. We already know that *capital* is a stock variable. We also know that *investment* is a flow into the capital stock, and that *depreciation* is a flow out of it. *Population* is a stock variable. Its level is affected by *the birth rate* (births are a flow into the pool of living, breathing people) and *the death rate* (deaths are a flow out of that pool). The *unemployment rate*, despite its name, is yet another stock variable.

REVIEW OF TECHNIQUE

Returns to Scale

A production function is said to exhibit **constant returns to scale (CRTS)** if, whenever we double every input, output doubles. All inputs must be increased in a balanced way for this to be the case—when we increase capital, labour must be increased by the same amount. The Cobb-Douglas production function has constant returns to scale—we can tell because its exponents add up to one (this is always a good, quick way to check).

We double K and L below to show, rigorously, that they cause output to double as well.

$$A(2K)^{\theta}(2L)^{1-\theta} = A(2)^{\theta}(2)^{1-\theta}(K)^{\theta}(L)^{1-\theta} = A(2)^{[\theta + (1-\theta)]}(K)^{\theta}(L)^{1-\theta}$$
$$= A(2)^{1}(K)^{\theta}(L)^{1-\theta} = (2)(AK^{\theta}L^{1-\theta}) = 2Y$$

A mathematical note may help you through the algebra above:

$$(x)^a (x)^b \text{ can also be written as } (x)^{a+b}$$

A production function has **increasing returns to scale** if doubling all inputs more than doubles output; if it is in a form similar to that of the Cobb-Douglas function (factors of production raised to some power and then multiplied together), its exponents will add up to a number greater than one.

FILL-IN QUESTIONS

1. We call the amount by which output increases when one more unit of labour is used the
   _____. It _____ as more labour is used in production.

2. When more output can be generated without using more inputs, it must be the case that
   _____ has increased.

3. We call the stock of machines and buildings used in production _____ capital.

4. The stock of knowledge and skills is called _____ capital.

5. If two countries have the same rate of population growth, and access to the same technologies, the rate at which their potential output grows will _____ over time, and be identical at the steady-state.

6. A major difference between the neo-classical model of growth and endogenous models of growth is whether the production function has constant or increasing _____.

7. The rate of technology growth, in the neo-classical model, is an _____ variable.

8. The rate of technology growth in endogenous growth models depends on the rate of capital accumulation, and therefore on the rate of _____.

9. Neo-classical growth theory predicts _____ convergence for countries with equal rates of saving, equal rates of population growth, and equal access to technology; it predicts _____ convergence for those with different rates of saving or population growth.

10. Empirical evidence suggests that, over long periods of time, countries converge _____.

TRUE-FALSE QUESTIONS

T F 1. An increase in the rate of population growth will change the rate at which per capita potential output grows in the steady-state.

T F 2. An increase in the rate of population growth will change the *level* of per capita potential output at the steady-state.

T F 3. An increase in the rate of population growth will change the rate at which *total* potential output grows in the steady-state.

T F 4. An increase in the savings rate will change the rate at which *total* potential output grows in the steady-state.

T F 5. Two countries with the same rate of population growth, and with access to the same technologies, will have the same level of output (and therefore income) at the steady-state.

T F 6. The presence of increasing returns to scale in the production function will create a tendency towards monopolization (will make one large firm more efficient than many smaller ones).

T F 7. Models of endogenous growth suggest that when countries have the same rates of depreciation and population growth, their potential output will grow at the same rate.

T F 8. The impact of higher saving on growth is transitory in the neo-classical model.

T F 9. The impact of higher saving on growth is transitory in models of endogenous growth.

T F 10. The low and negative rates of growth experienced by the formerly communist economies of Eastern Europe, during the early stages of reform, are a result of low and negative rates of saving.

MULTIPLE-CHOICE QUESTIONS

1. Which of the following *can* affect the growth rate of per capital potential output in the steady-state?

   a. savings rate   c. rate of depreciation
   b. rate of population growth   d. rate of productivity growth

2. Which of the following cannot affect the growth rate of total potential output in the steady-state?

   a. savings rate   c. rate of depreciation
   b. rate of population growth   d. (a) & (c)

3. Which of the following is a realistic estimate of capital's share of income (the fraction of total output that is used to pay capital's "wage") in Canada?

   a. 0.3   c. 0.75
   b. 0.5   d. .1

4. Which of the following *would not* increase labour's productivity (measured as Y/N)?

    a.   technological progress   c.   more natural resources

    b.   an increase in the capital-labour ratio   d.   an increase in the population growth rate

5. Which of the following *would not* increase capital's productivity (measured as Y/K)?

    a.   technological progress   c.   more natural resources

    b.   an increase in the capital-labour ratio   d.   an increase in the population growth rate

6. An increase in the rate of saving in neo-classical growth theory increases the steady-state

    a.   level of per capita output   c.   growth rate of per capita output

    b.   growth rate of technology   d.   rate of capital accumulation

7. In endogenous growth theory, the marginal product of capital is

    a.   constant   c.   decreasing in k

    b.   increasing in k   d.   variable

8. In neo-classical growth theory, the marginal product of capital is

    a.   constant   c.   decreasing in k

    b.   increasing in k   d.   variable

9. When two countries move toward steady-states which have the same level *and* growth rate of potential output, they are said to converge

    a.   absolutely   c.   relatively

    b.   partially   d.   conditionally

10. When two countries move toward steady-states with the same growth rate, but a different level of potential output, they are said to converge only

    a.   absolutely   c.   relatively

    b.   partially   d.   conditionally

CONCEPTUAL PROBLEMS

1. Name two important assumptions at the foundation of the neo-classical model of growth.

2. Which of the following are stock variables? flow variables?
   a) capital, b) depreciation, c) investment

3. What assumption changes when we move from neo-classical to endogenous growth theory?

4. Does this production function have constant returns to scale? $Y = K^{\theta}N^{1-\theta}$
   Does this one? $Y = K^{\theta}N^{2-\theta}$

5. How will an increase in the saving rate affect the growth rate of per capita output in an endogenous growth model?

6. How will an increase in the saving rate affect the growth rate of per capita output in the neo-classical growth model?

7. What can endogenous growth theory explain that neoclassical growth theory cannot? What *can't* endogenous growth theory explain?

WORKING WITH DATA

Many of the inhabitants of former communist countries in Eastern Europe have found, and are finding, the transition from a planned to a free market economy a painful one. In this exercise, you track the per capita GDP of a particular transition economy—the economy of Bulgaria. Table 4-1 provides the per capita GDP of Bulgaria between 1980 and 1992. Your job is to transform this data into rates of change, and to graph these rates of change during the sample period.

Can you guess, based on the information provided here, when Bulgaria began to make the transition to a market economy?

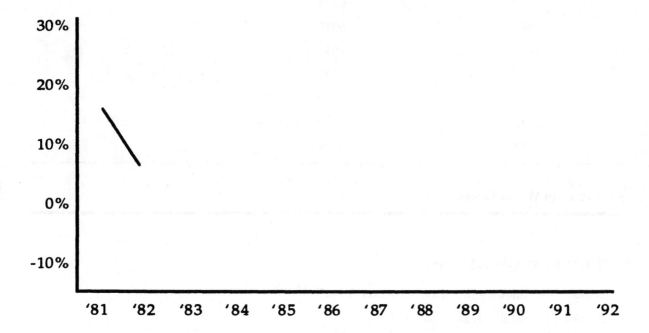

Figure 4-5

GROWTH RATE OF PER CAPITA GDP, BULGARIA

The Economy in the Very Long Run: The Economics of Growth

TABLE 4-1

Year	Per capita GDP of Bulgaria	Percent change from previous year
1980	3139	—
1981	3623	15.4
1982	3888	7.3
1983	4221	
1984	4366	
1985	4773	
1986	6284	
1987	6918	
1988	8030	
1989	8135	
1990	7529	
1991	6715	
1992	6774	

Source: Penn World Tables

APPLICATION QUESTIONS

1. Consider the following production function: $Y = K^{(1/4)}N^{3/4}$

   a) What is capital's share of income?

   b) Find an equation for the productivity of capital (Y/K).

   c) What is labour's share of income?

   d) Find an equation for the productivity of labour (Y/N).

   e) Does this production function have constant returns to scale? (Translation: Do the exponents add to 1?)

   f) Write this production function in per capita terms. (Translation: Divide both sides by N.)

2. If, in a fixed population, the number of people in the labour force doubles, what will happen to:

   a) the steady-state level of per capita potential output

   b) the steady-state growth rate of per capita potential output

   c) labour's share of income

   d) labour productivity

3. If, instead, the number of people in the population doubles (you may assume that the number of people in the labour force doubles as well) what will happen to:

   a) the steady-state level of per capita potential output

   b) the steady-state growth rate of per capita potential output

   c) labour's share of income

   d) labour productivity

4. Now suppose that, in an economy initially at steady-state, there is an exogenous increase in the savings rate. Show how per capita output changes over time.

5. Use the growth accounting equation to answer the following question:

   If capital's share of income is 25 percent and labour's share of income is 75 percent, the stocks of both capital and labour increase by 50 percent ($\Delta K/K = \Delta N/N = 0.5$), and there is no technology growth, at what rate will potential output grow? Will the capital-labour ratio increase at all?

6. Consider the following neo-classical production function: $Y = K^{1/2}N^{1/2}$

   a) Write this production function in per capita form

   b) Find the golden rule level of the (steady-state) capital-labour ratio, when the rate of depreciation is 0.05, and the (exogenous) rate of population growth is 0.20.

7. Find the rate of growth of the capital-labour ratio ($\Delta k/k$) for the endogenous growth production function: $f(k) - k$. Assume that the rate of saving is 0.3, that the rate of depreciation is 0.05, and that the rate of population growth is 0.20.

8. In this question you will verify that the growth accounting equation gives the same results as the Cobb-Douglas production function when expressed as growth rates. Let $\theta = .4$.

   a) Using the Cobb-Douglas production function, compute Y for the following values:

      i) A=5; K=10; N=40

      ii) A=5; K=11; N=40

      iii) A=5; K=10; N=43

      iv) A=5.5; K=10; N=40

      v) A=5.5; K=11; N=43

   b) Treating (i) as the starting year in each case, do the following calculations for each of (ii) to (v):

      — calculate $\Delta N/N$, $\Delta K/K$ and $\Delta A/A$.

      — use these growth rates along with the growth accounting equation to compute $\Delta Y/Y$.

The Economy in the Very Long Run: The Economics of Growth

c) Compute $\Delta Y/Y$ for each of parts (ii) to (v) as compared to (i), using the values of Y from (a). Compare them to the growth rates that come from the growth accounting equation in (b). (There should be small differences in some cases. This is because the growth accounting equation provides an approximation to the correct growth rates, which come from the Cobb-Douglas production function.)

9. a) Suppose that capital's share of income is 0.3. If the amount of labour increases by 20 percent, and the amount of output increases by 23 percent, while there has been no change in the level of technology, then by what percentage did the amount of capital increase?

b) Now suppose that capital's share of income still is 0.3, the amount of labour again increases by 20 percent, and the amount of output again increases by 23 percent, while this time there has been a 6 percent increase in the level of technology. By what percentage did the amount of capital increase?

10. a) Using the per capita production function: $y = 4k^{1/2}$, derive a formula for the steady-state levels of k and y as a function of s, n, and d from the neo-classical model.

b) What does the model predict would happen to k and y if: s=.1, n=.12, d=.08, and y = 6?

11. a) When the per capita production function is $y = 10k^{.4}$, the saving rate is s = .2, and the investment requirement function is: required investment = $(n + d)k$, where n = .02 and d = .08, what is the steady-state level of the per capita capital stock and output, k and y?

b) Now suppose that everything is the same as in (a) except that the per capita production function is $y = ak$ for some positive value of the parameter a.

i) For what value of a, if any, will there be a steady-state level of y and k?

ii) For what range of values of a will there be continuous long run growth in y and k?

5 INTERNATIONAL TRADE AND EXCHANGE RATES

FOCUS OF THE CHAPTER

A country's balance of payments is composed of the current account and the capital account. It depends on international flows of goods and services, existing assets, and returns on those assets.

An open economy does not necessarily have domestic saving equal to domestic investment in equilibrium. The relation between domestic saving and investment is related to net foreign lending and the balance of trade.

Purchasing power parity predicts that the exchange rate will move to keep relative prices across countries from changing in the long run.

SECTION SUMMARIES

1. The Balance of Payments Accounts

The balance of payments account summarizes a country's monetary transactions with the rest of the world. Outflows are transactions that result in the country's currency is exchanged for foreign currency, e.g., to buy an imported product. (The domestic currency is "flowing out" of the country – actually is just flowing out of circulation in the country.) Inflows are transactions that result in the foreign currency being exchanged for domestic currency, e.g., when exporting a product. (The foreign currency "flows in" to the country – actually flows somewhere into the financial sector and is exchanged for domestic currency which then enters circulation.) The balance of payments measures the difference between these two flows. Its two main components are the current account and the capital and finance account.

The current account measures the net flow of money resulting from purchases of goods and services (net exports), returns on financial investments (net income from assets) and transfers, gifts and foreign aid (net transfers).

The capital and financial account ("capital account" for short) measures the net flow resulting from trade in existing assets, such as business investment and inheritances. Another item in the balance of payments accounts is official reserves. This refers to transactions made by the Bank of Canada. If the Bank of Canada purchases foreign currency with Canadian currency, for example, this is recorded as an outflow in the official reserves part of the accounts. It is included in the capital account.

The capital and current account balances should add to zero in principle, but in fact there is often a substantial "statistical discrepancy."

2.   Savings and Investment in a Small Open Economy

When net exports, NX, are included in the national income accounting GDP identity:

$$Y = C + I + G + NX$$

then making the same substitutions as in chapter 3 gives a more general version of the "savings equals investment" result from that chapter:

$$S - I = NX$$

This result is related to the balance pf payments result from the previous section. Net exports NX is the same as the current account balance. $S - I$ is the excess of domestic saving over domestic investment. If positive, this is lent to foreigners (net capital outflow) and if negative, it is borrowed from foreigners (net capital inflow). $S - I$ then is the negative of the capital account balance. The equation $S - I = NX$ is just another way of saying that the current and capital account balances add to zero.

Next we account for the existence of world capital markets. Market forces should cause the real rate of interest to be similar across countries. Canada, a small open economy, is not big enough for its economic events to have an effect on this world interest rate. It can be taken as given, or exogenous, in a model of the Canadian economy. This rate will not necessarily ensure that savings equals investment as was the case in the closed economy model. There could be a trade deficit and net foreign borrowing (both S-I and NX are negative) or a trade surplus and net foreign lending (both S-I and NX are positive). The twin deficit problem occurs when the government budget deficit is large enough to cause S-I to be negative, resulting in a second deficit, as the trade balance must also be negative.

3.   Exchange Rates

An exchange rate is a price for exchanging the currency of one country for the currency of another county. Since this exchange involves two different currencies, the value of the exchange rate can be expressed in two ways. For instance, the Canada/U.S. exchange rate can be defined either as the Canadian dollar price of one U.S. dollar (e.g., $1.50 Canadian) or as the U.S. dollar price of a Canadian dollar ($0.67 U.S.). A *depreciation* of the domestic currency means that it becomes worth less in terms of foreign currency. This means that it would take more Canadian dollars to buy a U.S. dollar, or the Canadian dollar price *increases*. An *equivalent* statement of a depreciation is that it would take less U.S. dollars to buy one Canadian dollar, so the U.S. dollar price *decreases*. Conversely, an *appreciation* means that the domestic currency becomes worth more in terms of the foreign currency. An appreciation means that the Canadian dollar price of a U.S. dollar *decreases*, or equivalently the U.S. dollar price of a Canadian dollar *increases*.

Under a *fixed exchange rate* regime, central banks peg the prices of their currencies. For example, from 1962 to 1970 the Canadian dollar was fixed at 92.5 U.S. cents, so that the Bank of Canada was committed to buy or sell foreign currency to maintain that rate. If a country is in persistent deficit, it may run out of reserves, and it must either borrow reserves from other central banks or lower the value of its currency.

Under *flexible exchange rates*, the price of different currencies are determined by the laws of supply and demand. Since 1970 the value of the Canadian dollar has changed continually in the same manner as the prices of stocks on the stock exchange. In a *clean floating* system, the central banks allow supply and demand to operate without interference. In practice the world operates on a system of *managed* or *dirty floating*, in which central banks intervene in a limited way.

Occasionally, we wish to characterize the value of the Canadian dollar relative to several other currencies in a single index. This is known as a *multilateral exchange rate*.

4. The Exchange Rate in the Long Run: Purchasing Power Parity

Purchasing power parity (PPP) states that in the long run, the exchange rate moves to offset the effect of the difference in price level behaviour between the two countries. For example, suppose that prices in Canada increased by 10 percent per year over a long period, while prices in the U.S. increased by only 4 percent per year. If there was no change in the exchange rate during this period, the Canadian goods and services would be getting 6 percent more expensive each year relative to the U.S. goods and services. Since there is much trading in goods and services between Canada and the U.S., market forces should prevent this change in relative prices from happening. PPP says that this would take the form of a 6 percent annual depreciation of the Canadian dollar in order to offset the higher price increases in Canada.

PPP can be described as the long run constancy of the real exchange rate. The real exchange rate measures the relative prices of goods and services of two countries, expressing the two prices (or price indexes) in terms of a single country's currency. In this context we call the usual exchange rate a nominal exchange rate. Let e be the nominal exchange rate between Canada and the U.S., measured as the Canadian dollar price of one U.S. dollar. Let P_f be the price level of the foreign country (the U.S. here) and let P be the price level of the domestic country, Canada. Than eP_f is the U.S. price level converted into Canadian dollars. The real exchange rate is $R = eP/P$, the relative price of U.S. to Canadian goods, both expressed in Canadian dollars. If the Canadian inflation rate was higher than the U.S. inflation rate for a long period of time, P/P would fall. PPP predicts that would be offset by an increase in e of a similar percentage, to keep R constant. This would be a depreciation of the Canadian dollar as the U.S. dollar becomes more expensive.

5. Working with Data

The student is asked to take the Canadian and US. price index series from CANSIM along with the exchange rate, which is given, and construct a real exchange rate series.

LANGUAGE OF ECONOMICS

Key Terms

open economy	twin deficit
closed economy	flexible (or floating) exchange rate
balance of payments	currency appreciation or depreciation
current account	fixed rate
net exports	intervention
merchandise trade balance	managed, or dirty, floating
capital and financial account	multilateral exchange rate
official reserves	purchasing power parity (PPP)
net foreign investment	real exchange rate
foreign (or world) real rate of interest	

REVIEW OF TECHNIQUE

Logarithms, Proportional Changes, and Purchasing Power Parity

PPP states that the real exchange rate, $R = eP_f/P$, is constant in the long run. If eP_f/P is constant, a simple long run relationship between the exchange rate and domestic and foreign inflation rates can be established. One way to show it is to use logarithms, which are commonly used in many areas of economics. First, using the basic properties of logarithms that $\ln(1/x) = -\ln(x)$ and $\ln(xy) = \ln(x) + \ln(y)$, we can establish that

$$\ln(eP_f/P) = \ln(e) + \ln(P_f) - \ln(P)$$

PPP implies that the right hand side is constant, since if eP_f/P is constant then so is $\ln(eP_f/P)$.

To convert this fact into a statement about proportional changes, use the result that $\ln(e^*)$ approximately equals $\ln(e) + (e^* - e)/e$. (This can be shown using the Taylor series expansion formula $f(x^*) = f(x) + (x^* - x)(df(x)/dx)$, where in our case $f(x)$ is $\ln(e)$, and $df(x)/dx = 1/e$.) The logarithm of a variable changes approximately by the proportional change of the variable.

Applying this to the PPP formula, we see that if e, P_f, and P are all changing, and $\ln(e) + \ln(P_f) - \ln(P)$ remains constant, then it must be the case that (% change in e) + (% change in P_f) − (% change in P) equals zero, where we switch from proportions to percentages. Note that e is the price of one unit of the foreign currency measured in domestic currency units, so if e increases by 1 percent, that is a 1 percent decrease in the value of the domestic currency. Also, the percentage change in a price index is a measure of inflation. We can restate this PPP result as follows:

(% loss in value of domestic currency) + (foreign inflation rate) = domestic inflation rate

or

foreign inflation rate = (domestic inflation rate) + (% gain in value of domestic currency).

FILL-IN QUESTIONS

1. The value of foreign currency in terms of domestic currency is the _____ _____.

2. The net flow of goods and services and transfers from here abroad forms the _____ _____ of the balance of payments.

3. The net flow of investments from here to foreign countries forms the _____ _____.

4. The total flow of transactions between countries makes up the _____ _____.

5. A system in which the relative values of domestic and foreign currency are determined by the various governments involved is called a(n) _____.

6. When the relative values of domestic and foreign currency are determined by supply and demand, the system is called a(n) _____.

7. A system in which relative currency values are determined mostly through supply and demand but with some government intervention is called _____.

8. A decrease in the value of domestic currency vis-à-vis other currencies is called _____.

9. When initiated under fixed exchange rates, depreciation by the government is called _____.

10. The relative price of domestic to foreign goods, expressed in a common currency, is called the _____.

TRUE-FALSE QUESTIONS

T F   1. All purchases of foreign assets and collection of returns on those assets are counted in the capital and financial account.

T F   2. A decrease in the Canadian dollar price of a U.S. dollar is a depreciation of the Canadian currency.

T F   3. The merchandise trade balance is the difference between exports and imports of goods only.

T F   4. In general, a country that has a balance of payments surplus will have an increase in foreign reserves.

T F   5. In an open economy, the excess of domestic savings over domestic investment must equal net exports.

T F   6. In an open economy in equilibrium, net foreign investment must equal the trade balance plus the government budget deficit.

T F   7. A government budget deficit can cause a balance of trade surplus.

T F   8. In practice, the flexible exchange rate system has been one of "clean floating."

T F   9. One way of stating the theory of purchasing power parity is that in the long run the real exchange rate does not change.

MULTIPLE-CHOICE QUESTIONS

1. If the yen initially is worth 1.25 cents and Japan revalues its currency by 50 percent, the exchange rate

   a. rises
   b. falls

   c. remains unchanged
   d. cannot be determined from the information given

2. The current account includes

   a. net exports and change in official reserves only
   b. net transfers and net income from assets only

   c. net exports, net income from assets, net transfers, and change in official reserves
   d. net exports, net income from assets, and net transfers only

3. If the government budget deficit increases while investment spending remains unchanged, then

   a. net exports decreases and/or private saving decreases
   b. net exports increases and/or private saving decreases

   c. net exports decreases and/or private saving increases
   d. net exports increases and/or private saving increases

4. If net exports increases while the government budget deficit remains unchanged, then

   a. private saving decreases and/or investment spending decreases
   b. private saving increases and/or investment spending decreases

   c. private saving decreases and/or investment spending increases
   d. private saving increases and/or investment spending increases

5. A devaluation of a currency takes place when its value in terms of foreign exchange is

    a. reduced by forces in the foreign exchange market
    b. increased by forces in the foreign exchange market
    c. reduced by official action
    d. increased by official action

6. An appreciation of a currency takes place when its value in terms of foreign exchange is

    a. reduced by forces in the foreign exchange market
    b. increased by forces in the foreign exchange market
    c. reduced by official action
    d. increased by official action

7. If the price level in Canada increases by 50 percent, the price level in the U.S. increases by 30 percent, and the value of the Canadian dollar expressed in U.S. dollars increases by 20 percent, then the real exchange rate

    a. remains constant
    b. decreases, i.e., Canadian goods become more expensive
    c. increases, i.e., Canadian. goods become relatively less expensive
    d. not enough information is given

8. If the price level in Canada increases by 50 percent, the price level in the U.S. increases by 30 percent, and the value of the Canadian dollar expressed in U.S. dollars decreases by 20 percent, then the real exchange rate

    a. remains constant
    b. decreases, i.e., Canadian goods become more expensive
    c. increases, i.e., Canadian. goods become relatively less expensive
    d. not enough information is given

APPLICATION QUESTIONS

1. Initially, one Martian drooler is worth 25 cents. Suppose the Canadian dollar is devalued by 50 percent and then by an additional 20 percent. What is the new exchange rate?

2. Assume that purchasing power parity holds in the following questions:

   a) The Canadian inflation rate is 10 percent and the U.S. inflation rate is 7 percent. What is happening to the value of the Canadian dollar expressed in U.S. dollars?

   b) The Canadian dollar is appreciating by 4 percent per year, and the U.S. inflation rate is 6 percent. What is the Canadian inflation rate?

   c) The Canadian dollar is depreciating by 3 percent per year and the Canadian inflation rate is 4 percent. What is the U.S. inflation rate?

3. If there were no international capital flows, the equilibrium interest rate in a country would be 6 percent. But it is a small open economy, and the world interest rate is 10 percent. Does the country have a trade surplus or deficit?

6 BUSINESS CYCLES AND THE AGGREGATE DEMAND–AGGREGATE SUPPLY MODEL

FOCUS OF THE CHAPTER

We distinguish between long run trend changes in GDP and the more transitory changes, which are referred to as the business cycle.

We develop the aggregate supply/demand model to show how the supply and demand sides of the economy interact to uniquely determine output and the price level.

Supply side policies and the short and long run effects of tax cuts are discussed.

SECTION SUMMARIES

1. Business Cycles

It is useful to separate changes in GDP into two parts. First, there is a part resulting from the long run trend path of GDP. This is described by a change in the level of full employment GDP, which was discussed in Section 1 of Chapter 3. Also known as potential GDP, this usually is thought to grow smoothly with time, but is not observed directly. Second is the part resulting from fluctuations of GDP around this long run trend. The difference between actual and potential GDP is called the output gap. The movements of actual GDP around the long run trend form what is called the business cycle.

The behaviour of unemployment and inflation are closely connected to this cycle. The model of aggregate demand and supply is designed to explain this behaviour.

2. Introduction to Aggregate Demand and Aggregate Supply

The aggregate demand curve describes all of the combinations of output and the price level for which the goods and assets markets are <u>simultaneously</u> in equilibrium. It slopes downward because of the interaction between these markets: A decrease in the price level, because it increases the real money supply, causes the real interest rate to fall. Lower interest rates make investment less costly, so that more occurs. Aggregate demand increases.

The aggregate supply (AS) curve describes the amount of output that firms are willing to supply at different price levels. The fact that there is a relationship between output and the price level should be somewhat disturbing—if everyone is perfectly informed and all markets clear (so that supply equals demand in each of them), output should be fixed at the level of potential output whatever the price level.

In the long run, when markets clear and all inputs are fully employed, output is fixed at the level of potential output, and the AS curve is vertical. We call this the classical case.

If we characterize the short run as a period over which prices cannot adjust, the short-run AS curve must be horizontal. (We call this a Keynesian aggregate supply curve.)

3. Aggregate Demand Policy Under Alternative Supply Assumptions

Changes in aggregate demand only affect output in the short and medium run, when the AS curve is not vertical. When the AS curve is vertical (in the long run, or classical case), neither fiscal nor monetary policy can affect output. Shifts in the AD curve only change the price level. Output is fixed at potential output (Y^*).

An outward shift in the AD curve which results from increased government spending produces full crowding out in the classical case. See Figure 6-1. Private spending falls by exactly the amount that government spending increases. This must happen if output is to remain at its initial level.

When the AS curve is vertical, increases in the money supply translate directly into increases in the price level. As before, the outward shift in the AD curve affects neither output nor employment. Because it does not affect people's economic decisions, monetary policy is said to be neutral in the long run.

Demand management policies
(policies that shift only the
AD curve) cannot affect output
in the long run.

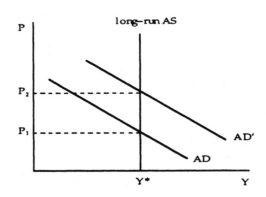

Figure 6-1

THE LONG-RUN (CLASSICAL CASE) EFFECT OF A SHIFT IN AD

4. Supply-Side Economics

Because the AS curve is vertical in the long run, only supply-side policies (policies which shift the aggregate supply curve) can produce long-run growth. Deregulating industries, making laws and regulations easier to comply with, and changing or removing unnecessary laws all have the capacity to do this.

You might wonder how the long-run AS curve can shift at all, as all factors of production are *fixed* in the long run by definition. The answer, of course, is that this shift does not occur because more inputs are being used. It occurs because these inputs are being used more effectively. It is similar, in this way, to technological improvement.

Chapter 6

The political meaning of the term "supply-side economics" is slightly different than the more general economic one. This term has been used, in recent years, to refer to the idea that tax cuts will increase output by so much that tax receipts will rise or remain constant, rather than fall.

The assumption that tax cuts increase aggregate supply as well as aggregate demand results from an incentive effect: Tax cuts, because they allow people to keep more of the money they earn, significantly increase the incentive to work, and therefore lower the natural rate of unemployment (raise potential output).

Economists don't argue about whether this incentive effect exists, or about whether a shift in long-run AS is likely to occur. What they do argue about is the magnitude of this shift — specifically, about whether the AS curve shifts far enough to the right to generate enough tax revenue to compensate for the negative effect on these revenues of the lower tax rate.

5. Working with Data

A potential GDP series is given. The student is asked to retrieve quarterly seasonally adjusted GDP data from CANSIM and asked to plot these series together to reproduce Figure 6-2 from the text.

THE LANGUAGE OF ECONOMICS

Key Terms

business cycle	aggregate supply (AS) curve
potential GDP	aggregate demand (AD) curve
expansion (recovery)	Keynesian aggregate supply curve
contraction (recession)	Classical aggregate supply curve
output gap	supply-side economics

Expansionary and Contractionary Policies

Monetary and fiscal policy can be either expansionary or contractionary—can either increase or decrease aggregate demand. The central bank (the Bank of Canada, in Canada) runs expansionary monetary policy when it increases the money stock. This drives down real interest rates, increases investment demand, and shifts AD to the right. It runs contractionary monetary policy when it reduces the real money supply, driving up interest rates and shifting AD to the left. This is pretty easy to remember, as contractionary monetary policy is nothing more than a contraction in the real money supply (it shrinks), and expansionary monetary policy nothing more than an expansion of the money stock (it grows).

Tax cuts and spending increases are both examples of expansionary fiscal policy, as they increase people's demand for consumption goods, and thus shift AD outward. Tax increases and spending cuts are both types of contractionary fiscal policy.

REVIEW OF TECHNIQUE

Working with Graphs

It is often easier to work with graphs instead of equations—especially, as will often be the case in this text, when a qualitative answer is all that is needed. (Take, for example, the question: Do interest rates rise or fall in response to a monetary expansion? As we only need to know the direction of change in this case, a graph is all that is needed to provide a complete answer.) To make sure you are comfortable working with graphs, we provide a brief review of some techniques here.

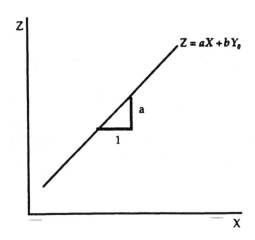

Figure 6-2

GRAPHING AN EQUATION

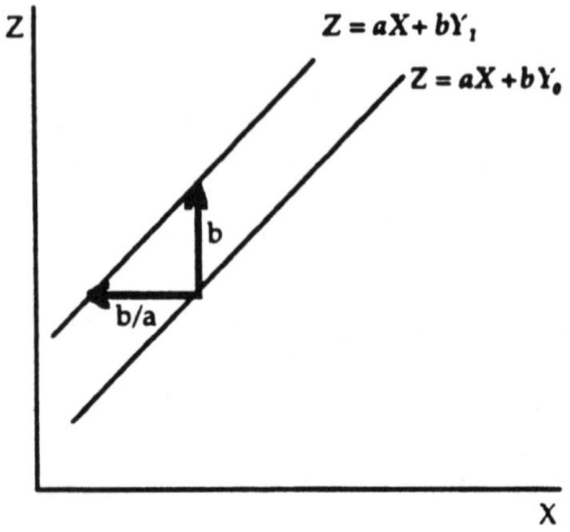

Figure 6-3

GRAPHING THE SHIFT OF A LINE

Suppose you have an equation of the form:

$$Z = aX + bY$$

where X, Y, and Z are three (unspecified) economic variables, and a and b are arbitrary constants, assumed to be greater than zero. First, a brief interpretation of this equation: the variable Z is a function of both X and Y. Because a and b are both assumed to be positive, Z will increase when either of these other variables increases, and will decrease when either falls.

Now, suppose we choose to graph this equation in Z and X. It is a convention that the dependent (endogenous) variable be on the vertical axis. For this reason, we place Z on the vertical axis, and X on the horizontal axis. We then find the slope of this equation—the amount that Z changes in response to a one unit change in X. In this case, our *slope* is the constant a (increase X by one, holding Y constant, and see for yourself), so we know that o   ine slopes upward and to the right.

It is important to remember that we are holding our "extra" variable, Y, constant throughout this entire process. Once Y changes, we have to pick up the line we've graphed and move it to a place that's consistent with the new value of Y. We do this in Figure 6-3.

Let's suppose, for example, that Y increases by 1 unit. What happens to our line? We know that for any given value of X, Z will increase by $(1 \times b)$ units. This tells us that our line must shift upward by an amount b.

Chapter 6

We could also hold **Z** constant in order to see how **X** could have to change to compensate for **Y**'s increase. This approach is a little more difficult—at least in this case. (As the vertical and horizontal shifts will produce the same final line, you should always just use whichever method is easiest, given the problem you're working on.) We work through an example below:

Suppose again that **Y** increases by one unit. To find how far (and in what direction) our line shifts *horizontally*, we hold **Z** constant and see how much **X** must change. (We denote this constant value of **Z** by $\overline{Z}$) We do this by first subtracting the quantity *"bY"* from both sides, so that

$$aX = \overline{Z} - bY$$

We then divide each side by **a** to isolate the variable **X**. We end up with the equation

$$X = \frac{1}{a}\,\overline{Z} - \frac{b}{a}\,Y$$

which tells us that in order to maintain a constant value $\overline{Z}$ of Z when Y increases by 1 unit, X must fall (this is because there's a minus sign) by exactly $(1 \times b/a)$ units. We must shift our curve exactly this far to the left to accommodate.

An increase in X, of course, is nothing more than a movement along the line we've already drawn.

FILL-IN QUESTIONS

1. The more or less regular pattern of expansion and contraction in economic activity is known as the
   _____.

2. The deviation of output from potential is referred to as the _____.

3. The recessions of the early 1980s and early 1990s caused the inflation rate to _____.

4. The _____ curve describes the combinations of output and the price level at which the goods market and the financial market are simultaneously in equilibrium.

5. In the long run, when markets have time to fully clear, the aggregate supply curve
   is_____ , and output is equal to _____.

6. In the short run, when prices do not have time to change at all, the aggregate supply curve
   is_____.

7. A 10 percent increase in the _____ will shift the aggregate demand curve up by 10%.

8. Under _____ supply assumptions, neither monetary nor fiscal policy can affect output. These assumptions are most appropriate in the _____ .

9. A decrease in tax rates will cause a relatively large shift to the _____ in the _____ curve and a relatively small shift to the _____ in the _____ curve.

TRUE-FALSE QUESTIONS

T F 1. Keynesian supply assumptions are most appropriate in the long run, when output is at its potential.

T F 2. The Keynesian aggregate supply curve is flat.

T F 3. In the long run, output is fixed.

T F 4. Under Keynesian supply assumptions, price is fixed.

T F 5. In the short run, a change in the money supply has no effect on real output.

T F 6. The AS/AD model explains how potential output changes in the short and medium run.

T F 7. The level of potential output is fixed in the short, medium, and long run—and hence in the AS/AD model. It is the difference between output and its potential that varies.

T F 8. When the AS curve is flat, a change in the level of government spending has no effect on real output.

T F 9. The assumption that the AS curve is flat in the short run is an oversimplification…it would be better modeled as being flat when output is below its potential, but when output is above potential, the slope of the AS curve rises sharply, as not much more can be produced without driving up the price level.

T F 10. Supply-side policies are useful only for short-term results.

MULTIPLE-CHOICE QUESTIONS

1. If government spending increases, the aggregate demand (AD) curve will

   a. shift in
   b. shift out
   c. not change
   d. change slope

2. If government spending increases, the aggregate supply (AS) curve will

   a. shift in
   b. shift out
   c. not change
   d. change slope

3. In the long run, when output is equal to potential output, an increase in government spending will raise

   a. output
   b. the price level
   c. taxes
   d. the money supply

4. Which of the following can shift the aggregate demand (AD) curve?

   a. only fiscal policy
   b. only monetary policy
   c. both fiscal and monetary policy
   d. none of the above

5. The classical _____ curve is vertical in the _____ run and horizontal in the _____ run.

   a. demand; short; long
   b. demand; long; short
   c. supply; short; long
   d. supply; long; short

Chapter 6

6. Over time, as prices adjust to bring markets into equilibrium, the slope of the aggregate supply (AS) curve will

    a.   increase   c.   remain constant
    b.   decrease   d.   fall to zero

7. Which of the following types of policy is most likely to increase output in the long run?

    a.   supply side   c.   neither
    b.   demand side   d.   both

8. An increase in the level of aggregate demand (AD) that exists at a given price level is represented, graphically, as _____ the AD curve

    a.   an inward (left) shift in   c.   a movement along
    b.   an outward (right) shift in   d.   a change in the slope of

9. On the AD curve, which markets are in equilibrium?

    a.   only the financial market   c.   both goods and financial markets
    b.   only the goods market   d.   neither goods nor financial markets

CONCEPTUAL PROBLEMS

1. Why does the AD curve slope downward?

2. Why is short-run AS best represented by an upward-sloping curve, as opposed to a horizontal line (as in the Keynesian case)?

3. How can supply-side policies increase long-run AS when we've assumed potential output to be fixed at this horizon? (Recall that we've assumed potential output to be fixed in the AS-AD model because all factor inputs are assumed to be fixed. This assumption has not changed... what has?)

4. Which of the following constitute expansionary fiscal policy? Which constitute contractionary fiscal policy? (For a review of expansionary and contractionary fiscal policy, see The Language of Economics, this chapter.)

    a)   an increase in the benefits paid to welfare recipients

    b)   a decrease in the capital gains tax

    c)   an increase in the inheritance tax

    d)   an increase in the number of available tax exemptions

    e)   a decrease in social insurance benefits

APPLICATION QUESTIONS

1. When we graph AD, what variables do we hold constant?

2. Suppose that the government increases its spending.

   a) What will happen to price and output in the short-run?

   b) What will happen to price and output in the long-run?

   c) In what way do your answers in parts (a) and (b) make use of an assumption?

3. a) What is the immediate effect on real interest rates when the money supply is reduced?

   b) How does this affect individuals' investment decisions, and, as a result, AD?

7 WAGE AND PRICE ADJUSTMENT: THE PHILLIPS CURVE AND AGGREGATE SUPPLY

FOCUS OF THE CHAPTER

The simple Phillips curve, describing the tradeoff between inflation and unemployment, is introduced.

The simple Phillips curve is modified to incorporate the effect on the inflation-unemployment tradeoff of inflation expectations.

The Phillips curve is used along with Okun's law to derive the short run aggregate supply curve.

SECTION SUMMARIES

1.   The Phillips Curve

In this chapter we consider the transition period between the short run and the long run. Since in this time frame prices and wages do not have time to fully adjust, unemployment can differ from its full employment level u^*, which we refer to as the natural unemployment rate. (This is greater than zero due to frictional unemployment.) If the unemployment rate is above u^*, then there is an excess supply of workers and the wage should be adjusting downward. This negative relationship is expressed as

$$g_w = -\varepsilon(u - u^*)$$

where g_w is the growth rate of the nominal wage. See Figure 7-1. This function is a simple Phillips curve. The slope coefficient ε relates to the speed of adjustment in the labour market. The higher ε is, the faster wages adjust in response to labour market disequilibria.

The term Phillips curve has come to refer to a curve relating price, rather than wage, inflation to the unemployment rate. This negative relation describes a short run policy tradeoff that has been an important part of macroeconomic policy analysis.

The inability to describe the behaviour of inflation and unemployment by a single Phillips curve in the 1970s led to the use of the expectations-augmented Phillips curve:

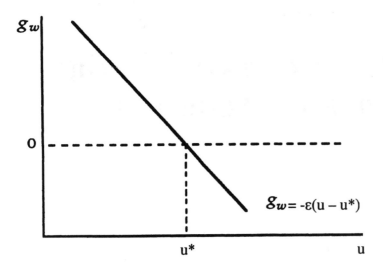

Figure 7-1

THE ORIGINAL PHILLIPS CURVE

(g_w = wage inflation)

$$\pi = \pi^e - \varepsilon\,(u - u^*),$$

where π is the (price) inflation rate and π^e is the expected inflation rate. A change in the level of expected inflation causes the Phillips curve to shift. There can be price (and wage) inflation at u^*. For example, if everyone expects inflation to be 6 percent, and wage and prices indeed rise by that rate, there are no surprises or reasons for u to differ from the equilibrium level u^*. This curve does a better job of describing Canadian data if we let π^e be higher during the high-inflation period 1972-1983.

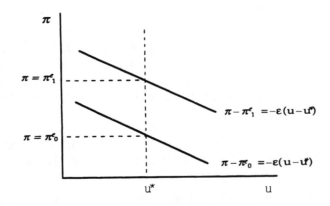

Figure 7-2

THE EXPECTATIONS-AUGMENTED PHILLIPS CURVE

2. From Phillips Curve to Aggregate Supply

The Phillips curve can be used to motivate an upward-sloping short run aggregate supply curve. In this time frame there is some price adjustment, but not enough to reach the full employment equilibrium implied by the vertical Classical aggregate supply curve.

Beginning with the naïve Phillips curve

$$\pi = \pi^e - \varepsilon(u - u^*)$$

we can substitute out the definition of inflation, at time t, $B_t = (P_t/P_{t-1}) - 1$, to obtain

$$P_t = P_{t-1}(1 - \varepsilon(u_t - u^*))$$

We can incorporate inflation expectations by replacing P_{t-1} with the expected price level P_t^e. Finally, we can arrive at a supply curve by using Okun's law, which relates unemployment to output. Okun's law can be written as

$$(Y_t - Y^*)/Y^* = -\gamma(u_t - u^*)$$

These two substitutions give

$$P_t = P_t^e\left(1 + \left(\frac{\varepsilon}{\gamma}\right)/()(Y_t - Y^*)/Y^*\right)$$

Letting $\lambda = \varepsilon/(\gamma Y^*)$, we have derived the short run aggregate supply curve (SRAS):

$$P_t = P_t^e(1 - \lambda(Y_t - Y^*))$$

The slope of this curve depends on ε, the speed-of-adjustment parameter from the Phillips curve. The faster is this speed of adjustment, the closer we are to the long run situation, and the steeper is the SRAS. The level of the SRAS depends on the expected price level P_t^e.

How are price and inflation expectations formed? One assumption is adaptive expectations, where the expectations are formed by looking at the recent past. A simple version of this is static expectations, where $P_t^e = P_{t-1}$ is assumed. This seems unreasonable in a period where inflation is ongoing and expected.

An alternative is rational expectations, where it is assumed that the errors made in forming the expectations are not systematic, and average out to be zero. An important implication can be seen from solving the SRAS for output:

$$Y_t = Y^* + \alpha(P_t - P_t^e),$$

where $\alpha = 1/\lambda$. Note that if expectations are correct, that is $P_t = P_t^e$, then $Y_t = Y^*$. The source of departures from the long run equilibrium is expectation errors.

3. Working with Data

The student is asked to fit a trend line to a plot of the rate of change of GDP against the change in the unemployment rate. The slope of this trend line should be close to -1.6, which was the slope suggested in Section 2 of this chapter for the Okun's law relationship.

LANGUAGE OF ECONOMICS

Key Terms

Phillips curve
policy trade-off
expected or anticipated inflation
expectations-augmented Phillips curve
Okun's law

short run aggregate supply (SRAS) curve
adaptive expectations
static expectations
rational expectations

Rational Expectations

Because none of us know what's going to happen in the future, we often have to base our decisions on what we *think* may happen; we form *expectations* about the future based on whatever information is currently available to us, and use those expectations to make decisions. (Should I go to the beach today? No. It's probably going to rain....)

People form expectations in any number of different ways. They might, perhaps, consult the stars. They might assume that whatever has happened in the recent past will continue to happen. They might try to adjust their previous expectations to correct what they now know was wrong with them.

A number of economists now believe, however, that it doesn't matter *how* people form their expectations as long as the errors that they make cannot be predicted. When this is the case, they say that expectations are *rational*—that all available information has been used to form them.

Imagine what it would mean if people made systematic predictable errors when forecasting future events. Workers who systematically underestimated future inflation would consistently negotiate wages that were too low. Runners who made systematic errors about the weather would consistently dress too warmly, or fail to prepare for predictable downpours. People able to forecast these errors—those able to form more accurate expectations—would be able to provide a valuable service to these folks. They could tell the workers what inflation is likely to be over the next three years, and the runners whether or not it is likely to rain on any given day. In fact, this service would be *so* valuable that they would probably be able to make a good bit of money. It is hard to imagine that such people would not exist.

When expectations are rational, it is assumed that systematic, predictable errors like the ones mentioned above do not occur. They should not be able to because, if they are predictable, someone is likely to come along and predict them. Once this happens, these errors will disappear.

REVIEW OF TECHNIQUE

Reading Equations

In Review of Technique 6, we discussed how to translate an equation into a graph. Graphing an equation is often the easiest and most useful way to make sense of it. It is also possible, however, to derive quite a bit of information from the visual inspection of an equation. As you begin to read more articles and learn more advanced theory, this skill—you can think of it as the ability to "read" equations—will become increasingly more valuable to you. For that reason, and because there *are* a few equations in this text, we work through an example for you here.

Let's use a simple Phillips curve:

$$g_w = -\varepsilon(u - u^*)$$

What does this equation tell us?

It tells us in general that there is a relationship between wage inflation and the rate of unemployment. It tells us more precisely that the further the rate of unemployment rises above its full-employment level, the more quickly wages will fall ($g_w < 0$ when $u > u^*$) and that the further the rate of unemployment falls below its full-employment level, the more quickly wages will rise ($g_w > 0$ when $u < u^*$).

This equation also tells us that there is no wage inflation when unemployment is at its natural rate ($g_w = 0$ when $u = u^*$). This is radically different than the result we find with the augmented Phillips curve—that wage inflation equals expected wage inflation at the natural rate of unemployment.

To complete our interpretation of this equation, we must be careful to explain the purpose of the parameter ε (pronounced "epsilon"). What is it? How does it affect the relationship between π and u? To answer these questions, we must look again at our original equation, which says that a one percentage point increase in the rate of unemployment will raise the rate of wage inflation by an amount ε, or that ε controls the degree to which output can be exchanged for wage inflation. When ε is high, a lot of inflation can be traded for a little unemployment. When ε is low, a little inflation must be traded for a lot of unemployment—an unattractive proposition if one is trying to reduce the rate of inflation. You can imagine why policy makers might want an estimate of this parameter.

Try interpreting other equations that you find in the text. In time, you will be able to do this very quickly.

FILL-IN QUESTIONS

1. In long run equilibrium, the unemployment is by definition equal to the _____.

2. If unemployment is below its natural rate, wages will _____.

3. When wages adjust slowly, over time, rather than being completely flexible, we say they are _____.

4. Sluggish wage adjustment can cause the _____ market to be out of equilibrium, and create _____.

5. Output and unemployment are related in the following way: when unemployment falls, output must _____.

6. The _____ curve illustrates the short run tradeoff between inflation and unemployment.

7. The _____ curve illustrates the short run tradeoff between output and the price level.

8. The conflict between the data and the simple Phillips curve can be largely resolved by considering the _____ Phillips curve.

9. The relationship between unemployment and output is referred to as _____.

10. The assumption that underlies rational expectations is that individuals do not make _____ in forming their expectations.

TRUE-FALSE QUESTIONS

T   F   1.   The economy is always at full employment.

T   F   2.   The economy is never at full employment.

T F   3. There is a tradeoff, in the short run, between inflation and unemployment.

T F   4. There is a tradeoff, in the long run, between inflation and unemployment.

T F   5. The tradeoff between inflation and unemployment easily can be exploited by politicians.

T F   6. In the expectations-augmented Phillips curve, inflation depends on people's expectations as well as on the level of unemployment.

T F   7. Unemployment is at its natural rate, on the augmented Phillips curve, when inflation is equal to expected inflation.

T F   8. In the expectations-augmented Phillips curve, expected inflation is translated only partially into actual inflation.

T F   9. Under adaptive expectations, individuals are assumed to not really form expectations, but instead to adapt their behaviour to their current circumstances without making any predictions of the future.

T F   10. Under rational expectations, individuals are assumed to make perfectly accurate predictions of the future inflation rate.

MULTIPLE-CHOICE QUESTIONS

1. Which of the following is *not* a necessary component of the price adjustment mechanism described by the aggregate supply curve?

    a. production function   c. price-cost relation
    b. rational expectations   d. Phillips curve

2. The expectations-augmented Philips curve predicts that if inflation is higher than it was expected to be, then

    a. unemployment will be above the   c. unemployment will be at the natural rate
        natural rate   regardless of the inflation rate
    b. unemployment will be below the   d. could be (a) or (b) depending on the
        natural rate   expectations assumption

3. Under the Classical fully flexible price assumption, the slope of the Phillips curve would be equal to

    a. infinity   c. one
    b. zero   d. minus one

4. The position of the short run aggregate supply (SRAS) curve depends on

    a. potential output   c. both
    b. past prices   d. neither

5. Which of the following is not one of the leading explanations for why there is wage stickiness?

    a. imperfect information   c. expected or anticipated inflation
    b. coordination problems   d. efficiency wages and costs of price change

6. Okun's law states that there is a relationship between

    a. GDP and inflation
    b. unemployment and inflation
    c. the price level and inflation
    d. GDP and unemployment

7. If the expected price level increases, the short run aggregate supply curve will

    a. shift to the left
    b. shift to the right
    c. become steeper
    d. become flatter

8. Static expectations says that individuals' expected price level

    a. is a perfectly accurate prediction
    b. is formed rationally
    c. equals last period's actual price level
    d. equals the long run equilibrium price level

9. Which of the following have the same long run equilibrium?

    a. the Classical model and the adaptive expectations model
    b. the Classical model and the rational expectations model
    c. the adaptive expectations model and the rational expectations model
    d. the Classical model, the adaptive expectations model and the rational expectations model

CONCEPTUAL PROBLEMS

1. How are output and unemployment connected?

2. What information does the parameter λ in the equation below give you?

$$P_{t+1} = P_t[1 + \lambda(Y_t - Y^*)]$$

What do you suppose would happen to the business cycle if λ increased? How would an increase in λ affect the government's decisions to use fiscal or monetary policy to stabilize the economy (that is, to keep output and employment close to their long-run values)?

WORKING WITH DATA

After the OPEC oil shock of 1973 drove output down and the price level up in Canada, people's inflationary expectations rose considerably. This increased the rate of inflation consistent with full-employment, shifting the augmented Phillips curve upward. This Graph It asks you to plot the rate of inflation against the rate of unemployment for Canada both before and after the OPEC oil shock, and to identify the inflationary-expectations augmented Phillips curve belonging to each period.

Data is provided in Table 7-1 for the years 1961 through 1969 and 1976 through 1978. We suggest that you graph each combination of inflation and unemployment, noting the year that each point is associated with. When connected, they should form two lines—the augmented Phillips curves for each of the periods we're considering. Assume that the natural rate of unemployment is 5.5 percent.

What must the expected rate of inflation have been during each period?

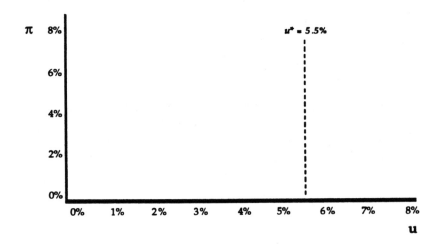

Chart 7-1

TABLE 7-1

Year	Rate of Inflation	Rate of Unemployment
1961	0.9%	7.1%
1962	1.2%	5.9%
1963	1.8%	5.5%
1964	1.8%	4.7%
1965	2.4%	3.9%
1966	3.7%	3.4%
1967	3.6%	3.8%
1968	4.0%	4.4%
1969	4.6%	4.4%
1976	7.5%	7.1%
1977	8.0%	8.1%
1978	8.9%	8.3%

APPLICATION QUESTIONS

minus

1. Given the expectations-augmented Phillips curve: $B_t = B^e_t - .5(u_t - u^*)$, where the natural unemployment rate is $u^* = .07$ and the static expectations assumption is used: $B^e_t = B_{t-1}$, where inflation in year 0 was $B_0 = .12$, compute the inflation rate for years t = 1, 2 and 3 when the unemployment rate u behaves as follows:

   a) $u = .07$ each year.

   b) $u = .09$ each year.

   c) $u = .05$ each year.

2. Repeat Question 1 with a modified adaptive expectations assumption. This time assume that inflation is expected to be the average of the inflation rates in the previous two years: $B^e_t = (B_{t-1} + B_{t-2})/2$, and assume that inflation in both years before year 1 was B = .12.

Wage and Price Adjustment: The Phillips Curve and Aggregate Supply

8 THE ANATOMY OF INFLATION AND UNEMPLOYMENT

FOCUS OF THE CHAPTER

In this chapter we take a closer look at the flows in and out of unemployment.

We examine the costs of both inflation and unemployment, and consider some of the policy questions that are raised by the tradeoff between them.

SECTION SUMMARIES

1. The Anatomy of Unemployment

There are three central facts about unemployment in Canada. These facts help us to understand who bears the cost of unemployment.

- Different groups in society have very different unemployment rates. Unemployment is higher in the 15 to 24 age group and, across regions, the Atlantic provinces have experienced the highest unemployment rates.

- There are substantial flows in and out of unemployment each month, and most people who become unemployed return to work very quickly.

- Much of the total number of unemployed persons is made up of people who are unemployed for long periods.

A person is unemployed if they are out of work and they have been: looking for work in the last four weeks, waiting to be recalled from lay off, or waiting to report to a new job within four weeks. Job loss accounts for about half of new unemployment. The other half comes from quits and entrants to the labour force.

While the latter two facts may seem to contradict each other, they do not. One concerns the flow of people into unemployment, while the other concerns the stock of unemployed, which depends on the flows of people in and out of unemployment.

Because the labour force is made up of a number of different groups, many of which have radically different rates of unemployment, we must take a weighted average of them in order to calculate the overall unemployment rate:

$$u = w_1 u_1 + n_2 u_2 + \cdots + w_n u_n$$

The w_i here are weights, equal to the fraction of the labour force represented by each group. The u_i are the unemployment rates for each group. The aggregate unemployment rate can change either because the unemployment rate of one or more groups changes, or because the fraction of the labour force that they represent changes.

Unemployment can be decomposed into frictional unemployment, which exists even when the economy is at full employment, and cyclical unemployment, which varies according to the business cycle.

2. Full Employment

The natural rate of unemployment depends on the frequency (the rate at which workers become unemployed) and the duration (once unemployed, how long do workers remain unemployed) of unemployment. The duration depends on labour market services such as employment agencies, demographic characteristics of workers, and the level of unemployment benefits. The frequency depends on the variability of the demand for labour across firms and the number of new workers entering the labour force. We do not observe the natural rate, but it is thought to have risen since the 1960s.

The tendency for unemployment to stay high for a while, even after a recession is over, is called hysteresis. This can also be described as an increase in the natural rate. It can result from changes in the behaviour of the unemployed after having been in that state for a while, and a change in the behaviour of employers toward them.

Proposals for reducing the natural rate include training programs, especially for teenaged workers, reducing the minimum wage, and adjusting unemployment benefit levels.

3. The Costs of Unemployment

Fewer employed workers means lower production (formalized in Okun's law). For example we estimate that the high unemployment in 1993 resulted in a $25 billion loss of output compared to full employment output. Further, the associated income loss from high unemployment tends to hit poorer people harder. An unemployment benefits system partially offsets this cost. Another cost is the loss of tax revenue following from the lower income of an unemployed worker. These costs are offset, but only slightly, by an increase in leisure time.

4. The Costs of Inflation

In determining the costs of inflation, we made a critical distinction between perfectly anticipated and imperfectly anticipated inflation. If everyone knew how much inflation there would be, all agreements and contracts would be written to reflect this inflation. The only costs of anticipated inflation arise because the interest rate on currency cannot be adjusted to inflation (since there is no interest on currency) and because people have to spend a lot of time remarking price tags. Both costs are trivial. When inflation is unanticipated or imperfectly anticipated, people who owe nominal debts repay them with cheaper dollars and people who are creditors are paid off in cheaper dollars. Thus debtors benefit and creditors lose. Of course, most people are both debtors and creditors. Unanticipated inflation helps some individuals and hurts others. The effect of unanticipated inflation is mostly distributional.

5. Inflation and Indexation: Inflation-Proofing the Economy

The major ways that unanticipated inflation redistributes income are through loans and wage contracts. An alternative to negotiating contracts in nominal terms and worrying about the level of future inflation is to index contracts — that is, tie their payoffs to the inflation rate. Wage contracts, for example, might include automatic cost of living adjustments, or COLA provisions, which tie nominal wages to the CPI. Interest rates might be adjusted for inflation as well. Of course, the CPI is not a perfect measure of inflation, and by tying wages and interest rates to this measure we may be trading one source of uncertainty for another. Indexation is used widely only in countries with extremely high rates of inflation.

THE LANGUAGE OF ECONOMICS

Key Terms

unemployed person	perfectly/imperfectly anticipated inflation
unemployment pool	menu costs
frictional unemployment	wealth redistribution
cyclical unemployment	indexation
natural rate of unemployment	cost-of-living adjustment (COLA)
sacrifice ratio	
Okun's law	

The Definition of Unemployment

To be considered unemployed, in the economic sense, one must be more than simply jobless. It is also necessary to be actively searching for employment—i.e., you must (1) have actively looked for work during the last four weeks, (2) be waiting to be recalled to a job after having been laid off, or (3) be waiting to report to a new job that will begin within the next four weeks.

Those who do not have jobs and are not actively seeking them are not considered to be a part of the labour force; they are neither considered employed nor considered unemployed. This is an important point to remember, as it highlights the fact that there are people without jobs, people who may have given up looking because they believe themselves unemployable, who, because of the way that we measure unemployment, are not captured by unemployment statistics. These discouraged workers represent a very real social problem—one which is not measured at all by unemployment statistics.

REVIEW OF TECHNIQUE

Weighting

In order to construct a statistic that provides information about a diverse population, it is necessary to account for differences across groups within that population. As the groups are likely to be different sizes, a statistic will best represent the population if the characteristics of small groups affect it less than those of larger ones. Weighting—multiplying the statistic for each individual group by the fraction of the population that group represents—is an effective way to guarantee this.

Let's suppose, for example, that there are two groups of people in our society with very different sleeping habits. People in group A tend to sleep an average of 4 hours a night; people in group B tend to sleep an average of 10. The unweighted average is $(4 + 10)/2 = 7$ hours a night. But if there are many more people in one group than the other, then this unweighted average is not a good indicator of the overall average. For example, if there are 10 people in group A and 40 in group B, the average number of hours that the 50 people in our society spend asleep will be equal to $((10/50) \times 4) + ((40/50) \times 10)$, or 8.8.

Multiplying each statistic by the fraction of the population it represents and then adding these statistics together is called taking a *weighted average*.

FILL-IN QUESTIONS

1. An unforeseen increase in the rate of inflation benefits _____, at the expense of _____.

2. An *expected* increase in the rate of inflation hurts people who hold _____.

3. The _____ is the amount of output (expressed in percentage terms) that is lost *for each one point reduction* in the inflation rate.

4. _____ is an empirical estimate of the amount of output (expressed, again, in percentage terms) which must be given up for each one percent decrease in the rate of unemployment.

5. To be considered unemployed, it is not enough to be without a job. An unemployed person must also count him/herself in the _____ (must be actively looking for work, waiting to return from a layoff, or waiting to start a new job).

6. The effects of unforeseen inflation are mostly _____.

7. If periods of high unemployment tended to raise the natural rate, there would be _____.

TRUE-FALSE QUESTIONS

T   F   1.   The rate of unemployment is a *flow variable*.

T   F   2.   A person is considered a part of the labour force as soon as they are old enough to work.

T   F   3.   People can move in and out of the labour force over their lifetimes.

T   F   4.   The effects of unemployment are mostly distributional.

T   F   5.   The effects of unanticipated inflation are mostly distributional.

T   F   6.   The costs of moderate (single digit) anticipated inflation are fairly trivial.

T   F   7.   The costs of *high* (triple & quadruple digit) anticipated inflation are quite serious.

T   F   8.   Optimally, the unemployment rate should be zero.

T   F   9.   The natural rate of unemployment cannot be changed by government policies.

MULTIPLE-CHOICE QUESTIONS

1.   Which of the following is present when the economy is at full-employment?

a.   cyclical unemployment   c.   both
b.   frictional unemployment   d.   neither

2.   Unemployment benefits allow/create

a.   longer job search   c.   both
b.   greater employment stability   d.   neither

3. Anticipated inflation transfers wealth from

    a.   creditors to debtors   c.   poor to rich
    b.   debtors to creditors   d.   none of the above

4. Unanticipated inflation transfers wealth from

    a.   creditors to debtors   c.   poor to rich
    b.   debtors to creditors   d.   none of the above

5. Wages and prices should most clearly be indexed in countries with

    a.   high inflation   c.   both
    b.   low inflation   d.   neither

CONCEPTUAL PROBLEMS

1. What costs are associated with unemployment?

2. Unemployment insurance, because it allows people to spend more time searching for a job than they would otherwise be able to, can increase the natural rate of unemployment. Is this something that policymakers should be concerned with? Explain.

3. Should zero unemployment be a goal? Why or why not?

4. Should zero inflation be a goal? Justify your answer.

WORKING WITH DATA

Although we generally use measures of output and output growth in order to determine whether the economy is doing well, we can also look at changes in the rate of unemployment. Here we ask you to chart the rate of unemployment in Canada between the years 1981 and 1998, and to compare your graph to the output growth graph you created in Chapter 1.

Can you see how changes in the rate of unemployment and in the growth rate of output are connected?

TABLE 8-1

Year	Unemployment Rate
1981	7.5
1982	11.0
1983	11.9
1984	11.3
1985	10.5
1986	9.6
1987	8.9
1988	7.8
1989	7.5
1990	8.1
1991	10.4
1992	11.3
1993	11.2
1994	10.4
1995	9.5
1996	9.7
1997	9.2
1998	8.3

Chart 8-1

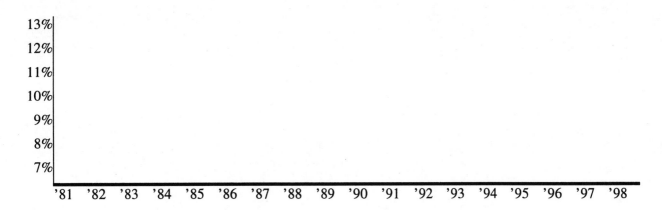

APPLICATION QUESTIONS

1. Suppose that the natural rate of unemployment is 5 percent for adults and 10 percent for teenagers. If teenagers make up 40 percent of the labour force (and adults the other 60 percent), what is the natural rate for the labour force as a whole?

    If the number of teenagers increased to 60 percent (and the number of adults fell to 40 percent), how would the overall natural rate change?

2. There are 100 labour force participants. Some are employed and some are unemployed. Each month, four people leave their jobs. Two of these people remain out of work for one month, one remains out of work for three months, and one remains out of work for one year, but they all remain in the labour force the entire time.

    a) What is the unemployment rate?

    b) What is the average duration of unemployment among the monthly flow of workers into unemployment?

    c) What is the average duration of unemployment among the stock of unemployed workers in any given month?

9 INTERNATIONAL ADJUSTMENT: AGGREGATE DEMAND AND SUPPLY IN AN OPEN ECONOMY

FOCUS OF THE CHAPTER

Policy options and problems are outlined for a fixed exchange rate economy.

We show that, with perfect capital mobility and flexible prices, monetary and fiscal policy cannot alter the long-run level of real income.

The relationships between the trade balance, the exchange rate, and the domestic price level can cause problems in adjusting to disturbances.

SECTION SUMMARIES

1. Adjustment Under Fixed Exchange Rates

First, note that under fixed exchange rates, there is a second reason for the domestic price level to affect the level of aggregate demand, beyond the effect on real balances. A higher domestic price will cause domestic goods and services to be more expensive relative to those in the rest of the world, for given foreign prices. Domestic exports will fall and imports will rise, causing a lower level of aggregate demand.

If a country has a current account deficit under fixed exchange rates, the imbalance in monetary flows (excess demand for foreign currency from the current account side) can be met by the central bank selling some of its foreign reserves. This solution will not work for very long. The economy must adjust, either automatically or through policy.

The sale of foreign reserves referred to above results in a decrease in the domestic money supply, since the foreign reserves are purchased by domestic money, which then leaves circulation (unless it is put back in circulation by the central bank, a practice known as sterilization). A decrease in the money supply will reduce aggregate demand, reducing the demand for imports and easing the current account deficit problem. This is an automatic adjustment.

Policy can also be used to reduce aggregate demand. For example, a tax increase or government spending decrease will reduce aggregate demand and thus import demand. This can also be seen to be likely to reduce the current account deficit through the national income accounting identity

$$NX = (S - I) + [TA - (G + TR)]$$

These policies would reduce the government budget deficit, increasing the term in square brackets. Unless there was an even larger shift in the opposite direction in the $(S - I)$ term, there also would be an increase in NX, implying a reduction in any current account deficit.

Another policy option is devaluation. This lowering of the value of the domestic currency should make imports more expensive and exports cheaper to the rest of the world, as long as this change dominates the effect of different inflation rates domestically and in the rest of the world. Specifically, an increase in the real exchange rate eP_f/P would be necessary. This should lead to a reduction of the current account deficit. If domestic inflation is consistently higher than foreign inflation, then the constant reduction of P_f/P must be offset by frequent increases in e (reductions in the value of the domestic currency, or frequent devaluations). This is called a crawling peg exchange rate policy.

2.   Exchange Rate Changes and Trade Adjustment: Empirical Issues

In order for a nominal devaluation to be successful (i.e., to resolve a payments imbalance), it must be accompanied by a real devaluation—a decline in the real exchange rate. This means that there can be no changes in foreign or domestic prices that negate the effect of the nominal devaluation. This section asks whether nominal devaluations are usually associated with real devaluations, and, on a slightly different subject, whether a decline in the relative price of domestic goods really does improve the trade balance.

The first question has a fairly straightforward answer: nominal devaluations do seem to cause real devaluations as long as the monetary authority resists the impulse to accommodate the price increases they create.

The answer to the second question is somewhat more complex: Because it takes some consumers—and some producers—time to adjust to changes in relative prices, the initial effect of a real devaluation is to *increase* the amount of money spent on imported goods. It is only later, after a year or so, that a decline in the relative price of domestic goods improves the trade balance.

3.   The Monetary Approach to the Balance of Payments

The monetary approach to the balance of payments is based on the belief that most balance of payments deficits are caused by excessive monetary growth. Sterilization operations may contribute to this problem, as they prevent the monetary contraction and subsequent rise in interest rates that would ordinarily result from the central bank's attempt to maintain an overvalued exchange rate. Higher real interest rates would, of course, attract foreign capital and add to the current account, reducing the balance of payments deficit.

Proponents of the monetary approach argue that devaluation can only reduce or eliminate a balance of payments deficit in the short run—that the increase in net exports it causes will lead to a monetary expansion, increasing aggregate demand, driving up the price level and causing a real appreciation of the currency so that the economy ends up right back where it started.

The authors of the textbook do not entirely agree with this analysis. They point out that when a currency is overvalued because of persistent deficits and a high rate of unemployment, a devaluation may actually speed up the adjustment process.

4.   Flexible Exchange Rates, Money, and Prices

This section argues that monetary policy can affect output only temporarily. Eventually, prices will adjust to bring the economy back into internal balance. Real money balances will rise or fall, returning to their original level, as will the real exchange rate. The adjustment process works first through interest rates and then through the price level. For example, consider a monetary contraction, causing output to fall below its long run equilibrium, with higher domestic real interest rates. First this causes an exchange rate appreciation due to an increased net capital inflow. The more expensive domestic currency will reduce net exports. In the long run, the lower domestic prices will restore competitiveness, and net exports will increase. The price change in the long run will match the exchange rate movement, leaving relative prices unchanged.

Because prices and exchange rates do not change at the same rate, there are some interesting effects that occur during the adjustment process. One of these is exchange rate overshooting—a tendency of the exchange rate to move beyond the point of its long–run equilibrium and then, after time, gradually return. Imagine a rubber band. You stretch it—perturb it from its equilibrium—and then let go and allow it to snap back. Anyone who has spent enough of their childhood playing with rubber bands knows that the rubber band will snap too far backwards, and will hit their finger. The rubber band, like the exchange rate, overshoots its equilibrium position… much to the dismay of whoever is holding it.

5.   Exchange Rate Fluctuations and Interdependence

It used to be argued that floating exchange rates allowed nations to pursue totally independent macroeconomic policies. We now know that spillover effects are caused by the changes in a nation's competitive position. This interdependence suggests that countries can benefit from coordination of macroeconomic policies across countries.

6.   Working with Data

Using the data from Chapter 5, the student is asked to graph the real and nominal exchange rates together. Their close co-movements suggest that PPP does not hold, at least in the short run.

THE LANGUAGE OF ECONOMICS

Key Terms

automatic adjustment mechanisms
classical adjustment process
expenditure-switching policies
expenditure-reducing (-increasing) policies
internal and external balance
tariff
World Trade Organization (WTO)
International Monetary Fund (IMF)

devaluation
real devaluation
J-curve effect
monetary approach
(exchange rate) overshooting
purchasing power parity (PPP)
spillover (interdependence) effects

REVIEW OF TECHNIQUE

Units of Measurement

Generally we write our equations and variables without reference to the units in which they are measured. Care must be taken, however, to see that these units are consistent throughout an equation.

Consider, for example, the formula used to calculate the real exchange rate:

$$R = eP_f/P$$

We know that e represents the nominal exchange rate, and that P and P_f represent the domestic and foreign price levels, respectively. How do we know what units the nominal exchange rate is measured in? What units are the real exchange rate measured in?

P_f, we know, is measured in units of foreign currency. Euros, perhaps. If we use a price index to measure it, its units will be Euros per European basket of goods. P will be written in units of domestic currency, say Canadian dollars. When it is measured by a price index like the CPI, its units will be dollars per Canadian basket. If the units in which the nominal exchange rate is measured are to be consistent with the units in which the domestic and foreign price levels are measured, e must be written in units of domestic currency per unit of foreign currency—not in the conventional way.

Some of the units of measurement on the right hand side of this formula cancel:

[(units of domestic currency)/(units of foreign currency)]/[(units of foreign currency)/(foreign basket of goods and services)] ÷

      [(units of domestic currency)/(domestic basket of goods and services)]

= [(units of domestic currency)/(foreign basket of goods and services)] ÷

      [(units of domestic currency)/(domestic basket of goods and services)]

= (domestic basket of goods and services)/(foreign basket of goods and services)

The real exchange rate isn't measured in terms of any currency. It measures the quantity of domestic baskets for which a foreign basket of goods can be exchanged. An increase means that a foreign basket can be traded for more domestic baskets, and represents an improvement in the terms of trade.

The variable whose units are most often confused is the interest rate. We can write an interest rate as 5% or 0.05, or even as 500 "basis points" (a basis point is $1/100$ of a percentage point). It is understood in all of these cases that the rate is 5 percent *per year*. Obviously, our units don't matter so long as we are consistent. The statement "the interest rate rose 10 percent" can be another source of confusion. It does not (or, at least, should not) mean the same thing as the statement "the interest rate rose 10 percentage points" …from 5 percent to 15 percent in our example. A 10 percent rise in the interest rate is much smaller, 1/2 a percentage point in this case. A 10 percent increase in the interest rate only raises it from 5 percent to 5.5 percent.

FILL-IN QUESTIONS

1. The _____ show the relative prices of imports as compared with domestically produced goods.

2. With fixed exchange rates and no sterilization the economy reaches internal and external balance via the _____ adjustment process.

3. The fixed exchange rate system that was established after World War II was called the

    _____ .

4. If the relative prices of goods in two countries, adjusted for the exchange rate, are constant, we say there is _____ .

5. The _____ shows the response over time of imports to a devaluation.

6. A policy intended to encourage consumption of domestically-produced goods and discourage consumption of goods produced in other countries is called an expenditure _____ policy.

7. A policy intended to decrease overall aggregate demand is called an expenditure _____ policy.

8. Devaluing the nominal exchange rate is only effective if it causes a _____.

TRUE-FALSE QUESTIONS

T F 1. An increase in the domestic price level improves the balance of trade.

T F 2. Sterilization operations break the link between the balance of payments and the money supply.

T F 3. Devaluation of the currency causes a recession.

T F 4. The long-run effect of an increase in the money supply is a proportional increase in the price level and the exchange rate e.

T F 5. With perfect capital mobility, income must always be at the full-employment level.

T F 6. If purchasing power parity holds, differences in inflation rates between countries are offset by exchange rate changes.

T F 7. Tariffs and devaluation are both expenditure switching policies.

MULTIPLE-CHOICE QUESTIONS

1. If the typical European good costs 1000 Euros and the typical Canadian good costs $250, and if the exchange rate is 25 cents to 1 Euro, the real exchange rate is

   a. ¼   c. 1
   b. 4   d. 1/16

2. If U.S. prices increase 10 percent while the Canadian dollar depreciates by 10 percent relative to the U.S. dollar, then constant Canadian prices would imply that relative prices (U.S., relative to Canadian)

   a. increased 10 percent   c. remained constant
   b. increased 20 percent   d. fell 20 percent

3. With flexible prices, perfect capital mobility, and a flexible exchange rate, expansionary monetary policy will result in

   a. an increase in real income in the long   c. a decrease in the price level in the long
       run, but not in the short run   run
   b. an increase in real income in the short   d. an appreciation of the nominal exchange
       run, but not in the long run   rate in the long run

4. With flexible prices, perfect capital mobility, and a fixed exchange rate, expansionary fiscal policy will result in

   a. an increase in real income in the long   c. a decrease in the price level in the long
       run, but not in the short run   run
   b. no change in the real exchange rate in   d. an appreciation of the nominal exchange
       the long run   rate in the long run

5. Empirical evidence shows that following a devaluation, the dollar value of imports

    a. rises, then falls   c. remains unchanged

    b. falls, then rises   d. rises

6. Capital will flow into a country when its interest rate, adjusted for expected changes in the exchange rate, is _____ foreign interest rates.

    a. the same as   c. higher than

    b. lower than   d. no relation to interest rates

APPLICATION QUESTIONS

1. Consider an economy in equilibrium, with perfect capital mobility and a flexible exchange rate. Describe what happens, before and after full price adjustment, when:

a) government spending is reduced permanently.

b) the money supply is reduced permanently.

Chapter 9

10 POLICY

FOCUS OF THE CHAPTER

This chapter highlights three factors that hinder policymakers: lags, expectations, and uncertainty.

It also considers the choice of targets and implementation strategies for particular policy goals.

SECTION SUMMARIES

1. Lags in the Effects of Policy

In practice, it is very difficult to use fiscal policy to stabilize output. First, it is necessary to determine whether a disturbance is temporary or permanent (or at least very persistent). If it is temporary, it may be best to do nothing at all; the effects of the disturbance may have worn off before a policy change is felt. The policy change may actually *destabilize* output.

After a disturbance has been deemed worthy of a policy response, there are more delays. We must first decide what policy to use; that policy must then be implemented. We must then wait for the policy to take effect. All of these delays have names: the time required to recognize that a policy response is necessary is called the *recognition lag*; the time required to choose the appropriate policy response is referred to as the *decision lag*; and the length of time required to implement a policy once it has been decided upon is called the *action lag*. These three lags are grouped together, and the amount of time between the point at which a disturbance hits the economy and the point at which a policy response is implemented is referred to, generally, as the *inside lag*. The amount of time required for a policy to have its full effect, once it has been implemented, is called the *outside lag*.

The inside lag is a *discrete lag*—an amount of time that passes before *anything* happens. The outside lag, on the other hand, is a *distributed lag*; the effects are cumulative, and only gradually take effect.

Inside lags are avoided with *automatic stabilizers*, which are mechanisms that reduce the size of output changes in response to changes in autonomous demand. Examples are income tax and unemployment benefits.

Monetary policy has a very short inside lag. Open market operations can be undertaken almost as soon as the decision to use them is made. Fiscal policy has a fairly long inside lag. For this reason, monetary policy is used more frequently than fiscal policy to stabilize output. The outside lag associated with monetary policy is longer than the outside lag associated with fiscal policy.

2. Expectations and Reactions

Policymakers do not know the precise values of the multipliers which tell them how strongly their policy will affect aggregate demand. They also do not know how people will react to the implementation of their policy: Will consumers believe that a "permanent" tax cut is really temporary? That a temporary tax cut will last longer than policymakers claim?

The implementation of a policy may itself affect expectations. Lucas, in his *econometric policy evaluation critique* (often referred to simply as the *Lucas critique*), argues that many existing macroeconomic models cannot be used to study the effects of policy changes because the way that people respond to those changes depends on the policy that is being followed.

Credibility can also be a problem for policymakers. If people do not believe the announcements that a government makes, their expectations will be unaffected and they may not respond to policy changes the way that policymakers anticipate.

3. Uncertainty and Economic Policy

Stabilization policy could fail because an unforeseen event, such as a natural disaster or change in consumer preferences, occurs. It could fail also if policymakers use the wrong model to analyze the impact of their policy, or because they use the right model, but with badly estimated parameters. None of us know enough about the true structure and workings of the economy to accurately and confidently predict all of the effects of any policy.

When we are uncertain about the size of the multipliers associated with different policies, it may be a good idea to use a mix of different policies—mildly expansionary fiscal policy for example, with mildly expansionary monetary policy. With luck, the unexpected effects of both policies will cancel each other out.

The more uncertain we are, the less willing we should be to use activist policy. A combination of active policy and poor information runs the risk of introducing unnecessary fluctuations into the economy.

4. Dynamic Policy and Information Feedback

A policymaker can use either *gradualist* or *cold-turkey* policies to reach an objective. Each has its advantages and disadvantages.

Gradualist policies move the economy slowly toward its target. This is a drawback if you're in a hurry, but it does allow policymakers to monitor a policy's effects as they roll through the economy, and to fine-tune their policy as new information becomes available. Contractionary policies also tend to produce fewer recessionary side effects when they are implemented gradually, as the effects of the contraction are spread out over a longer period of time. Unfortunately gradualist policies can also lack credibility; often they move so slowly it doesn't look as if the government is doing anything at all. People's expectations can play an important role in determining a policy's success or failure.

Cold-turkey policies solve the credibility problem. That is the main reason for using them. They can produce severe side effects, however, so authorities will usually choose another strategy if one is available.

Policymakers divide variables into several different classes when they formulate and implement policy: *targets*, or a set of variables with some desired value (a real interest rate of 4 percent, for example, or an inflation rate of 2 percent); *instruments*, or the variables whose value a policymaker manipulates to achieve these targets (nominal money balances are an example); and *indicators*, a set of variables whose value signals the policy's success or failure. A particular variable, the nominal interest rate for example, can switch categories as policymakers' tactics change—sometimes used as an indicator, other times used as a target.

Chapter 10

There are two types of targets: *ultimate* and *intermediate*. An ultimate target is just what it sounds like—the goal we hope to achieve through the implementation of a policy (2 percent inflation, for example, or 5 percent output growth). An intermediate target is something a little trickier; because sometimes these ultimate targets are a little hard to shoot for, an intermediate target is less directly important but easier to measure and attain (2 percent money growth to correspond to that ultimate goal of 2 percent inflation, for example).

5. Activist Policy

Proponents of activist policy argue that we should use monetary and fiscal policy to reduce economic fluctuations. While some economists argue against the use of active policy entirely, the authors feel that active policy is appropriate as long as policymakers recognize the uncertainty involved, take into account the lags associated with their policy, and are appropriately modest in their attempts to counteract the effects of disturbances.

Critics of activist monetary policy argue that the monetary authority should be forced to follow the rules rather than being able to use policy at its discretion.

6. Dynamic Inconsistency and Rules Versus Discretion

This section argues that well-intentioned policymakers who have the discretion to implement activist policies will be tempted to act, in the short run, in a way that is not consistent with the long-run goals and interests of the economy. They may, for example, be tempted to raise output and reduce unemployment in the short run, only to cause inflation in the long run.

This problem is referred to as dynamic inconsistency, as rational, well-intended policymakers find it optimal to deviate from policies (e.g., low inflation) they have committed to.

7. Working with Data: Recent Monetary Policy

Students are asked to plot unemployment, inflation, and interest data for Canada for the years 1977–2000 and examine them in light of the policy discussion in Box 10-1 of the text.

THE LANGUAGE OF ECONOMICS

Key Terms

permanent disturbance
transitory disturbance
inside lag
outside lag
recognition lag
decision lag
action lag
automatic stabilizer
discrete lag
distributed lag
econometric model
credibility
econometric policy evaluation critique
multiplier uncertainty

portfolio of policy instruments (diversification)
loss function
marginal loss function
certainty equivalence policy
targets
instruments
indicators
activist policies
fine tuning
rules vs. discretion
activist rules
dynamic inconsistency
dynamic programming

Stabilization

Usually when economists talk about "stabilizing" the economy, they mean that they want to dampen output fluctuations—reduce the size of recessions and booms, so that the path of output over time is smoother. In an AS-AD framework, this means using fiscal and monetary policy to keep output as close as possible to potential, or full-employment, output.

FILL-IN QUESTIONS

1. The time required for policymakers to realize the need for, develop, and implement a policy to counteract an economic disturbance is referred to as the _____ lag.

2. The length of time for this policy, once implemented, to have its full effect is called the _____ lag.

3. The three handicaps of policy making are _____, _____, _____.

4. The amount of time required for policymakers to evaluate and choose a policy that will counteract an economic disturbance is referred to as the _____ lag.

5. Countercyclical policies that require no discretionary action on the part of policymakers are called _____.

6. The _____ lag is much longer for fiscal than for monetary policy.

7. The _____ lag is much shorter for fiscal than for monetary policy.

8. The _____ suggests that the implementation of a policy may itself affect expectations.

9. Economic variables that are the identified goals of policy are known as _____ .

10. Economic variables that are the tools that the policymaker manipulates directly are known as _____.

TRUE-FALSE QUESTIONS

T F 1. It is quite simple to use monetary and fiscal policies to stabilize output.

T F 2. The world is no more complicated than our models suggest.

T F 3. The decision lag is shorter for monetary policy than it is for fiscal policy.

T F 4. Most economists agree that the best way for policymakers to reach ultimate targets is to avoid being distracted by "indicators" and to pay attention only to target variables.

T F 5. An automatic stabilizer is any mechanism in the economy that makes output more sensitive to changes in autonomous demand.

T F 6. The implementation of a policy may itself affect people's expectations.

T F 7. If we are uncertain about the size of the multipliers associated with different policies, we should *not* mix the policies.

T F 8. Even well-intentioned policymakers who have the discretion to implement activist policies will be tempted to act, in the short run, in a way that is not consistent with the long-run goals and interests of the economy.

MULTIPLE-CHOICE QUESTIONS

1. A policymaker should be more willing to act when he or she believes a shock is:

   a. temporary
   b. discrete

   c. permanent
   d. contractionary

2. Which of the following types of uncertainty hinder effective policy implementation?

   a. multiplier uncertainty
   b. uncertainty about a shock's permanence

   c. model uncertainty
   d. all of the above

3. A policymaker might choose to adopt a "cold-turkey" policy because

   a. it has a shorter inside lag
   b. it may give the policymaker more credibility

   c. it reduces multiplier uncertainty
   d. the indicators are more reliable

4. Which of the following does *not* make it difficult for policymakers to stabilize output with fiscal policy?

   a. long inside lag
   b. short outside lag

   c. multiplier uncertainty
   d. long decision lag

5. The outside lag associated with monetary policy is

   a. discrete
   b. distributed

   c. diversified
   d. activist

6. The inside lag associated with fiscal policy is

   a. discrete
   b. distributed

   c. diversified
   d. activist

CONCEPTUAL PROBLEMS

1. What do you think about the "rules vs. discretion" debate? Do you favour rules or discretion?

2. Do you think policymakers should try to "fine-tune" the economy? Why or why not?

WORKING WITH DATA

Does tight monetary policy put people out of work? You might think that we could answer such a question by simply graphing the unemployment rate against the level of real money balances. This would be a dangerous way to answer the question because it ignores the influence of fiscal policy on unemployment. Nevertheless, in this section we will do it anyway.

Table 10-1 provides data on the level of unemployment, the nominal money supply, and the price level for the years 1990–1998. You will have to calculate the level of real money balances by hand. This isn't so bad; it just involves dividing some measure of the nominal money supply (we use M1) by another measure of the price level (we use the CPI). After you have calculated the level of real money balances, you should plot the rate of unemployment against it for each year in the sample. We've plotted the first two data points to get you started (see Table 10-1 and Chart 10-1). You do the rest.

Does it look like an increase in the real money supply will reduce the rate of unemployment? (If you fit a line to the points you have drawn, would it slope downward? If so, your answer should be yes.)

TABLE 10-1

Year	Unemployment	M1	CPI	Real Money Balances
1990	8.1	40.9	93.3	0.438
1991	10.4	42.4	98.5	0.430
1992	11.3	47.5	100.0	
1993	11.2	53.7	101.8	
1994	10.4	56.7	102.0	
1995	9.5	61.5	104.2	
1996	9.7	70.1	105.9	
1997	9.2	80.0	107.6	
1998	8.3	86.1	108.6	

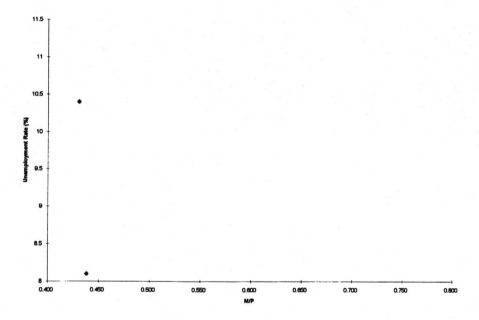

Chart 10-1

APPLICATION QUESTIONS

1. Suppose we know that $Y = \beta M$, where Y is output (the target variable), M is the money supply, (the policy variable), and β is the monetary policy multiplier. The policymaker's target value for Y is $Y^* = 10$. The loss function is $L = .5(Y - Y^*)^2$. Find the value of M that minimizes the expected loss function (that is, sets the weighted average marginal loss function to zero) in the following cases. In each case, the expected value of β is equal to 2.

   a) $\beta = 2$

   b) $\beta = 1.5$ with probability .5 and $\beta = 2.5$ with probability .5

   c) $\beta = 1$ with probability 2/3 and $\beta = 4$ with probability 1/3

2. A policymaker faced with an inflation-unemployment tradeoff decides to minimize the loss function $L = a(u - u^*) + \beta^2$ where the expected inflation and natural unemployment rates are such that the expectations-augmented Phillips curve is $\beta = .06 + 2(.08 - u)$ (note $u^* = .08$). Determine the loss-minimizing inflation and unemployment rates for the following values of the policy tradeoff coefficient.

   a) $a = .4$

   b) $a = .2$

   c) $a = .1$

11 INCOME AND SPENDING

FOCUS OF THE CHAPTER

This chapter takes a closer look at the way that changes in the goods market affect aggregate demand by examining the link between income and spending—i.e., we use the fundamental national income identity $(Y = C + I + G + NX)$ to analyze the way in which changes in consumption affect output, but treat both income and consumption as endogenous variables.

A basic result is that an increase in autonomous spending will increase output by an amount greater than the spending increase.

SECTION SUMMARIES

1. Aggregate Demand and Equilibrium Output

The fundamental national income accounting identity, $Y = C + I + G$, states that the *actual* level of output must always equal the sum of all the different sources of aggregate demand. (Notice that we're ignoring net exports, NX, for the moment; we'll talk about how to incorporate these into our analysis in Section 7.) It is easy, however, to imagine a situation in which *planned* levels of output differ from *planned* levels of consumption, investment, and government spending. When this happens, the goods market is not in equilibrium: the quantity of output produced does not equal the quantity demanded. Unintended changes in inventories occur.

These unplanned inventory changes cause firms to increase or decrease their production. The level of output rises or falls accordingly, and brings the goods market back into equilibrium.

2. The Consumption Function and Aggregate Demand

Increased income causes increased consumption. This relationship is captured by the *consumption function*:

$$C = \bar{C} + cY$$

where c is a number between zero and one, and $\bar{C}$ is positive.

The fraction of each additional dollar of income that is consumed is represented by the variable c in the equation above and called the *marginal propensity to consume* (mpc). The fraction that is saved is equal to $(1 - c)$, and is called the **marginal propensity to save** (mps). Neither the mpc or mps can be greater than 1; that would mean that people were increasing consumption or saving by an amount greater than the increase in income. The amount that people choose to consume when their income is zero—the variable $\overline{C}$ — is positive because people consume out of wealth as well as income.

Since saving $(Y - C)$ is just the difference between income and consumption, saving and consumption cannot be looked at independently. A specific consumption function implies a specific savings function.

If we add a government sector to this model and force individuals to pay taxes $(\overline{T})$, the consumption function changes slightly:

$$C = \overline{C} + c(Y - \overline{T})$$

so that consumption now depends on **disposable**, or after tax, **income (YD)**. If we assume that investment and government spending are exogenously determined, we can now write aggregate demand as

$$AD = C + \overline{I} + \overline{G} = \overline{C} + c(Y - \overline{T}) + \overline{I} + \overline{G}$$

or, defining a new variable $\overline{A} = \overline{C} + \overline{I} + \overline{G} - c\overline{T}$, as

$$AD = \overline{A} + cY$$

We can find the level of output for which the goods market is in equilibrium (Y_0) by imposing the requirement $Y = AD$. This can be accomplished graphically, as in Figure 11-1, by finding the point at which the lines $Y = AD$ and $AD = \overline{A} \times cY$ intersect. It can also be accomplished algebraically, by solving the equation $Y_0 = AD = \overline{A} + cY_0$.

(It turns out that $Y_0 = \dfrac{1}{1 - c} \overline{A}$.)

We can also get this result by setting total saving (government + personal) in our economy equal to planned investment $((\overline{T} - G) + S = \overline{I}$, where $S = Y - C)$.

3. The Multiplier

A \$1 increase in *autonomous* spending (the term $\overline{A}$ introduced in the previous section), in general, increases GDP by more than \$1.

> *The goods market is in equilibrium when the quantity of output produced is equal to the quantity demanded, or when Y = AD.*

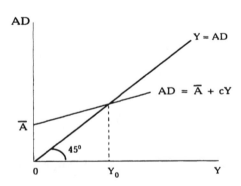

Figure 11-1

A GRAPHIC REPRESENTATION OF THE GOODS MARKET EQUILIBRIUM

Let's follow this $1 of spending through the economy: The first thing it does is to create one additional dollar of income for those people who helped to produce and sell the goods and services it purchased. Once in their pockets, a fraction c of it is spent and a fraction $(1 - c)$ is saved, so that an amount $(c \times \$1)$, or $\$c$, goes on to become income for others. They, in turn, spend a fraction c and save a fraction $(1 - c)$; an amount $(c \times c \times \$1)$, or $\$c^2$, moves on to become income for still others.

As this process continues, the original $1 spending increase generates an increase in income (and output) of $(1 + c + c^2 + c^3 + ...) \times \$1$, or $(1/(1 - c)) \times \$1$, as the **infinite geometric series** $(1 + c + c^2 + c^3 + ...)$ can be written as $1/(1 - c)$ when $c < 1$. (This chapter's "Review of Technique" shows why this is the case.)

We call the number $1/(1- c)$ **the multiplier**, as it describes the amount by which that initial $1 is multiplied as it changes hands, and is spent again and again. Note than an increase in the mpc (the variable c) makes this multiplier larger.

4. The Government Sector

In this section we develop a more complete government sector. We assume, first of all, that the government can transfer money directly to households. We also assume that it collects a proportional income tax. Everyone pays the government a constant fraction t of their income, and keeps a fraction $1 - t$. Disposable income is equal to $(Y + TR - tY)$, where TR represents a fixed government transfer.

The consumption function becomes

$$C = \bar{C} + c\overline{TR} + c(1 - t)Y$$

reducing the multiplier to:

$$\alpha_G = \frac{1}{1 - c(1 - t)}$$

Because it makes the multiplier smaller, so that shocks to autonomous spending have less of an impact on the output and unemployment, the income tax is considered an **automatic stabilizer.**

Transfers, because they initially increase aggregate demand by only $c\overline{TR}$ (some of the transfer is saved), have a smaller multiplier: $c\alpha_G$.

5. The Budget

The **budget surplus** (BS) is defined as the difference between the money that the government takes in and the money that the government spends:

$$BS = TA - G - TR$$

When a proportional income tax is assumed, as in the previous section, measures of the budget surplus change both because of changes in government policy (G, t, TR) and because the level of output changes. We should, therefore, not be surprised to see the budget surplus shrink (or become more negative) in recessions, when output falls.

A negative budget surplus is called a **budget deficit**.

6. The Full-Employment Budget Surplus

The *full-employment budget surplus* (BS*) is a measure of what the budget surplus would be if the economy were at full-employment. It responds to only changes in government policy, and is not affected by the business cycle. For this reason it can be an indicator of fiscal policy: A full-employment budget deficit, for example, would suggest that fiscal policy is expansionary—tending to increase output.

7. The Foreign Sector

Including net exports, NX, in the basic accounting identity gives $AD = C + I + G + NX$. We treat exports as fixed, $X = \overline{X}$, and imports depend positively on income, $Q = \overline{Q} + mY$, so that $NX = \overline{X} - \overline{Q} - mY$. Combining the equilibrium condition $Y = AD$ with the consumption function and this net export function gives $Y = \overline{A} + [c(1 - t) - m]Y$, where now $\overline{A}$ is redefined as $\overline{A} = \overline{C} + c\overline{TR} + \overline{I} + \overline{G} + \overline{X} - \overline{Q}$.

The equilibrium condition is now $Y_0 = [1/(1 - c(1 - t) + m)]\ \overline{A}$.

Countries' income levels are interrelated. For example, an increase in income in the U.S. will increase the demand in the U.S. for Canada's exports, which in turn increases income in Canada. Three factors that influence the size of these effects are: the sizes of the economies, their openness to trade, and the extent to which they trade with each other.

8. Working with Data

The student is asked to reproduce a time series plot of the Canadian federal government's actual and cyclically adjusted budget deficits.

THE LANGUAGE OF ECONOMICS

Key Terms

aggregate demand	multiplier
equilibrium level of output	fiscal policy
consumption function	automatic stabilizer
marginal propensity to consume	budget surplus/deficit
budget constraint	balanced budget multiplier
marginal propensity to save	full-employment budget surplus
disposable income	marginal propensity to import

Autonomous Spending

Autonomous spending is spending that is *exogenously determined*—that is, it is not affected by any of the other variables in our model. In this chapter, this means specifically that it must be independent of income. In the next, we will find that it must be independent of interest rates as well.

Even when a variable itself is endogenously determined—consumption, in this chapter's model, is an example—it may have an exogenous, or autonomous, component.

REVIEW OF TECHNIQUE

Infinite Geometric Series

This section shows you how to calculate the sum of an infinite geometric series—a series of the form

$$S = 1 + c + c^2 + c^3 + c^4 + \dots$$

that goes on forever (i.e., the exponents approach infinity).

Suppose that c is a number between zero and one. When this is the case, there is a useful trick that we can use to find the value of S (the series' sum): We multiply every term in our geometric series by c, creating a new series

$$cS = c + c^2 + c^3 + c^4 + c^5 + \dots$$

and then subtract this new series from our original one

$$S - cS = 1 + (c - c) + (c^2 - c^2) + (c^3 - c^3) + \dots$$

This allows us to solve for S, the sum of the original series:

$$S - cS = 1 + (c - c) + (c^2 - c^2) + (c^3 - c^3) + \dots$$

$$S - cS = 1 + 0 + 0 + 0 + \dots = 1$$

$$S(1 - c) = 1$$

or,

$$S = \frac{1}{1 - c}$$

IN QUESTIONS 1 TO 10 BELOW, WE INCLUDE A GOVERNMENT SECTOR BUT NOT A FOREIGN SECTOR.

FILL-IN QUESTIONS

1. When planned and actual spending are equal, the goods market is in _____.

2. In this chapter's model of aggregate demand, consumption is an _____ variable.

3. A $1 increase in income will increase consumption by $1 times the _____ , in the absence of income taxes.

4. Consumption, in this chapter, is assumed to be a function of _____.

5. Output increases by a greater amount than autonomous spending because of the _____.

6. The complement of the marginal propensity to consume is the _____.

7. The difference between government expenditure and taxes is called the _____.

8. A(n) _____ is a program, such as unemployment insurance, that reduces the impact of shocks on the economy without any direct government intervention.

9. The difference between the taxes that *would* be taken in, if the economy were at full-employment, and government expenditure is called the _____.

10. The balanced budget multiplier is always equal to _____.

11. A higher marginal propensity to import leads to a _____ multiplier.

12. The model assumes that one of exports and imports depends on income. Which one? _____.

TRUE-FALSE QUESTIONS

T F   1. Raising the income tax rate should increase GDP.

T F   2. An increase in the marginal propensity to consume (mpc) should decrease GDP.

T F   3. An increase in the mpc should decrease the mps.

T F   4. An increase in the mpc should increase the equilibrium level of investment.

T F   5. The mpc is an endogenous variable.

T F   6. An increase in disposable income will increase consumption.

T F   7. An increase in disposable income will increase the mpc.

T F   8. An increase in autonomous spending will have no effect on the equilibrium level of output.

T F   9. An increase in the mpc will increase autonomous spending.

T F   10. Output should fluctuate less when automatic stabilizers are present than when they aren't.

MULTIPLE-CHOICE QUESTIONS

1. When we say that investment and government spending are *autonomous*, we mean that they are

    a. exogenous variables   c. automatic stabilizers
    b. endogenous variables   d. none of the above

2. When aggregate demand is greater than output, there is unplanned

    a. inventory accumulation   c. saving
    b. inventory reduction   d. consumption

3. An increase in the mpc will _____ the multiplier.

    a. increase   c. not affect
    b. decrease   d. who knows?

4. An increase in the mpc will _____ the mps (marginal propensity to save).

    a. increase   c. not affect
    b. decrease   d. who knows?

5. Income taxes _____ the multiplier.

    a. increase   c. do not affect
    b. decrease   d. who knows?

6. Government purchases will have _____ effect on output in an economy *without* income taxes than it will have in an economy with them.

    a. a greater   c. it depends on the tax rate
    b. less of an   d. it depends on the mpc

7. If the mpc = 0.8 and there are no income taxes, the multiplier will be

   a. 1   c. 5
   b. 2   d. 10

8. If the mpc = 0.8 and there are no income taxes, the multiplier relating changes in *transfer payments* to changes in national income will be

   a. 4   c. 6
   b. 5   d. 8

9. If the mpc = 0.8 and there is a $0.375 tax levied on each dollar of income, the multiplier will be

   a. 1   c. 5
   b. 2   d. 10

10. If the mpc = 0.8 and there is a $0.375 tax levied on each dollar of income, a $40 increase in government purchases will cause the budget surplus to

    a. increase by $10   c. increase by $40
    b. decrease by $10   d. decrease by $40

11. If the mpc = 0.8, there is a $0.25 tax levied on each dollar of income, and the marginal propensity to import is 0.2, then the multiplier will be

    a. 1.7   c. 2.5
    b. 2   d. 5

12. If the mpc = 0.8, there is a $0.25 tax levied on each dollar of income, and the marginal propensity to import is 0.2, then a $60 increase in government purchases will cause the budget surplus to

    a. increase by $60   c. decrease by $35
    b. increase by $100   d. decrease by $60

CONCEPTUAL PROBLEMS

1. Which will increase output more: a $1 million increase in government spending, or a $1 million increase in government transfers? Why?

2. Which of the following variables are endogenously determined in this chapter's model of aggregate demand? Which are exogenously determined? *(See "The Language of Economics" in Chapter 1 for a review of endogenous and exogenous variables.)*

   a) income   d) consumption
   b) output   e) investment
   c) disposable income   f) autonomous spending

3. Why might the budget deficit be a bad measure of the direction of fiscal policy?

4. In what way is the full-employment budget surplus a better measure of the direction of fiscal policy than is the actual budget surplus?

APPLICATION QUESTIONS

1. Find the savings function that is implied by the following consumption function:
   (*Hint: Remember that S = Y – C.*)

   $$C = \overline{C} + cY$$

2. Consider an economy with no income taxes or net exports where the mpc = 0.9.

   a) What is the value of the multiplier associated with autonomous spending (αG)?

   b) How much will output in this economy increase if government expenditures are increased by $100.

   c) How much will output in this economy increase if government transfers are increased by $100?

3. Now suppose that this economy imposes a proportional income tax, $t = 1/3$.

   a) What is the value of the multiplier (αG) now?

   b) How much will output in this economy increase if government spending rises by $100?

   c) How will this affect the government budget surplus/deficit?

4. Now suppose that, in addition to the income tax of Question 3, there is also a marginal propensity to import equal to 0.1.

   a) What is the value of the multiplier now?

   b) How much will output in this economy increase if government spending rises by $100?

   c) How will this affect the government budget surplus/deficit?

QUESTIONS 5 TO 10 REFER TO THE FOLLOWING MODEL:

$AD = C + I + G + NX$	(aggregate demand)
$IU = Y - AD = 0$	(unplanned additions to inventories equals zero)
$C = 10 + .8(Y + TR - TA)$	(consumption)
$TR = 20$	(government transfers)
$TA = .25Y$	(tax revenue)
$BS = TA - TR - G$	(government budget surplus)
$I = 20$	(investment)
$G = 30$	(government spending on goods and services)
$NX = 0$	(net exports equals zero)

5. Divide the variables into two groups: exogenous and endogenous.

6. Solve for the numerical values of all of the endogenous variables. (Do not substitute the numerical values for G and TR until near the end of your solution. This will make it much easier to answer some of the following questions.)

7. Find the value of the multiplier.

8. Compare the effect on output of increasing government spending G by two units with the effect on output of increasing transfers TR.

9. Solve for the value of government spending G that would be necessary, given the values of the other exogenous variables, for the government budget surplus to equal zero (a balanced budget).

10. Suppose that the full employment output level was $Y^* = 202$, and that at the originally given values of G and TR, there was a change in net exports NX sufficient to achieve an output level $Y = 202$.

   a) What is the new value of NX?

   b) Solve for BS in this new situation. This is BS*, the full-employment budget surplus.

12 MONEY, INTEREST, AND INCOME

FOCUS OF THE CHAPTER

This chapter introduces the IS-LM model—the heart of short-run macroeconomic theory.

The simple model of Chapter 11 is extended to include the interaction of goods and money markets, which, together, uniquely determine both the interest rate and the position of the AD curve.

Both investment and the interest rate are now endogenous variables: Investment is a function of the interest rate, which is determined by the equilibrium conditions for goods and money markets.

SECTION SUMMARIES

1.   The Goods Market and the *IS* Curve

This section derives the **IS curve**. The IS curve shows all of the combinations of income and the interest rate for which the goods market is in equilibrium (Y = AD). This equilibrium turns out to be a function of the interest rate because AD is now a function of the interest rate. We develop an investment function, which shows that the level of investment falls when interest rates increase.

Our investment function is written as follows:

$$I = \overline{I} - bi$$

where i is the real interest rate, $\overline{I}$ is a constant which represents **autonomous investment**, and b is a coefficient which measures the responsiveness of investment spending to changes in the interest rate.

If we imagine that firms borrow the money that they use for investment, it is easy to see why their investment decisions should be affected by the interest rate: higher real interest rates mean more expensive loans, and therefore lower returns on investment opportunities.

When we incorporate this investment function into our AD schedule from Section 11-7, we find that AD is now a function of the interest rate as well:

$$AD = (\overline{C} + cY) + (\overline{I} - bi) + \overline{G} + \overline{NX}$$

or, allowing both income taxes and transfers,

$$AD = (\overline{C} + c[(1-t)Y + \overline{TR}] + (\overline{I} - bi) + \overline{G} + \overline{NX}$$
$$= A + c(1-t)Y - bi$$

where $\bar{A} = \bar{C} + c\bar{TR} + \bar{I} + \bar{G} + \bar{NX}$. $\bar{A}$, as before, represents autonomous spending. Here we assume net exports $\bar{NX}$ are exogenous, to simplify a bit.

As before, we can find the level of output for which the goods market is in equilibrium by imposing the requirement $Y = AD$. The only difference now is that there will be one of these equilibria for each value of i, the real interest rate. We derive the IS curve by allowing the interest rate to vary, and plotting the combinations of i and Y for which the goods market is in equilibrium. This is done graphically in Figure 12-1. It is also done algebraically, below:

$$Y = \bar{A} + c(1 - t)Y - bi$$
$$Y - c(1 - t)Y = \bar{A} - bi$$
$$(1 - c(1 - t))Y = \bar{A} - bi$$

or,

$$Y = \frac{1}{1 - c(1 - t)} \, (\bar{A} - bi)$$

which tells us that the IS curve is negatively sloped. Notice that the term $\dfrac{1}{1 - c(1 - t)}$ is the multiplier (α_G) that we found in Chapter 11. An increase in this multiplier—caused either by an increase in the mpc or a decrease in the tax rate—makes the IS curve flatter.*

Just as in Chapter 11 a change in the autonomous spending changed the equilibrium level of output, a change in autonomous spending here shifts the IS curve—changes the equilibrium level of output for each interest rate. An increase shifts the IS curve outward; a decrease shifts it inward.

---

* The slope of the IS curve is $- \dfrac{(1 - c(1 - t))}{b}$, or $\dfrac{-1}{b\alpha_G}$.

You can show this for yourself by simply writing i as a function of Y (the IS curve is drawn with the interest rate, rather than the level of output, on the vertical axis).

Chapter 12

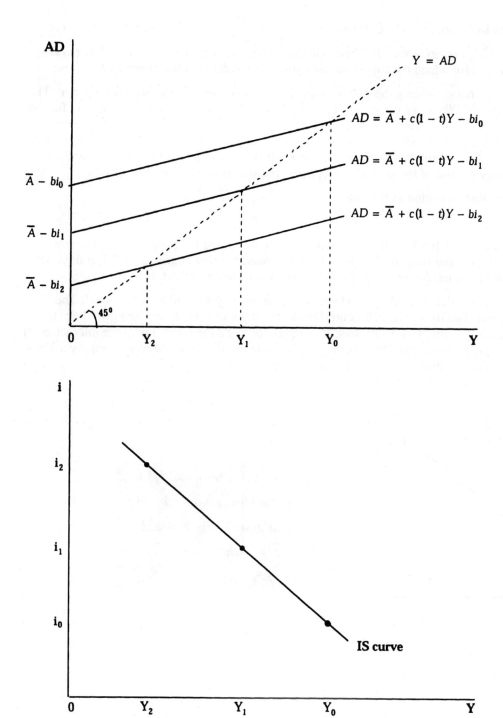

Figure 12-1

DERIVING THE IS CURVE

2. The Money Market and the *LM* Curve

This section reviews the requirements for equilibrium in the money market, and derives the ***LM curve***— the combinations of *i* and *Y* for which the supply of money equals the demand for money.

The demand for money increases when people's incomes rise, and decreases when interest rates rise. The reason for the first is simple: When our incomes rise, we need to hold more money in order to pay for the extra goods we buy. The reason we want to hold less money when interest rates rise has to do with the ***opportunity cost of holding money***: when we choose to hold money, rather than keeping our money in an interest bearing asset, we fail to earn the market rate of interest. When real interest rates rise, therefore, the cost of holding money instead of these other assets rises, and we choose to hold less money.

The money demand function is written as follows:

$$L = kY - hi$$

where k and h are constants which reflect the sensitivity of money demand to changes in income and in the interest rate, respectively. The function *L* represents the demand for ***real balances*** (M/P). It does not represent the demand for ***nominal balances*** (M); simple inflation shouldn't affect it.

The supply of real balances is determined by two factors: the money supply, and the price level. The money supply (M) is controlled by a country's central bank (the Bank of Canada in Canada). The price level (P), as we have already learned, is determined in both the long and the short run by the interaction of aggregate supply and aggregate demand. We assume, for the moment, that both the money supply and the price level are fixed, so that the supply of real balances is constant at the level $\overline{M}/\overline{P}$

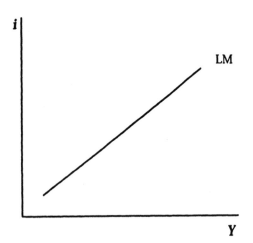

> *The LM curve shows all of the combinations of output and the real interest rate for which the market for real money balances is in equilibrium.*

Figure 12-2

THE LM CURVE

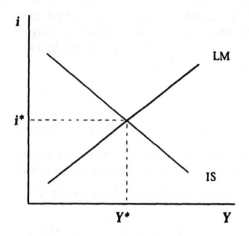

The combination of output and the interest rate at which the IS and LM curves intersect is the only one that brings both the goods market and the money market into equilibrium

Figure 12-3

IS-LM EQUILIBRIUM

We can write the equilibrium condition for the money market (the demand for real balances must equal the supply of real balances) as

$$\overline{M}/\overline{P} = kY - hi$$

Solving this for i gives us the equation for the LM curve:

$$i = \frac{1}{h}\left[kY - \frac{\overline{M}}{\overline{P}}\right]$$

Notice first that the LM curve is upward-sloping in Y, as the constants k and h are positive.

Notice also that an increase in real money balances ($\overline{M}/\overline{P}$) will shift it outward, or downward, and that a decrease in real balances will shift it inward (upward).

Real balances can change either because nominal balances change (the money supply changes), or because the price level changes. Because the AD curve is graphed in P and Y, however, a change in the price level causes movement along the AD curve rather than a shift in it.

3. Equilibrium in the Goods and Money Markets

The levels of output and the interest rate at which the IS and LM curves intersect are the only ones for which both the goods market and the money market are in equilibrium.

A shift in either curve will change the combination of i and Y at which this equilibrium occurs.

4. Deriving the Aggregate Demand Schedule

This section derives the AD curve by varying the price level for which the LM curve is drawn, and observing the way that this changes the IS-LM equilibrium. The combinations of P and Y that result sketch out a downward-sloping AD curve.

Application Question 3 of the text gives you the opportunity to see this for yourself. As you change the price level in order to generate the AD relationship, notice that you are holding the money supply and the level of autonomous spending constant. Any change in these variables, therefore, will cause the AD curve to shift—inward, if the level of income that brings goods and money markets into equilibrium falls, and outward if this level falls.

A change in the price level will just cause a movement along the AD curve.

5. A Formal Treatment of the *IS-LM* Model (optional section)

Since both the IS and the LM curves are described by linear equations, we can solve these equations simultaneously to find the equilibrium levels of output and the interest rate.

Combining the equations for the IS and LM curves and solving for both Y and i, we find that

$$Y = \frac{\alpha_G}{1 + k\alpha_G\,(b/h)}\,\bar{A} + \frac{b\alpha_G}{h + kb\alpha_G}\left[\frac{\bar{M}}{\bar{P}}\right]$$

and

$$i = \frac{k\alpha_G}{h + kb\alpha_G}\,\bar{A} + \frac{1}{h + kb\alpha_G}\left[\frac{\bar{M}}{\bar{P}}\right]$$

The fraction $\dfrac{\alpha_G}{1 + k\alpha_G(b/h)}$ is called the *fiscal policy multiplier*. The fraction $\dfrac{b\alpha_G}{h + kb\alpha_G}$ is called the *monetary policy multiplier*. The equation for Y is also the equation for the AD curve.

6. Working with Data

The student is asked to plot the three variables from Figure 12-1 of the text, real money growth, the interest rate and real output growth, two at a time.

THE LANGUAGE OF ECONOMICS

Key Terms

IS-LM model
IS curve goods market equilibrium schedule
LM curve money market equilibrium schedule
demand for real balances

central bank
aggregate demand schedule
fiscal policy multiplier
monetary policy multiplier

Endogenous Variables Revisited

When we first made the distinction between endogenous and exogenous variables, we had not yet worked with two equation systems. To make sure you are still comfortable with this distinction in the more complicated models you now work with, we provide this brief review.

Endogenous variables, you may remember, are determined *within* a particular model. Typically, the more equations a model involves, the more endogenous variables it is likely to have—the more variables it will determine.

Consider the IS-LM model: We take the price level as given (exogenously determined), and find the levels of output and the real interest rate for which both goods and money markets are in equilibrium. The levels of output and the interest rate are determined endogenously—by the interaction of all the other variables in the model. *Their values can never change unless one of these other variables changes*.

The same is true for the AS-AD model—the price level and the level of output are determined by the level of government spending, the taxes people are required to pay, and the size of the money supply. They are also determined by the position and slope of the AS curve. It is interesting to notice that the interest rate, which varies along the AD curve, is also endogenously determined; we cannot change it without first changing the value of some other exogenous variable. Consumption and investment also are endogenous.

REVIEW OF TECHNIQUE

Solving a Two Equation System Graphically and Algebraically

In Review of Technique 6 we learned how to graph a linear equation. In this Review of Technique, we discuss how to find the solution to two linear equations, graphically and algebraically.

Consider the following two equations:

$$Y = aX + b, \text{ and } X = -cY + d$$

If we were to graph these, we would draw two curves—one for each equation. In this instance, we would have one upward-sloping and one downward-sloping curve, which, because of their different slopes, would be guaranteed to intersect. (See Figure 12-4 below.)

We would have a very easy time solving these equations graphically: we would simply find the point at which our lines crossed, and the values of X and Y that defined that point. That would be our solution.

Solving these equations algebraically doesn't involve much more than this: We impose the assumption (or the requirement) that the values of X and Y are the same in both equations. Once we do this, we can substitute the value of X (or, if we prefer, the value of Y) from one equation into the other, and solve for the remaining variable. For example, we could write:

$$Y = a(-cY + d) + b = -acY + ad + b$$

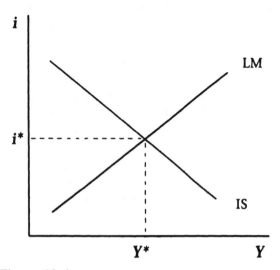

Figure 12-4

IS-LM EQUILIBRIUM

and solve as follows:

$$Y + (ac)Y = ad + b$$
$$(1 + ac)Y = ad + b$$
$$Y = (ad + b)/(1 + ac)$$

We could then plug this value of Y into either equation to find the solution for X:

$$X = -c((ad + b)/(1 + ac)) + d$$
$$X = -c((ad + b)/(1 + ac)) + d((1 + ac)/(1 + ac))$$
$$X = ((-cad - bc) + (d + cad))/(1 + ac)$$
$$X = (d - bc)/(1 + ac)$$

Algebraic solutions are particularly useful when we need to find a quantitative, rather than qualitative, solution—numbers, rather than just directions of change.

FILL-IN QUESTIONS

1. The IS curve describes all of the combinations of output and the interest rate for which the
    _____ market is in equilibrium.

2. The IS curve is downward-sloping because a decrease in the interest rate increases
    _____.

3. An increase in the marginal propensity to consume (mpc), and hence an *increase* in the multiplier α_G
    will make the IS curve _____.

4. The LM curve describes all of the combinations of output and the interest rate for which the
    _____ market is in equilibrium.

5. The LM curve is upward-sloping because when people's income rises, they want to hold more
    _____. The increase in money demand drives up the interest rate.

6. If money demand is relatively *insensitive* to the interest rate, the LM curve will be quite _____.

7. If money demand is very *sensitive* to the interest rate, the LM curve will be nearly _____.

8. _____ policy shifts the IS curve; _____ policy shifts the LM curve.

9. The interest rate and level of output (under the assumption of a fixed price level) are jointly determined by _____ for goods and money markets.

10. Any change in the equilibrium level of income in the IS-LM model, with the exception of a change in the price level, will cause the _____ curve to shift.

TRUE-FALSE QUESTIONS

T F 1. A change in the price level will shift the IS curve.

T F 2. For a given level of real money balances, there is a positive relationship between interest rates and income along the LM curve.

T F 3. An increase in government spending will shift the IS curve outward (*up and to the right*).

T F 4. An increase in the money supply will shift the LM curve outward (*down and to the right*).

T F 5. Decreasing the money supply increases investment.

T F 6. For a given level of output, there can be more than one interest rate for which the goods market is in equilibrium.

T F 7. For a given level of output there can be more than one interest rate for which the money market is in equilibrium.

T F 8. An increase in the tax rate reduces the multiplier.

T F 9. The slope of the IS curve cannot be affected by policy decisions.

T F 10. Equal increases in government purchases and transfers will shift the IS curve by the same amount.

MULTIPLE-CHOICE QUESTIONS

1. Which component of aggregate demand is the main link between goods and money markets?

   a. consumption
   b. investment
   c. government spending
   d. none of the above

2. Which of the following variables can shift the IS curve?

   a. price level
   b. money supply
   c. government spending
   d. none of the above

3. A change in the tax rate will

   a. shift the IS curve
   b. change the slope of the IS curve
   c. both
   d. neither

4. An increase in the price level will

   a. increase real money balances
   b. decrease real money balances
   c. increase nominal money balances
   d. decrease nominal money balances

5. Which of the following variables can shift the LM curve?

   a. price level
   b. money supply
   c. real money balances
   d. all of the above

6. For a fixed price level, a lower money supply leads to

   a. higher income
   b. higher interest rate
   c. both
   d. neither

7. An increase in the mpc will

   a. make the IS curve steeper
   b. make the IS curve flatter
   c. shift the IS curve outward
   d. have no effect on the IS curve

8. When investment is very sensitive to the interest rate, there will be a relatively

   a. steep IS curve
   b. flat IS curve
   c. steep LM curve
   d. flat LM curve

9. The less sensitive money demand is to changes in the interest rate, the more an increase in the money stock will

   a. increase AD
   b. lower interest rates
   c. both
   d. neither

10. Quick adjustment in the money market means that the economy is always on

   a. the IS curve
   b. the LM curve
   c. both
   d. neither

CONCEPTUAL PROBLEMS

1. Name all of the endogenous variables in the AS-AD model.

2. How are the IS-LM and AS-AD models related to each other?

3. What determines the slope of the IS curve? Will it be steeper or flatter in the presence of a proportional income tax?

4. What determines the slope of the LM curve?

APPLICATION QUESTIONS

1. Suppose that the following equations describe the economy:

$$C = 100 + .8(Y - \overline{T}) \qquad \text{(consumption)}$$

$$I = 200 - 1000i \qquad \text{(investment)}$$

$$L = \tfrac{1}{2} Y - 7000i \qquad \text{(demand for real money balances)}$$

   Suppose also that government spending (G) is $550, taxes (T) are $500, real money balances (M/P) are $900, and net exports (NX) are $0.

a) Write the formula for the IS curve.
   (Hint: When the goods market is in equilibrium, $Y = C + I + G$.)

b) Write the formula for the LM curve.
   (Hint: When the money market is in equilibrium, the supply of real money balances is equal to the demand for real money balances.)

c) What are the equilibrium levels of output (Y), the real interest rate (i), consumption (C), and investment (I)?

2. Now suppose that the government imposes a proportional income tax, so that

$$C = 100 + .8(Y - \overline{T}) \qquad \text{(consumption)}$$

$$I = 200 - 1000i \qquad \text{(investment)}$$

$$L = \tfrac{1}{2} Y - 7000i \qquad \text{(demand for real money balances)}$$

If $t = .33$ (there is a 33% income tax), government purchases (G) are \$700, net exports (NX) are \$0, and the real supply (M/P) is \$900.

a) What is the formula for the IS curve?

b) What is the formula for the LM curve?

c) What is the initial value of the budget deficit?

d) How large a change in the money supply would be necessary in order to balance the budget?

e) Why might this be a dangerous strategy for keeping the budget balanced in the long run?

3. Chart 12-1 below lines up an IS-LM diagram with an aggregate demand diagram. The IS curve, the LM curve based on the price level P_1, and the equilibrium level of income (Y_1^*) which they mutually determine on the IS-LM diagram, have been drawn. This same combination of income (Y_1^*) and the price level (P_1) are given on the AS-AD diagram below it, giving one point on the AD curve.

Draw two more LM curves on the top graph—one for a price level (P_2) greater than P_1, and another for a price level (P_0) less than P_1, and mark the equilibrium levels of output that they, and the IS curve, determine.

Drop vertical lines to mark the points (P_0, Y_0^*) and (P_2, Y_2^*) on the aggregate demand diagram. Connect the three points on the lower graph, to form an AD curve.

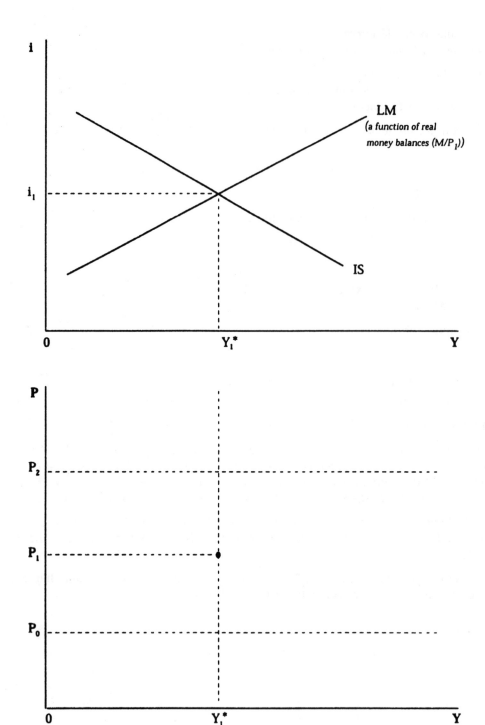

Chart 12-1

DERIVING THE AD CURVE

13 MONETARY AND FISCAL POLICY IN THE SHORT RUN

FOCUS OF THE CHAPTER

This chapter uses the IS-LM model to look at the ways that fiscal and monetary policy can be used to stabilize the economy. We find that the effectiveness of monetary and fiscal policy depends on the slopes of the IS and LM curves.

The combination of fiscal and monetary policy in an economy determines both the composition of output and the position of the AD curve.

SECTION SUMMARIES

1. Monetary Policy

The central bank conducts monetary policy by engaging in **open market operations**—by buying and selling bonds. When the Bank of Canada sells bonds, it reduces the money supply. People send money to the central bank, which it takes out of circulation; in return, they receive a piece of paper they cannot spend. When the Bank of Canada buys bonds, it increases the money supply: people exchange those pieces of paper for money.

An increase in the money supply does not initially affect people's disposable income, or the autonomous component of AD; its initial effect is to lower the interest rate. Because this raises the level of investment without reducing consumption or government spending, aggregate demand then increases. Figure 13-1 uses an IS-LM diagram to show the short-run effect of a monetary expansion.

Monetary policy is most effective when the LM curve is relatively steep, or when the demand for real money balances is not very sensitive to the interest rate (the parameter h in the money demand equation is small). It is also more effective when investment is highly sensitive to changes in the interest rate (the parameter b in the investment function is large), and when the marginal propensity to consume, c, is small—i.e., when the IS curve is relatively flat.

There are two polar cases that have received a lot of attention: The first, called a **liquidity trap**, occurs when people are willing to hold as much money as is supplied (when the money demand curve is horizontal, so that an increase in the supply of real money balances does not affect the interest rate). When the economy is in a liquidity trap, the LM curve is perfectly flat, and changes in the supply of money do not cause it to shift. Because the interest rate does not change, investment demand remains constant, and the level of aggregate demand is not affected.

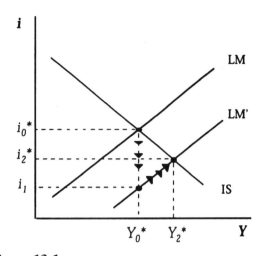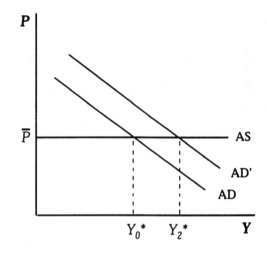

Figure 13-1

A MONETARY EXPANSION LOWERS THE INTEREST RATE, INCREASING AD.

The second—the *Classical case*—occurs when the LM curve is vertical, or when the demand for money is not a function of the interest rate. In this instance, monetary policy is most effective, and fiscal policy cannot affect the level of output at all.

2. Fiscal Policy and Crowding Out

A fiscal expansion—a decrease in taxes, or an increase in either government spending or transfers—directly increases AD, although by less than we might initially expect. An increase in autonomous demand makes people want to purchase more goods and services at any given interest rate, shifting the IS curve outward. The resulting increase in money demand, however, drives up the interest rate, which, in turn, reduces the level of investment. One force acts to increase AD; the other pushes back, preventing it from increasing as much as otherwise it would. Figure 13-2 illustrates this.

When a fiscal expansion increases the interest rate and, therefore, reduces investment demand, we say there is *crowding out*. In the classical case (when the LM curve is vertical) there is *full crowding out*—any increase in autonomous spending raises interest rates so much that the corresponding fall in investment prevents AD from increasing at all. Fiscal policy has no effect on output.

There is no crowding out when the economy is in a liquidity trap; an increase in autonomous spending has no effect on the interest rate, and thus no impact on investment. There also need not be any crowding out if the central bank *accommodates* a fiscal expansion by increasing the money supply enough to keep the interest rate at its current level. When the central bank accommodates a fiscal expansion, we also say that they are *monetizing* the budget deficit: it uses some of the money it has taken out of circulation to buy the bonds that the federal government uses to finance its deficit. Figure 13-3 provides an example.

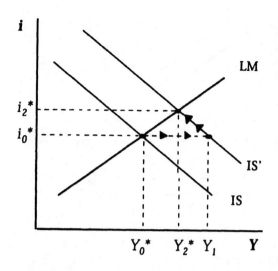
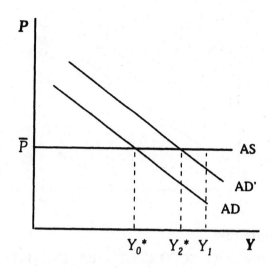

Figure 13-2

A FISCAL EXPANSION RAISES THE INTEREST RATE, CROWDING OUT INVESTMENT.
AD INCREASES, BUT NOT BY AS MUCH AS IT WOULD WITH NO CROWDING OUT.

3. The Composition of Output and the Policy Mix

Either fiscal policy or monetary policy can be used to expand aggregate demand. Expansionary fiscal policy, however, discourages investment, while expansionary monetary policy encourages it. Different methods of fiscal expansion affect the composition of output differently. The choice of policy mix—particularly the choice between spending and tax policy—can be made in such a way that other political objectives are accomplished.

4. The Policy Mix in Action

This section provides several historical examples of the ways that the policy mix decision has been made in the real world. It discusses, in particular, the combination of loose (expansionary) fiscal policy with tight (contractionary) monetary policy, and highlights the central bank's ability to combat anticipated as well as existing problems. The connection between the policy and the current or anticipated rate of inflation is discussed.

We are reminded of the difference between real and nominal interest rates: The real rate is roughly equal to the nominal rate minus the rate of inflation.

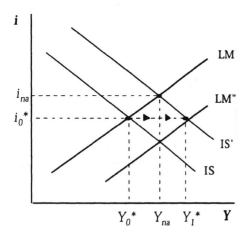
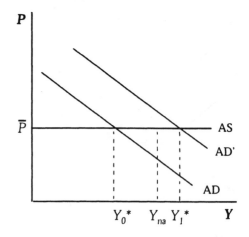

Figure 13-3

MONETARY ACCOMMODATION PREVENTS CROWDING OUT.
THE AD CURVE SHIFTS OUTWARD BY THE FULL AMOUNT.

5. Working with Data

The student is asked to graph the real interest rate against output growth, and look for a negative relationship between them.

THE LANGUAGE OF ECONOMICS

Key Terms

open market operations
transmission mechanism
portfolio disequilibrium
liquidity trap
Classical case
crowding out

monetary accommodation
investment subsidy
investment tax credit
policy mix
real interest rate

Stabilization

Usually when economists talk about "stabilizing" the economy, they mean that they want to dampen output fluctuations—reduce the size of recessions and booms, so that the path of output over time is smoother. In an AS-AD framework, this means using fiscal and monetary policy to keep output as close as possible to potential, or full-employment, output.

REVIEW OF TECHNIQUE

Working with Multipliers

A multiplier, in general, tells you the amount that some endogenously determined variable increases in response to a one unit change in some other exogenously determined variable; i.e., it tells you how far a particular curve shifts in response to a change in one of the variables that was held constant when it was drawn.

Take the multiplier

$$\alpha_G = \frac{1}{1 - c(1 - t)}$$

from Chapter 11 for example. Chapter 11 tells us that a \$1 increase in autonomous spending $(\overline{A})$ will increase output by $(\$1) \times (\alpha_G)$, or $\$\left[\dfrac{1}{1-c(1-t)}\right]$, when the level of investment is held constant.

We can interpret this as a curve shift if we recall from Chapter 12 that investment can only remain constant when the interest rate does not change. A \$1 increase in autonomous demand, therefore, will increase output by this amount, at each possible level of the interest rate. The IS curve will shift outward by an amount α_G.

However, unless the economy is in a liquidity trap, the AD curve will not shift out this far. This is because the multiplier above does not consider the effect that increased demand will have on the interest rate, and therefore on investment.

While multipliers do tell you how far, and in what direction, to shift various curves, they do *not* say anything about how these shifts affect the equilibrium values of the models' endogenous variables.

FILL-IN QUESTIONS

1. Monetary policy cannot affect output or the interest rate when the economy is in a _____.

2. Fiscal policy causes complete crowding out in the _____.

3. When money demand is relatively insensitive to the interest rate, the LM curve is _____.

4. When investment is very sensitive to the interest rate, the IS curve is _____.
   (*Hint: when investment is sensitive to the interest rate, is b large or small? Chapter 11 tells you how b affects the slope of the IS curve.*)

5. When expansionary fiscal policy raises the real interest rate and reduces investment, we say there is _____.

6. The central bank can prevent a fiscal expansion from raising the real interest rate by _____ it.

7. The real interest rate is the _____ minus _____.

8. The extent of crowding out is greater the more the _____ increases when government spending rises.

9. A fiscal expansion _____ investment.

10. The central bank can change the money supply by engaging in _____.

TRUE-FALSE QUESTIONS

T F 1. Monetary policy is more effective when the LM curve is relatively steep.

T F 2. Fiscal policy is more effective when the LM curve is relatively flat.

T F 3. Monetary policy is always more effective than fiscal policy.

T F 4. The effectiveness of monetary policy depends only on the slope of the LM curve.

T F 5. Monetary policy first affects AD, and only indirectly affects the interest rate.

T F 6. Expansionary monetary and fiscal policy affect investment differently.

T F 7. A combination of expansionary fiscal and expansionary monetary policy can be used to prevent crowding out.

T F 8. An increase of equal size in transfers and in government spending will shift the IS curve the same distance.

T F 9. An increase in the mpc will make the LM curve steeper.

T F 10. An increase in the mpc will make the IS curve flatter.

MULTIPLE-CHOICE QUESTIONS

1. Fiscal policy is most effective in

    a. the Classical case   c. France
    b. a liquidity trap   d. the long run

2. Monetary policy is most effective in

    a. the Classical case   c. Belgium
    b. a liquidity trap   d. the neo-classical growth model

3. Fiscal policy is more effective when

    a. investment is relatively sensitive to the   c. investment is relatively insensitive to the
        interest rate   interest rate
    b. sensitivity doesn't matter   d. fiscal policy is never effective

4. Monetary policy is more effective when

    a. the IS curve is steep   c. slope of IS curve doesn't matter
    b. the IS curve is flat   d. it's never effective

5. Expansionary fiscal policy generally

    a. encourages investment   c. has no effect on investment
    b. discourages investment   d. lowers the interest rate

6. Expansionary monetary policy generally

    a. encourages investment   c. has no effect on investment
    b. discourages investment   d. raises the interest rate

7. A combination of loose (expansionary) fiscal policy and tight (contractionary) monetary policy

    a. raises Y, lowers i c. raises Y, can't predict effect on i
    b. raises i, lowers Y d. raises i, can't predict effect on Y

8. Contractionary monetary policy has been used in the past to combat

   a. inflation   c. unemployment
   b. recession   d. famine

9. The central bank is able to choose whether or not to _____ a fiscal expansion.

   a. illuminate   c. accommodate
   b. prevent   d. run

10. The multiplier $\alpha_G = \dfrac{1}{1 - c(1 - t)}$ tells us how far the ____ curve shifts in response to an increase in autonomous spending.

   a. IS   c. AS
   b. LM   d. AD

CONCEPTUAL PROBLEMS

1. Will proportional income taxes make monetary policy more effective, less effective, or will their presence have no effect?

2. Will proportional income taxes increase, decrease, or not affect the expansionary effect of an increase in government spending (the amount it raises output) in the short run?

TABLE 13-1

Year	Unemployment	M1	CPI	Real Money Balances
1990	8.1	40.9	93.3	0.438
1991	10.4	42.4	98.5	0.430
1992	11.3	47.5	100.0	
1993	11.2	53.7	101.8	
1994	10.4	56.7	102.0	
1995	9.5	61.5	104.2	
1996	9.7	70.1	105.9	
1997	9.2	80.0	107.6	
1998	8.3	86.1	108.6	

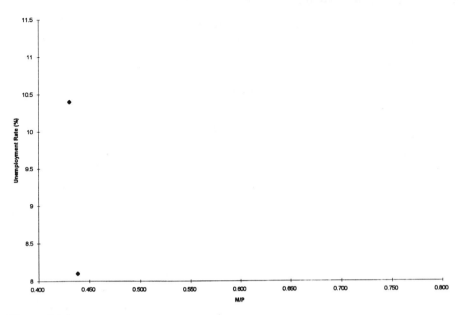

Chart 13-1

WORKING WITH DATA

Does tight monetary policy put people out of work? You might think that we could answer such a question by simply graphing the unemployment rate against the level of real money balances. This could be a misleading way to answer the question because it ignores the influence of fiscal policy on unemployment. As monetary policy seems to have been dominant in recent years, however, we'll throw caution to the winds and do it anyway.

Table 13-1 provides data on the level of unemployment, the nominal money supply, and the price level for the years 1990–1998. You will have to calculate the level of real money balances by hand. This involves dividing some measure of the nominal money supply (we use M1) by a measure of the price level (we use the CPI). After you have calculated the level of real money balances, you should plot the rate of unemployment against it for each year in the sample. The first two data points already have been plotted (see Table 13-1 and Chart 13-1).

Does it look like an increase in the real money supply will reduce the rate of unemployment? (If you fit a line to the points you have drawn, would it slope downward? If so, your answer should be yes.)

APPLICATION QUESTIONS

1. How far, and in what direction, will the IS curve shift in response to a $100 increase in government spending?

2. How far, and in what direction, will the AD curve shift in response to a $100 increase in government spending? If the LM curve is upward-sloping, should this AD shift be bigger or smaller than the IS shift in Question 1?

3. How far, and in what direction, will the LM curve shift if the money supply (M) increases $100? (Assume that the price level is constant.) *Hint: Use the equation for the LM curve: $M/P = kY - hi$. If you hold i constant and find how much Y changes, this will tell you how far (horizontally) the LM curve shifts.*

4. How far, and in what direction, will the AD curve shift in response to this $100 increase in the money supply? Should this AD shift be bigger or smaller than the LM shift in Question 3?

5. Under what conditions will the level of output increase by exactly the same amount as the shift in the AD curve?

6. Under what conditions will the level of output not be affected by changes in aggregate demand (AD shifts)?

7. Suppose that government spending were not simply exogenous. If it increased and decreased with the output gap (the difference between potential output (Y_p) and actual output (Y)) according to the rule

$$G = \bar{G} + d(Yp - Y)$$

where $d > 0$, what would happen to the slope of the IS curve? Would this make monetary policy more effective or less effective?

8. The IS part of an economy is:

    $Y = C + I + G + NX$
    $C = 30 + .9(Y - TA)$ (TR = 0)
    $TA = .2Y$
    $I = 200 - 200i$
    $NX = 300 - .12Y - 200i$

    and the LM part is:

    $M/P = 2Y - 10000i$

    The price level is P = 110. What combination of fiscal and monetary policy (values of G and M) will achieve a level of real GDP of Y = 2515 and an interest rate of I = .06?

9. The following equations describe the "IS" part of an ISLM model:

    $Y = C + I + G + NX$

    $C = 50 + .9(Y - TA)$ (TR = 0)

    $TA = .3Y$

    $I = 100 - 100i$

    $NX = 200 - .113Y - 100i$

    $G = 500$

    a) Derive the IS curve. (Express Y as a function of i only. It may help to express Y first as a function of i and G to make it easier to do part (c).)

    b) Suppose that the LM curve is $M/P = Y - 1600i$, the money supply is M = 154,000, and P = 100. What are the values of i and Y?

    c) What level of government spending G is necessary to make real output equal to Y = 1684? (M and P are the same as in part (b).)

14 INTERNATIONAL TRADE, CAPITAL MOBILITY, AND THE ECONOMY IN THE SHORT RUN

FOCUS OF THE CHAPTER

We study the relationship between capital flows and interest rates.

We show how monetary and fiscal policy operate under fixed and flexible exchange rates under the perfect capital mobility assumption, using the Mundell-Fleming model.

We look at how the presence of differences in interest rates across countries, with perfect capital mobility, can be explained by expected changes in the exchange rate.

SECTION SUMMARIES

1. Trade in Goods, Market Equilibrium, and the Balance of Trade

This section adds net exports (NX) to the IS-LM model. Domestic spending no longer determines domestic output. Instead, it depends on spending by both domestic residents and residents of other countries on domestically produced goods and services.

Spending by domestic residents (A = C + I + G) includes spending on imported goods by consumers, by investors, and by the government, and excludes the value of the goods that we export. This makes our previous measure of aggregate demand (AD = C + I + G) inadequate. To convert this into a measure of spending on domestic goods and services, we have to include the value of the goods that we export to other countries, and exclude the value of the goods and services that we import from other countries. This is done by adding net exports (exports minus imports) to the aggregate demand equation:

$$AD = C + I + G + NX$$

We assume, as in Chapter 11, that spending by domestic residents depends on their income (Y) and on the real interest rate (i). This is denoted by the domestic spending function A(Y,i). Also, these assumptions are made about exports and imports:

- Exports (X) increase when other countries' income (Y_f) rises, and when there is a real depreciation in the home country (when the real exchange rate R rises). The exports function is then $X(Y_f, R)$.

- Imports (Q) increase when the home country's income (Y) rises, and imports fall when the country experiences a real depreciation, resulting in the imports function $Q(Y,R)$.

These assumptions allow us to conclude that net exports rise when the real exchange rate rises, fall when domestic income rises, and rise when foreign income rises. The net exports function is

$$NX(Y, Y_f, R) = X(Y_f, R) - Q(Y,R)$$

We now can write a more precise equation for aggregate demand:

$$AD = A(Y,i) + NX(Y, Y_f, R)$$

Imposing the requirement for equilibrium in the goods and services market gives the IS curve:

$$Y = A(Y,i) + NX(Y, Y_f, R)$$

The fact that a fraction of domestic income is spent on foreign goods reduces the multiplier α_G and makes the IS curve steeper than it would be in a closed economy. As before, expansionary fiscal policy will shift the IS curve outward. It will not shift as far as it did in Chapter 13, because now the multiplier is smaller. An increase in foreign income also will cause an outward shift in the IS curve, as will a real depreciation.

Domestic policies have *repercussion effects*. They can affect income in other countries as well as domestic income. Expansionary fiscal policy increases income both at home and abroad. When our income rises, we import more goods from other countries. This causes their incomes to rise, so that they, in turn, import more of our goods. Everyone shares in the expansion. This is not true of changes in the real exchange rate. A real depreciation of our currency increases our income and reduces income abroad. The size of these effects depends on three chief factors: the size of the country, its openness to trade, and the extent to which trade patterns are reflected in the multipliers.

2. Capital Mobility

Once they have been adjusted for the risk associated with changes in the exchange rate, interest rates tend to be very similar across countries with well-developed capital markets when capital is highly mobile (able to flow easily across borders). If they get very far out of line, they crease an opportunity for speculators to make a substantial profit by taking their money out of countries with low interest rates and investing it in countries with high interest rates. This causes the higher interest rates to fall, as more funds become available to investors, and the lower rates to rise, as the funds that local investors in the low interest rate countries have been using are sent abroad.

We assume in this chapter that capital is *perfectly mobile*, that is, it is able to move quickly between countries, with low transaction costs, in unlimited amounts. Capital will then flow into a country whenever its interest rate is even a little above the world interest rate, and will flow out of it whenever its interest rate is below the world interest rate. This affects the capital account and therefore the balance of payments, and has implications for the use of fiscal and monetary policy.

The economy is in *external balance* when its balance of payments surplus is zero:

$$BP = NX(Y, Y_f, R) + CF(i - i_f) = 0$$

Net exports represent the current account surplus in this equation. Net capital flows (flows into the country minus flows out of the country) measure the capital account surplus. By choosing an appropriate real interest rate, the capital account surplus (or deficit) can be made to offset the current account deficit (or surplus).

The economy is in *internal balance* when output is at its full-employment level. The next two sections look at how fiscal and monetary policy can be used to keep the economy in both internal and external balance under different exchange rate regimes.

3.   Perfect Capital Mobility and Fixed Exchange Rates

As noted previously, when capital is mobile, small differences between domestic and international interest rates can generate immense capital flows, which force the interest rates to become closer. The Mundell-Fleming model imposes on the IS-LM model the requirement that domestic interest rates be fixed at the prevailing world rate, or that the balance of payments surplus be zero. By requiring that the country be in external balance, we are able to see which policies also are able to bring it into internal balance, that is to bring output as close as possible to its full employment level.

Under fixed exchange rates, the central bank must intervene in the foreign exchange market to keep the exchange rate at its agreed-upon level. In a small open economy, when capital is perfectly mobile, this means that the central bank must keep the domestic interest rate at the same level as the world interest rate at all times, so that the amounts of capital flowing in or out of the country stay in balance. This obligation prevents the central bank from using monetary policy to stabilize output, since monetary policy can affect output only by changing the interest rate.

Fiscal policy is thus the only tool the government of a small open economy can use to bring its economy into internal balance, when its exchange rate is fixed relative to that of some other country.

4.   Perfect Capital Mobility and Flexible Exchange Rates

The Mundell-Fleming model can be used with flexible as well as fixed exchange rates. The major difference is that when nominal exchange rates are flexible, the central bank has no obligation to keep the domestic interest rate equal to foreign ones. The LM curve does not adjust to keep the balance of payments surplus equal to zero. Instead, capital flows into and out of the country in search of the highest return, raising demand for domestic currency when real interest rates at home exceed those abroad, and lowering it when real interest rates at home are less than those abroad. Any change in currency demand will cause the nominal exchange rate to change. This, in turn, will change net exports and therefore the position of the IS curve. Thus it is the IS curve that shifts to keep domestic interest rates equal to foreign ones, when capital is perfectly mobile and exchange rates are flexible.

For example, consider a country that is in both internal and external balance, so that output is equal to potential output and the balance of payments surplus is equal to zero. If the central bank increases the money supply, the LM curve will shift outward and domestic interest rates will fall below foreign interest rates. This situation cannot continue. Capital immediately flows out of the country, increasing the demand for other currencies and decreasing the demand for domestic currency. As a result, the domestic currency will depreciate. Goods and services produced abroad will look more expensive to domestic residents. Goods and services produced domestically will appear less expensive to foreigners. Imports will fall and exports will rise. The IS curve will shift outwards. Output is now greater than potential output, and the balance of payments surplus is still zero.

While net exports rise at home, they fall for the rest of the world. We improve our standard of living at the expense of everyone else's. For this reason, depreciation-induced output growth has been called a **beggar-thy-neighbour policy**. Despite its less-than-flattering nickname, this sort of depreciation can be mutually beneficial when countries are at different stages in the business cycle. Increasing AD at home and decreasing it abroad may not be a bad thing, if the home country is in a recession and the affected foreign countries are under inflationary pressures. However, when countries have highly synchronized business cycles, the contractionary effect of this policy on other countries is unwelcome. Then they may retaliate, resulting in a cycle of **competitive depreciation**, as each country tries to reduce the value of its own currency in order to increase its exports and raise output.

Unlike the fixed exchange rate case, now fiscal policy cannot affect output unless the central bank chooses to accommodate it. This is because expansionary fiscal policy raises the domestic interest rate, causing the domestic currency to appreciate and net exports to fall, reversing the initial IS shift and leaving output at its original level, with a higher nominal exchange rate.

5. Interest Differentials and Exchange Rate Expectations

We have argued that capital mobility should prevent interest differentials from developing. How then can we explain why there *are* differences in tax- and risk-adjusted real interest rates across countries?

The answer is that real interest rates are not the only component of an asset's return, because its holder ultimately is concerned with its return valued in his or her own currency, and therefore is affected by changes in the exchange rate during the time they own the asset.

The return on a foreign asset is equal to the rate of interest that it pays (i_f), measured in units of the foreign currency, plus the proportional change in the value of that currency $(-\Delta e/e)$. With perfect capital mobility, we should then expect:

$$i = i_f - \Delta e/e.$$

Because the change in the exchange rate, $\Delta e/e$, refers to the future change, it is unknown. Thus $\Delta e/e$ in the above equation refers to the *expected* proportional change in the exchange rate, and $i_f - \Delta e/e$ is the expected rate of return of the foreign asset, expressed in terms of the domestic currency.

Interest rates can differ across countries because of anticipated changes in the exchange rate. Because of the way that interest rates affect international capital flows and, therefore, actual exchange rates, exchange rate expectations can be self-fulfilling. For example, if enough people expect the Canadian dollar to depreciate, money will flow out of Canada in search of higher expected returns, causing the Canadian dollar to depreciate.

6. Working with Data

The student is asked to make a scatter diagram, plotting the Canada-U.S. interest rate differential against the proportional change in the exchange rate.

THE LANGUAGE OF ECONOMICS

Key Terms

marginal propensity to import
repercussion effects
perfect capital mobility
interest differential
external balance

internal balance
Mundell-Fleming model
beggar-thy-neighbour policy
competitive depreciation
exchange rate expectations

Accommodation

Typically, when we refer to a policy as "accommodating," we mean that it relaxes whatever barriers prevent a shock from having its full effect. Monetary policy can be used to accommodate a fiscal expansion. By increasing the money supply just enough to prevent interest rates from rising, the central bank can prevent the crowding out that a fiscal expansion otherwise would cause. When exchange rates are fixed, the central bank is required to accommodate both expansionary and contractionary fiscal policy, whereas when exchange rates are floating, it can choose whether or not to accommodate.

REVIEW OF TECHNIQUE

The Real Exchange Rate and the Conventional Nominal Exchange Rate

The real interest rate R referred to in this book differs in two ways from the nominal exchange rate as it is normally written. The nominal exchange rate normally is written in units of foreign currency per unit of domestic currency. For example, Canada's nominal exchange rate with the U.S. might be .65, meaning $0.65 U.S. per $1 C.

The first difference comes from the definition of e, the nominal exchange rate used in the book, in terms of the number of units of domestic currency required to purchase one unit of foreign currency. In other words e is the reciprocal of the usual exchange rate. For example, if the Canadian exchange rate as normally expressed was $0.65 U.S., then $e = \$(1/.65) = \$1.54$ C per $1 U.S.

The second difference between R and the conventional nominal exchange rate comes from the fact that R is relating the purchasing power, or units of goods and services, across countries, whereas the conventional nominal exchange rate is purely a comparison of their currency values. We define

$$R = eP_f/P$$

R can change due to a change in the nominal exchange rate e, or due to a difference in the inflation rates, which would cause a change in the ratio P_f/P.

FILL-IN QUESTIONS

1. A depreciation of the currency leads to a gain in _____.

2. _____ _____ implies that there will be very large capital flows when the domestic rate deviates from foreign rates.

3. A(n) _____ policy is an attempt to increase domestic income at the expense of income in other countries.

4. If domestic interest rates are higher than foreign rates, investors must be expecting a currency _____.

5. An increase in the domestic money supply leads to exchange rate _____ in the short run.

6. Economic linkages between different countries can cause _____, or _____ effects.

7. When the expected real rate of return is higher in one country than in the rest of the world, capital will flow _____ that country, _____ the demand for its currency and causing its exchange rate (expressed in units of foreign currency per unit of domestic currency) to _____.

8. When a country's currency depreciates, we expect that country's imports to _____ and its exports to _____.

TRUE-FALSE QUESTIONS

T F   1. Fiscal policy is ineffective under fixed exchange rates and perfect capital mobility.

T F   2. An increase in the U.S. interest rate leads to an improvement in Canada's balance of payments.

T F   3. An increase in the exchange rate (when defined as e) increases domestic aggregate demand.

T F   4. Under perfect capital mobility the LM curve is horizontal.

T F 5. An increase in Canadian government spending causes the Canadian dollar to appreciate.

T F 6. With perfect capital mobility and flexible exchange rates, an increase in Canadian government spending increases Canadian GDP.

T F 7. With perfect capital mobility, an increase in government spending increases net exports.

T F 8. Under flexible exchange rates, the central bank has no control over the money supply.

T F 9. With perfect capital mobility, an increase in the money supply increases aggregate demand.

T F 10. With perfect capital mobility, an increase in the money supply causes the currency to depreciate.

MULTIPLE-CHOICE QUESTIONS

1. An economy is in internal balance when (the)

   a. balance of payments surplus is zero
   b. output equals potential output

   c. domestic and foreign interest rates are equal
   d. the current account equals the capital account

2. With fixed exchange rates and perfect capital mobility

   a. only fiscal policy is effective
   b. only monetary policy is effective

   c. both are effective
   d. neither is effective

3. An increase in foreign demand for our exports

   a. causes an appreciation of the currency
   b. causes a depreciation of the currency

   c. has no effect on the currency
   d. causes an equal increase in imports

4. Under perfect capital mobility, an increase in government spending crowds out private spending as a result of

   a. a decrease in the foreign interest rate
   b. an increase in the foreign interest rate

   c. an appreciation of the currency
   d. a depreciation of the currency

5. Under perfect capital mobility, an increase in the money supply increases aggregate demand through

   a. a fall in the domestic interest rate
   b. a fall in the foreign interest rate

   c. an appreciation of the currency
   d. a depreciation of the currency

6. An increase in the money supply increases

   a. exports
   b. capital inflow

   c. government spending
   d. none of the above

7. The central bank has no control over the money supply under

   a. perfect capital mobility and a fixed exchange rate
   b. imperfect capital mobility and a flexible rate

   c. perfect capital mobility and a flexible rate
   d. imperfect capital mobility and a fixed rate

8. Capital flows into Canada when the Canadian interest rate (adjusted for expected changes in the exchange rate) is _____ foreign interest rates.

   a. greater than
   b. equal to

   c. less than
   d. either greater than or less than

9. Contractionary monetary policy increases

    a. the current account surplus
    b. the capital account surplus
    c. both types of surplus
    d. neither type of surplus

10. Imperfect capital mobility suggests that the Canadian interest rate _____ foreign interest rates.

    a. is greater than
    b. equals
    c. is less than
    d. may be greater than, equal to, or less than

CONCEPTUAL PROBLEMS

1. When capital is perfectly mobile and exchange rates are perfectly flexible, by what mechanism does an increase in the money stock raise GDP?

2. With perfect capital mobility and fixed exchange rates, how will the domestic economy be affected by an increase in government spending and an increase in the money stock so as to keep interest rates constant?

WORKING WITH DATA

The 12-month period beginning in the fourth quarter of 1979 was one of unusual swings in U.S. interest rates and the spread between Canadian and U.S. rates. To see the effects on the exchange rate, plot on Chart 14-1 a graph of the interest differential against the exchange rate.

The interest parity condition states a relationship between the interest differential and the expected future change in the exchange rate. Indicate which quadrant in your graph corresponds to an expected appreciation and which corresponds to an expected depreciation.

TABLE 14-1

| | | | Interest Rates | | |
Year and Quarter		Exchange Rate	U.S.	Canada	Differential
1979	4	116.7	14.20	13.97	0.23
1980	1	119.6	15.25	17.93	−2.68
	2	115.1	11.50	8.30	3.20
	3	117.0	10.90	11.51	−0.61

Source: Bank of Canada Review.

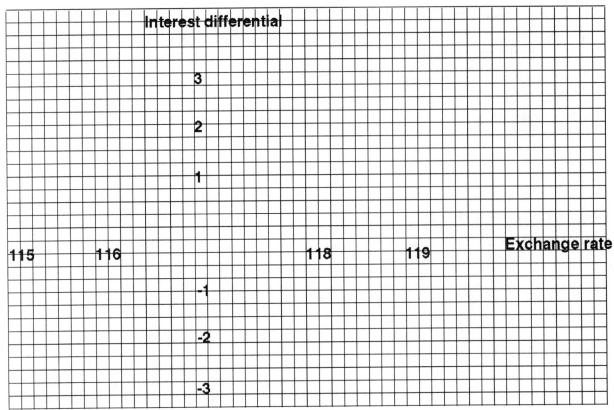

Chart 14-1

APPLICATION QUESTIONS

1. Suppose the interest rate in the U.S. is 4 percent and the interest rate in Canada is 6 percent. If the current value of the Canadian dollar is 60 U.S. cents, what is the value of the Canadian dollar expected to be a year from now?

$AD = C + I + G + NX$	(aggregate demand)
$IU = Y - AD = 0$	(unplanned additions to inventories equals zero)
$C = 10 + .8(Y + TR - TA)$	(consumption)
$TR = 20$	(government transfers)
$TA = .25Y$	(tax revenue)
$BS = TA - TR - G$	(government budget surplus)
$I = 20$	(investment)
$G = 30$	(government spending on goods and services)
$NX = X - Q$	(net exports)
$X = 30$	(exports)
$Q = 10 + .1Y$	(imports)

THIS IS THE SAME AS THE MODEL IN QUESTIONS 5 TO 10 OF CHAPTER 11, EXCEPT THAT NOW NET EXPORTS HAVE BEEN ADJUSTED SO THAT IMPORTS ARE SENSITIVE TO INCOME. AS PART OF YOUR ANSWERS, NOTE ANY DIFFERENCES BETWEEN THESE ANSWERS AND THE ANSWERS TO THE CORRESPONDING QUESTION FROM CHAPTER 11, IF THERE IS ONE.

2. Divide the variables into two groups: exogenous and endogenous.

3. Solve for the numerical values of all of the endogenous variables. (Do not substitute the numerical values for G and TR until near the end of your solution. This will make it much easier to answer some of the following questions.)

4. Find the value of the multiplier.

5. Compare the effect on output of increasing government spending G by two units with the effect on output of increasing transfers TR.

6. Solve for the value of government spending G that would be necessary, given the values of the other exogenous variables, for the government budget surplus to equal zero (a balanced budget).

7. Solve for the value of government spending that would be necessary for net exports to equal zero.

8. Suppose that the full employment output level was $Y^* = 202$, and that at the originally given values of G and TR, there was a change in exports X sufficient to achieve an output level $Y = 202$.

   a) What is the new value of X?

   b) Solve for BS in this new situation. This is BS*, the full-employment budget surplus.

15

CONSUMPTION AND SAVING

FOCUS OF THE CHAPTER

Consumption is the largest component of aggregate demand.

The amount that we consume today depends not only on our current income, but also on our wealth and our expectations of future income.

Because people try to spread their resources out over their lifetimes, transitory changes in income do not affect their consumption as much as permanent changes.

SECTION SUMMARIES

1. The Life-Cycle/Permanent-Income Theory of Consumption and Saving

The life-cycle and permanent-income theories tell a very similar story, and for that reason have been grouped together in this textbook. Both are based on the notion that people try to smooth consumption over their lifetimes—that they borrow when their income is low and save when their income is high in order to maintain a constant level of consumption over the years. They really only differ in the way that they model the decision-making involved in this process.

The *life-cycle theory* of consumption assumes that consumption is a function of both wealth and our average lifetime income, and that we have different *marginal propensities to consume* out of each: a high marginal propensity to consume out of income, and a low marginal propensity to consume out of wealth, which we try to spread out evenly over our lifetimes. It emphasizes the demographic aspect of saving behaviour—people's tendency to borrow against their future income when they are young, save for retirement when they are older, and to live off of their savings after they retire.

The *permanent income theory* suggests that people form expectations of the income they will receive over their lifetime, divide it by the number of years during which they expect to live, and consume an amount equal to that each period. When their actual income is below their *permanent income*, they borrow or draw down their savings. When their actual income exceeds their permanent income, they save. For this reason temporary changes in people's incomes do not affect their consumption very much; the benefits of a windfall gain today get spread out over an entire lifetime.

It is interesting to note that, in both of these models, changes in people's expectations—either their expectations regarding their future income or their expectations regarding their time of death—can strongly influence their consumption patterns.

2. Consumption Under Uncertainty: The Modern Approach

Modern consumption theory both emphasizes the link between income uncertainty and changes in consumption and takes a slightly more formal approach to modelling the way that people decide how much to consume. Here, consumption does not change unless something causes people's *expectations* to change. Changes in people's consumption, as a result, should not be predictable.

The empirical predictions of modern consumption theory have not been validated. Consumption seems to respond both too strongly to predictable (read *expected*) changes in income, and not strongly enough to unexpected changes in income. These characteristics are referred to, respectively, as *excess sensitivity* and *excess smoothness*.

Excess sensitivity could well be the result of *liquidity constraints*, which are constraints on people's ability to borrow money that force them to finance their consumption entirely out of current income. It could also result from *myopia*, a tendency for some people to not know or care as much about the future as we assume in our models.

3. Further Aspects of Consumption Behaviour

In Chapter 3 we saw that the savings rate is an important determinant of output growth. Do higher interest rates cause a higher saving rate? Not necessarily. One might think that a higher rate of return on savings would make saving more attractive, but it also makes it less necessary. Less saving is required to provide a given amount of money at some fixed future date. Researchers have not found a strong effect of interest rates on the saving rate when examining data from several countries.

The Barro-Ricardo problem concerns whether tax cuts should have any impact on consumption. While the standard aggregate demand model suggests that a tax cut should increase consumption, it ignores the effect of expectations and permanent income. Barro, and Ricardo before him, pointed out that without any corresponding cut in government spending, a tax cut now implies a future tax increase. Forward-looking consumers would take this into account now. They would not increase their spending, saving more instead to finance the anticipated higher future taxes. Two theoretical objections to this argument are: (1) people may not feel that the future higher taxes will affect them because they will be dead by then, and (2) some consumers are liquidity constrained, and would happily spend more money now if they could, even if their expected future disposable income is lower.

4. Working with Data

The student is asked to construct and plot the saving rate and the real rate of interest and look for a relationship between them.

THE LANGUAGE OF ECONOMICS

Key Terms

life-cycle hypothesis
permanent-income hypothesis
permanent income
lifetime utility
lifetime budget constraint
marginal utility of consumption
random-walk model of consumption
excess sensitivity

excess smoothness
liquidity constraints
myopia
buffer stock
Barro-Ricardo equivalence proposition
(Ricardian equivalence)
operational bequest motive

Theories and Hypotheses

All theories begin as hypotheses, that is, ideas, proposed relationships, or statements about what might be true. If you told a friend, for example, that you believed there were life on other planets, you would be making a *hypothesis*. If you thought that perhaps humans had evolved from seaweed, you would be making another hypothesis.

Not all hypotheses are true, and not all hypotheses become theories. A theory is nothing more than a hypothesis, or set of hypotheses, that seem to provide a good description of the world. The theory of general relativity was once a hypothesis, so was the belief that the sun orbited the Earth. The latter, obviously, would not be considered a theory by most people today.

REVIEW OF TECHNIQUE

Errors in Variables

"Errors in variables" is a phrase borrowed from statistics to describe a problem that arises when we try to test theories and hypotheses. Often we cannot find precise measures of the variables that we wish to look at; there are no universal accepted measures of the depreciation rate, for example, and there are so many different measures of the interest rate and the money supply that it is hard to know which one to use. Often there are no good measures: think of trying to measure intelligence or courage, for example.

An errors-in-variables problem occurs when we use a variable that we *can* measure in place of a more appropriate variable that we can't—actual instead of permanent income, for example, or scores on IQ tests in place of intelligence. Substituting variables in this way can *bias*—introduce systematic errors into—our estimates when those variables are systematically related to one another.

Consider the consumption function: The permanent-income hypothesis suggests that consumption is most appropriately expressed as a function of permanent income (YP)

$$C = cYP$$

If we substitute actual income for permanent income when actual income (Y) is given by the function

$$Y = YP + YT$$

where YT is the transitory deviation of actual income from permanent income, and try to estimate c (the marginal propensity to consume), our estimate $\bar{c}$ will be *biased downwards*:

$$C = \bar{c}Y = \bar{c}(YP + YT)$$

Note that $\bar{c}$ here will be a weighted average of the marginal propensities to consume out of permanent and transitory income and therefore, because the marginal propensity to consume out of transitory income is small, $\bar{c}$ will tend to be too low.

FILL-IN QUESTIONS

1. The _____ theory of consumption assumes that people try to smooth consumption over their lifetimes, and make consumption decisions based on the income they expect to earn over their lifetimes.

2. When people's actual income exceeds their permanent income, they _____.

3. The marginal propensity to consume out of permanent income is _____ than the marginal propensity to consume out of transitory income.

4. The life-cycle hypothesis suggests that the marginal propensity to consume out of income is _____ than the marginal propensity to consume out of wealth.

5. The life-cycle/permanent-income theory of consumption implies that consumption should follow a _____.

6. The marginal propensity to consume depends on the number of years spent _____ relative to the number of years spent _____.

7. The _____ hypothesis highlights the way that demographic changes affect national saving.

8. Purchases of _____ are very sensitive to changes in the interest rate.

9. The permanent-income hypothesis suggests that saving should change over the business cycle, rising in _____ and falling in _____.

10. The theory of _____ postulates that consumption will be unaffected by changes in disposable income that are due to changes in the government deficit.

TRUE-FALSE QUESTIONS

T F   1. Consumption is the largest component of aggregate demand.

T F   2. The life-cycle and permanent-income hypotheses make very different claims about the way that people make consumption decisions.

T F   3. The long-run mpc appears to be higher than the short-run mpc.

T F   4. Consumption appears to change too much (compared to the predictions of the life-cycle permanent-income hypothesis) in response to predictable changes in income.

T F   5. Consumption appears to change too much in response to *unpredictable* changes in income.

T F   6. The life-cycle hypothesis suggests that countries with higher proportions of retired individuals should see savings rise.

T F   7. People may save more than the life-cycle/permanent-income theory suggests because they wish to leave inheritances for their children.

T F   8. People may not be able to smooth consumption as much as the life-cycle/permanent-income theory suggests because they are liquidity constrained.

T F   9. Changes in the rate of interest paid by savings accounts have a strong impact on household savings.

T F   10. If the theory of Ricardian equivalence were true, then an income tax cut by the government would have no impact on current consumption.

MULTIPLE-CHOICE QUESTIONS

1. An estimate of long-term consumption opportunities based on expectations of lifetime income is called _____ income.

    a. disposable   c. permanent
    b. adjusted   d. transitory

2. The observation that consumption changes too much in response to predictable changes in income, is referred to as

    a. liquidity constraint   c. excess smoothness
    b. excess sensitivity   d. myopia

3. The observation that consumption does not change enough in response to unpredictable changes in income, is referred to as

    a. liquidity constraint   c. excess smoothness
    b. excess sensitivity   d. myopia

4. Constraints on people's ability to borrow money at the market interest rate are referred to as

    a. liquidity constraints   c. myopia
    b. budget constraints   d. bequests

5. Which of the following is the largest component of aggregate demand?

    a. consumption   c. government spending
    b. investment   d. net exports

6. The life-cycle/permanent-income theory of consumption is associated with the

    a. Keynesian school   c. neither
    b. Monetarist school   d. both

7. The life-cycle hypothesis suggests that wealth during a person's working years should

    a. increase   c. not change, on average
    b. decrease   d. all be spent

8. Which of the following groups of people should have the highest rate of saving?

    a. college students   c. people who have retired
    b. children   d. people approaching the end of their working lives

CONCEPTUAL PROBLEMS

1. Why do modern theorists argue that, if the life-cycle/permanent-income theory of consumption is correct, consumption should follow a random walk?

2. How do you think longer life-spans will affect people's saving patterns? Explain.

3. How should an increase in the interest rate affect people's permanent income?

4. Are you liquidity constrained?

APPLICATION QUESTIONS

1. If the typical urban consumer expects to work for 30 more years and live 10 years beyond retirement, how should a $100 tax cut on his or her labour income affect consumption? Does your answer depend on whether the tax cut is temporary or permanent? Disregard any multiplier effects.

2. Will expansionary fiscal policy be more or less effective when people are liquidity constrained? Justify your answer.

3. In this question you construct a graph to see why the marginal propensity to consume might appear to be too small in estimates based on cross-sectional data (data that takes a "slice" of the current population instead of following a few select individuals through time).

    Table 15-1 provides data for a hypothetical cross-section of the population. There are six individuals in our sample; three have one level of permanent income, and three have another. Each person is experiencing a different level of good or bad fortune, so that their actual income does not equal their permanent income.

    Graph each point in the sample, and find the line that best fits the group as a whole. Does the mpc appear too small? Does the consumption function appear to have a positive intercept? This is an example of what statisticians call an "errors in variables" problem. Our estimate of the marginal propensity to consume is biased (wrong) because we have plotted consumption against the wrong variable. What variable does life-cycle/permanent-income theory suggest we should have plotted consumption against?

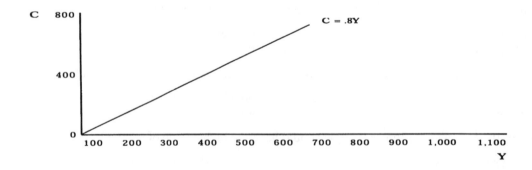

Chart 15 - 1

TABLE 15-1

Permanent Income (YP)	Total Income (Y)	Consumption* (C = cYP)
$500	$400	$400
$500	$500	$400
$500	$600	$400
$1,000	$900	$800
$1,000	$1,000	$800
$1,000	$1,100	$800

* We assume that c, the marginal propensity to consume, is 0.8.

16 INVESTMENT SPENDING

FOCUS OF THE CHAPTER

Investment is the most volatile sector of aggregate demand; changes in investment account for much of the change in GDP.

The three types of investment are *business fixed investment, residential investment,* and *inventory investment.*

Investment is the flow of spending that adds to the physical stock of capital.

Investment demand is the primary link between monetary policy and aggregate demand. Increased interest rates reduce investment because capital becomes more expensive.

SECTION SUMMARIES

1.   The Stock Demand for Capital and the Flow of Investment

This section develops a theory of the demand for capital, which is the capital stock that businesses and consumers would like to have in the long run. Because it takes time to order and install new capital, firms and consumers do not always have this desired capital stock. Investment, which is the flow of new capital (e.g., machinery, private homes) into the capital stock, closes the gap between the desired and the actual capital stock.

Investment is the main route through which monetary policy affects aggregate demand. With lower interest rates, the holding of one's wealth in the form of capital, rather than interest-bearing assets, becomes more attractive. Similarly, it becomes more attractive to borrow to finance capital investment with lower interest rates. Investment can also be affected by fiscal policy through taxes on capital.

Firms consider three factors when they decide how much capital they want to have: the amount of output they expect to sell, the amount that one more unit of capital will increase their output (the *marginal product of capital*), and the amount that it will cost them to use that unit of capital (the *rental*, or *user, cost of capital*).

More capital always enables more output to be produced. Each additional unit of capital costs the same amount to use, but each additional unit also contributes less and less to production. This combination of constant marginal cost and diminishing marginal product means that there will be some point at which it is no longer sensible for firms to buy capital; eventually, the marginal benefit that they derive from their capital will fall below the marginal cost of employing it. Firms will then accumulate capital as long as the marginal benefit of their doing so exceeds the marginal cost. The capital stock will be at its desired level when the marginal benefit of employing an additional unit of capital (i.e., the marginal product of capital) is exactly equal to the marginal cost.

The rental cost of capital is little more than the expected real interest rate (r)—the opportunity cost associated with using their funds to buy capital instead of bonds. There is also a cost, however, that firms must incur if they wish to keep the capital they have already installed in good working order; capital *depreciates*, or wears out, over time. Letting d be the rate of depreciation, we write the rental cost of capital (rc), as

$$rc = r + d = (i - \pi^e) + d$$

where we use the definition of the expected real interest rate as the difference between the nominal interest rate i and the expected inflation rate π^e.

We use the expected real interest rate instead of the actual one because uncertainty regarding future inflation translates into uncertainty regarding the real rate of interest that assets pay when they are held over time; we only ever really *know* that real interest rate when we look back on it and can measure the difference between the nominal rate of interest and the rate of inflation.

This rental cost must be adjusted to account for the effect of taxes. The capital stock will really be at its optimal level when the *after-tax marginal product of capital* is equal to the *after-tax rental cost*. Interest payments are deducted from a firm's income before its taxes are calculated, however, so when investment is entirely bond financed or when the company's stock does not pay dividends, the optimal, *or desired capital stock is not affected by corporate taxes*.

When a company is publicly held and its stock pays dividends, this is no longer true: Because the dividends paid out to stockholders are not deducted from the firm's income for tax purposes, the rental cost of capital is affected by the corporate tax rate. Higher corporate tax rates raise the rental cost of capital, and, as a result, reduce the desired capital stock. Investment tax credits do the opposite: Because they allow firms to deduct a fraction of their investment expenditures each year, they *reduce* firms' rental cost of capital.

Fiscal policy therefore can affect the desired capital stock by changing either the corporate tax rate or the investment tax credit. Both monetary and fiscal policy can also affect the desired capital stock through their effect on the real interest rate.

The *q theory of investment* restates the marginal benefit equals marginal cost rule in more easily quantifiable terms. It points out that that the price of a company's stock, because it represents a claim on the stream of profits that its capital is expected to generate, is a measure of the value of that capital. Likewise, the amount of money that would be required to replace all of the capital that a firm owns is a measure of that firm's cost of capital.

Looking at the ratio of the market value of a firm (the number of shares of stock it has issued times the market value of those shares) to that firm's replacement cost of capital,

$$q = \frac{market\ value\ of\ firm}{replacement\ cost\ of\ firm's\ capital}$$

should tell us something about ratio of marginal benefits to marginal costs: A q greater than one suggests that the benefit of acquiring new capital exceeds the cost, or that the firm should invest more. A q smaller than one suggests that the cost of acquiring new capital is greater than the benefit, or that the firm should *disinvest*—allow its capital stock to fall. A q exactly equal to one suggests that the firm has exactly the right amount of capital, or capital is at its desired level.

The rate of investment depends on the difference between the actual capital stock (K) and the desired capital stock (K^*). The *flexible accelerator model* is based on the notion that firms with larger gaps between their actual and desired capital stocks should be investing more than firms whose actual capital stock is closer to its desired level. It assumes that firms try to close some fraction, λ, of this gap each period, or that

$$I = K - K_{-1} = \lambda\,(K^* - K_{-1}),$$

where K_{-1} represents the capital stock that the firm had at the end of the previous period. If you're not comfortable working with lagged terms, consult this chapter's Review of Technique section.

2. Investment Subsectors – Business Fixed, Residential, and Inventory

Business fixed investment is strongly procyclical. As firms assess which of their many projects to undertake, they compare the discounted cash flow (discounted by the expected future interest rate) to the cost of the project. Since a lower expected future interest rate increases the discounted cash flow, it should result in a larger number of projects and higher fixed investment demand.

The price and quantity of housing depend on the supply and demand for homes. Investment in housing occurs when the quantity of homes demanded exceeds the existing stock of housing, driving up the price of buying or renting a home. Housing demand falls when interest rates—especially mortgage rates—rise, and when people's incomes fall. For the latter reason, housing demand also tends to move with the business cycle, rising in booms and falling in recessions.

Inventories consist of raw materials held for use in production, unfinished goods currently in the middle of the production process, and finished goods held by firms in anticipation of future sale. Unintended inventory accumulation occurs when sales fall unexpectedly, and is a signal to firms to decrease production. Intended inventory accumulates when firms anticipate an increase in the demand for their good in the near future. Unintended inventory accumulation occurs when there is an unanticipated fall in aggregate demand, or when the economy falls into recession.

To reduce the cost of storing inventories, many firms have been adopting *just-in-time inventory management* techniques, bringing production more closely into line with sales and keeping fewer inventories on hand. Inventories are moving less over the business cycle as a result.

3. Investment and Aggregate Supply

As we learned in Chapters 4 and 5, investment, because it adds to the capital stock, increases the level of potential output. Countries that typically invest a substantial fraction of their output grow faster than countries that do not. However, a one-time increase in investment, even a large one, likely would not result in much gain in long-term productivity.

4. Working with Data

The student is asked to plot the real rate of interest against investment spending in Canada to look for a negative relationship.

THE LANGUAGE OF ECONOMICS

Key Terms

business fixed investment
residential investment
inventory investment
flow of investment
stock of capital
marginal product of capital
rental (user) cost of capital
opportunity cost
expected inflation rate

expected real interest rate
diminishing marginal product
capital gains
q theory of investment
flexible accelerator model
dynamic behaviour
accelerator model
inventory cycle
just-in-time inventory management

Investment

Investment, as it is used in macroeconomics, does *not* refer to the accumulation of interest-bearing assets. It does *not* refer to the purchase of stocks and bonds.

Investment is the accumulation of physical, and sometimes human, capital. New home construction, the purchase of new machinery, and the accumulation of inventories are all types of physical investment. Education and health maintenance are both types of investment in *human capital* (not discussed in this chapter). Investment in human capital is not usually measured by national income accounts.

REVIEW OF TECHNIQUE

Working with Lagged Variables

When we introduce lags into a model, it becomes *dynamic* instead of *static*. Past events can affect the values of present variables; current events can affect the values of future variables.

A **lagged variable** is just a variable valued in an earlier period. Lags are represented by time subscripts: Last period's income, for example, might be represented by Y_{-1}. The "–1" indicates a one-period lag. It tells us to use last period's value instead of this period's. Last period's capital stock can be represented by K_{-1}. The difference between last period's capital stock and the desired capital stock is $K^* - K_{-1}$.

Although you may not know it, you've already worked with lags. You've found the rates of change of a number of variables by applying the formula

$$\left[\frac{x - x_{-1}}{x_{-1}} \right] \times 100$$

You've seen the random walk model in Chapter 15, which is characterized, in its simplest form, by the equation

$$y = y_{-1} + \varepsilon$$

Here are some other examples of dynamic processes that you may have worked through: deriving the government purchases multiplier; the way that capital accumulates over time in the neo-classical growth model; and the way that past and expected future income interact to determine people's permanent income.

FILL-IN QUESTIONS

1. The three principal types of investment are _____, _____, and _____.

2. The machinery, equipment, and structures used in production are a part of _____ investment.

3. The rental cost of capital is equal to the real interest rate plus the rate of _____.

4. The rental cost of capital is also called the _____ cost of capital.

5. The _____ model assumes that firms try to close some fraction of the gap between their desired and actual capital stock each period.

6. _____ inventory management techniques reduce the number of inventories kept on hand, bringing production more closely into line with sales.

7. The government can subsidize firms' investment by giving them _____.

8. The _____ theory of investment restates the "marginal benefit equals marginal cost" rule in more easily quantifiable terms.

9. _____ consist of raw materials held for use in production, unfinished goods, and finished goods held by firms in anticipation of future sale.

10. Investment, because it adds to the capital stock, increases _____.

TRUE-FALSE QUESTIONS

T F   1. Investment is the most volatile sector of aggregate demand.

T F   2. Rising interest rates increase investment.

T F   3. Rising GDP increases investment.

T F   4. Investment is a stock variable.

T F   5. Investment is the primary link between monetary policy and aggregate demand.

T F   6. Expansionary monetary policy increases investment.

T F   7. Rising interest rates increase investment.

T F   8. Unexpectedly high sales cause inventories to fall.

T F   9. The actual capital stock adjusts gradually to the desired capital stock.

T F   10. The adoption of just-in-time inventory management techniques has caused inventories to fluctuate less over the business cycle.

MULTIPLE-CHOICE QUESTIONS

1. An increase in the corporate tax rate _____ investment when firms are at least partially financed through equity.

   a. increases
   b. decreases
   c. has no effect
   d. could be any of the above

2. An increase in the investment tax credit _____ investment.

   a. increases
   b. decreases
   c. has no effect
   d. could be any of the above

3. Which of the following is not a type of investment?

   a. purchase of a machine
   b. accumulation of inventories
   c. construction of new home
   d. purchase of stock or bond

4. An increase in the rate of depreciation _____ the rental cost of capital.

   a. increases
   b. decreases
   c. has no effect
   d. who knows?

5. An increase in the rate of depreciation _____ the desired capital stock.

   a. increases
   b. decreases
   c. has no effect
   d. who knows?

6. An increase in the real interest rate _____ the rental cost of capital.

   a. increases
   b. decreases
   c. has no effect
   d. could be any of the above

7. An increase in the real interest rate _____ the desired capital stock.

   a. increases
   b. decreases
   c. has no effect
   d. could be any of the above

8. Which of the following measures the benefit to a firm of acquiring capital?

   a. market value of firm
   b. replacement cost of capital
   c. user cost of capital
   d. rate of depreciation

9. Expansionary monetary policy _____ investment.

   a. increases
   b. decreases
   c. does not effect
   d. who knows?

10. Expansionary fiscal policy, *when* it is accommodated, _____ investment.

    a. increases
    b. decreases
    c. does not affect
    d. who knows?

CONCEPTUAL PROBLEMS

1. Why does an increase in the real interest rate reduce the desired capital stock?

2. Why does an increase in the rate at which capital depreciates reduce the desired capital stock?

3. Why do we use real instead of nominal interest rates in our formula for the rental cost of capital?

WORKING WITH DATA

Investment is a small but volatile sector; its changes are responsible for much of the variation in aggregate demand. This Graph It asks you to show that changes in aggregate demand closely follow changes in investment—that the relationship between investment volatility and aggregate demand volatility is very strong.

Table 16-1 provides data on GDP and gross investment. Your task is to find the amount that each of these variables changes from year to year (note that the change is in absolute and not percentage terms), and to plot each, individually, on Chart 16-1.

TABLE 16-1

Year	Real GDP	Gross Investment	Annual Change in Real GDP	Annual Change in Investment
1985	496.7	85.5		
1986	511.8	91.6	15.1	6.1
1987	532.8	102.9		
1988	558.7	113.2		
1989	572.9	120.9		
1990	574.4	109.7		
1991	563.6	104.6		
1992	568.8	101.4		
1993	581.8	106.8		
1994	609.3	115.6		
1995	625.3	116.8		

Source: Bank of Canada Review.

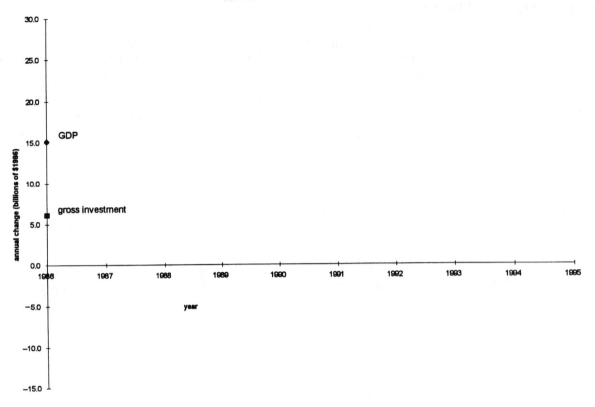

GDP and Gross Investment Growth

Chart 16-1

APPLICATION QUESTIONS

1. If the desired capital stock is $20,000, the current level of the capital stock is $12,000, and a firm wishes to close half of the gap between them each period, what does the flexible accelerator model suggest will be next period's level of net investment? What will be the level of net investment the year after that?

2. Assume that the desired capital stock is determined by the equation $K^* = 0.25Y/rd$. The nominal interest rate is 12 percent. The rate of inflation is 6 percent. Capital depreciates at a rate of 10 percent per year ($d = .1$).

   a) If income is $16,000, what is the desired capital stock?

   b) What will be the desired capital stock if income doubles?

   c) What will be the desired capital stock if, instead, the rental cost of capital doubles?

3. Let net investment be determined by the flexible accelerator model: net $I = K - K_{-1} = .6(K - K_{-1})$. The depreciation rate is 10 percent. The desired capital stock is $K^* = 240$. In year 0 the capital stock is 200. Work out the net and gross investment levels in years 1 and 2.

4. An economy has a GDP of $600 billion. In which case would you expect it to have the highest level of investment spending? Last year's GDP was: (i) $570 billion, (ii) $600 billion, (iii) $630 billion.

17 THE DEMAND FOR MONEY

FOCUS OF THE CHAPTER

We all hold money—either in currency, in our pockets, or as deposits in a bank. In studying the demand for money, we try to discover why people hold money, and what determines the amount of money they hold.

Our mail goal is to find some function that tells us the amount of money people will hold for a known level of income and a known interest rate. We need to know this in order to form the LM curve.

Both theory and empirical evidence suggest that an increase in people's incomes makes them want to hold more money, and that an increase in the interest rate makes them want to hold less.

SECTION SUMMARIES

1.   Components of the Money Stock

Money consists of the stock of assets held as cash, chequing accounts, and other, closely related assets, *not* generic wealth or income. There are four different measures of the money supply: *M1, M2, M3,* and *M2+*. *M1* consists of those assets that are the most *liquid*—most easily used to pay for goods and services. *M3* consists of those assets that are least liquid, but which can still be converted into a form that creditors will accept. The components of each measure of money are listed below:

M1	currency and demand deposits
M2	M1 plus personal savings deposits and nonpersonal notice deposits
M3	M2 plus nonpersonal term deposits plus foreign currency deposits
M2+	M2 plus deposits at other deposit-taking institutions

2.   The Functions of Money

Money has traditionally been thought to have four functions:

A medium of exchange. Money is used to pay for goods and services, and enables us to avoid the "double coincidence of wants" required in a barter economy.

A store of value. Money retains its value over time; money we receive today can be stuck under our mattresses or placed in our chequing account and used to purchase goods and services at a later date.

A unit of account. Prices are quoted in dollars and cents rather than chickens, avocados, or visits to the dentist.

A standard of deferred payment. Money is used in long-term transactions; you might borrow $100 from a friend, for example, and promise to pay him back $105 at a later date.

The most important thing to know about money is that *it is whatever people generally accept as a payment for goods and services*. As such, it can take many forms.

3.   The Demand for Money: Theory

Why would we ever choose to hold money instead of some other, interest-bearing asset? Keynes suggested three different motives:

The transactions motive. We wish to avoid having to cash in another asset every time we make a purchase. (Imagine what a nuisance that would be!)

The precautionary motive. "Just in case." We never know our spending plans exactly: it pays to keep a little extra money around in case the urge for a hot fudge sundae hits at a time when your stock broker is playing golf and cannot liquidate any of your assets.

The speculative motive. While money doesn't have a very high return, it is less risky than other assets. Speculative demand for money is actually demand for a safe asset.

An increase in the rate of return on other assets reduces the demand for money, whatever one's motive for holding it. An increase in the amount of uncertainty we have about our future spending plans increases the people's demand for money, when that demand is based on the precautionary motive.

We model the demand for real rather than nominal money balances here (*M/P* rather than *M*); we assume that, because people hold money for its purchasing power, they do not care about their nominal money holdings. For this to be true, people must be free of *money illusion*—the belief that changes in nominal wages and prices are meaningful.

4.   Empirical Evidence

Empirical research has settled four key points about money demand:

1)   When the real interest rate increases, the demand for real money balances falls.

2)   When income increases, money demand also increases.

3)   It takes time for money demand to fully adjust to changes in income and the interest rate.

4)   If the price level doubles, so will nominal money demand. Real money demand will be unaffected; there is no money illusion.

High inflation can also induce people to hold less money. With sufficiently high rates of inflation, people may not wish to hold financial assets at all, holding food and other goods instead. This is called a *flight out of money*.

5. The Income Velocity of Money

The *income velocity of money* is the number of times the stock of money is turned over, or reused each year to finance all of the purchases that occur. If people purchased $1,000,000 of goods and services in a particular year, and the (nominal) money supply were $1,000,000, for example, the velocity of money would be equal to 1; each dollar would be used an average of one time. If people purchased $1,000,000 of goods and services in a particular year, and the (nominal) money supply were $500,000, the velocity of money would be equal to 2; each dollar would be used an average of two times.

The income velocity of money is defined as:

$$V = \frac{P \times Y}{M} = \frac{Y}{M/P}$$

6. Working with Data

The student is asked to calculate and plot the velocity of M2, M2+, M3 and the treasury bill rate.

Appendix

The Baumol-Tobin formula for the transactions demand for money,

$$\frac{M}{P} = \sqrt{\frac{tcY}{2i}}$$

uses some basic intuition and some math to find a formula for the amount of money people want to hold for the purpose of buying goods and services.

First, notice that a person's average real balance (*M/P*) over a given period will be equal to 1/2 the amount of money they spend over that period divided by the number of times (*n*) they convert their other assets into money (e.g., withdraw cash from their savings account):

$$\frac{M}{P} = \frac{Y}{2n}$$

Next, observe that the opportunity cost of holding money is equal to the value of the next best opportunity—the rate of interest (*i*) paid by other assets. Each transfer is also assumed to cost an amount *tc*.

The total cost of holding average balances *Y /(2n)*, then is:

$$(n \times tc) + \frac{iY}{2n}$$

The best number of transactions is, of course, the one that minimizes this total cost. That number ($n*$), it turns out, is given by the following formula:

$$n* = \sqrt{\frac{iY}{2tc}}$$

Plugging this into our original equation $M/P = Y / 2n$, we find that people will find it optimal, or best to hold average real money balances.

$$\frac{M}{P} = \sqrt{\frac{tcY}{2i}}$$

THE LANGUAGE OF ECONOMICS

Key Terms

money	real balances
M1	money illusion
liquid asset	transactions motive
M2	precautionary motive
M3	speculative motive
M2+	portfolio
medium of exchange	risky asset
store of value	interest elasticity
unit of account	income elasticity
standard of deferred payment	income velocity of money

Liquidity

An asset is *liquid* when it can be converted into goods or services quickly, at low cost, and with low risk. Cash is the ultimate liquid asset; it can be directly exchanged for goods and services anywhere. Chequing accounts, also known as "demand deposits," are liquid too.

Stocks and bonds are less liquid. Both take time to sell, and therefore cannot as easily be used to buy goods and services. The prices of stocks and bonds also fluctuate. Imagine having to sell a share of stock every time you get a haircut or buy groceries; you might have to sell at a loss, simply to finance your purchases. Having to regularly convert either of these assets into goods and services would involve considerable risk.

REVIEW OF TECHNIQUE

Working with Natural Logarithms

Before the days of calculators, tables of logarithms were used to speed up calculations. Today that is no longer necessary; few of us do our calculations by hand.

Natural logarithms are still useful, however, because they are intimately connected to percentage changes. *The change in the natural log of a variable is approximately equal to the percentage change of that variable*. This is particularly useful when graphing one variable against another. If you graph the natural log of y (ln y) against the natural log of x (ln x), for example, the slope of your line will tell you the amount that y changes, in percentage terms, when x rises by 1 percent, which is the elasticity of y with respect to x.

A natural logarithm is formally defined as follows:

$$X = \ln Y \quad \text{if and only if} \quad Y = e^X,$$

where e is an irrational number (i.e., it cannot be expressed as a fraction) approximately equal to 2.71828. Taking the natural log of the function e^x gives you x; raising e to the power ln x also gives you x (e^x and ln x are *inverse functions*).

There are some rules that will help you to work with natural logs:

1) $\ln (xy) = \ln x + \ln y$

2) $\ln (x / y) = \ln x - \ln y$

3) $\ln (x^y) = y \times \ln x$

4) $\ln (1 + x) \cong x$ (the symbol $\cong$ means "approximately equal to") when x is close to zero

FILL-IN QUESTIONS

1. The assets which form M1 are _____ liquid than the assets which form M2.

2. Savings accounts are _____ liquid than Canada Savings Bonds.

3. Holding money to reduce the risk associated with your portfolio of assets is an example of the _____ motive.

4. Holding money because you're worried that something may come up that requires you to spend it is an example of the _____ motive.

5. Holding money in order to use it to buy goods and services is an example of the _____ motive.

6. Ice cubes would not be a very good form of money because they would be a terrible _____.

7. Giant stone slabs might not be the best form of money because they would not be a very convenient _____.

8. When high inflation induces people to hold goods instead of assets, we say there is a _____.

9. Usually the money unit is also the _____, that is, the unit in which prices are quoted and books kept.

10. The _____ of money measures number of times the average dollar changes hands each year.

TRUE-FALSE QUESTIONS

T F 1. Cash is the most liquid asset of all.

T F 2. Stocks are the most liquid asset of all.

T F 3. An increase in income raises money demand.

T F 4. Money demand adjusts immediately to changes in both income and the interest rate.

T F 5. M1 is more liquid than M3.

T F 6. M2 is more liquid than M3.

T F 7. People will hold as much money as they can get their hands on.

T F 8. It is always better to hold more money than less.

T F 9. If the money supply grows more quickly than output, it will cause inflation.

T F 10. When the real interest rate increases, the demand for real money balances falls.

MULTIPLE-CHOICE QUESTIONS

1. Currency is contained in

    a. M1
    b. M2
    c. M3
    d. all of the above

2. Foreign currency deposits are contained in

    a. M1
    b. M2
    c. M3
    d. all of the above

3. Which of the following is the most liquid?

    a. M1
    b. M2
    c. M3
    d. M2+

4. Which of the following is the least liquid?

    a. M1
    b. M2
    c. M3
    d. M2+

5. The measure of money demand that is meaningful to people is *not*:

    a. real balances
    b. nominal money holdings
    c. purchasing power
    d. the amount of goods that can be purchased with it

6. Which of the following is not a function of money?

    a. medium of exchange
    b. unit of account
    c. store of value
    d. measure of greed

7. People will want to hold less money if there is/are

    a. high inflation
    b. low interest rates
    c. money illusion
    d. all of the above

Chapter 17

8.   In the long run, an increase in the money supply causes

    a.   high real interest rates   c.   inflation
    b.   high output   d.   all of the above

9.   Money is

    a.   bills and coins   c.   anything people can exchange for goods
    b.   bills, coins, and bank accounts   and services

10.   The income velocity of money is equal to the ratio of the nominal _____ to the nominal _____.

    a.   money stock; disposable income   c.   money stock; price level
    b.   M2; M1   d.   GDP; money stock

CONCEPTUAL PROBLEMS

1.   Why do you hold money? (How many of the motives for holding money identified by Keynes can you identify with?)

2.   What do you know of, aside from bills and coins, that has been used as money over the years?

APPLICATION QUESTIONS

1.   If nominal GDP is $1,000,000 and the money supply (as measured by M2) is $500,000, what is the income velocity of money?

2.   If you earn $100,000 per year, you pay (including the cost of your time) $1.50 to withdraw money from your bank account, and the interest rate is 6 percent, how much money, on average, does the Baumol-Tobin model of the transactions demand for money suggest you will want to hold? (Set $P = 1$.)

3.   If the velocity of money is 10, then the average dollar gets spent ten times in a year, roughly speaking. One would expect then that the average cent also is spent ten times in a year. But if we measure the nominal money stock in cents instead of dollars, the number is 100 times larger. Is this a contradiction? Are there two different velocities, one for dollars and one for cents?

18

THE MONEY SUPPLY PROCESS AND FINANCIAL MARKETS

FOCUS OF THE CHAPTER

In previous chapters, the money supply has been taken to be exogenous. We now explore the process by which the Bank of Canada, the chartered banks, and the public interact in determining the stock of money.

We also examine the way in which the Bank of Canada operates monetary policy.

This chapter also examines the behaviour of the bond market and the stock market.

SECTION SUMMARIES

1.   The Money Supply and the Banking System

The sum of currency in circulation plus chartered bank deposits at the Bank of Canada (known as *reserves*) constitutes the ***monetary base***, which is also known as high-powered money. The Bank of Canada controls the money supply indirectly by controlling the monetary base. High-powered money is the principal liability of the Bank of Canada. Its main asset is government bonds.

Three sectors play a role in determining the money supply: the non-bank public, the chartered banks, and the Bank of Canada. The Bank of Canada creates more money through an ***open market purchase***, in which it buys bonds by writing a cheque on itself. The amount of the cheque is added to the total reserves available to the public and the banking system.

The federal government has bank accounts at the Bank of Canada and at the chartered banks. Transferring these deposits between the Bank of Canada and the chartered banks is an alternative to open market operations as a means of changing the monetary base.

2.   The Money Supply and the Monetary Base

The money supply multiplier is equal to the ratio of the money supply to the monetary base. The money supply multiplier depends on the ***currency-deposit ratio*** chosen by the public and by the ***reserve-deposit ratio*** of the chartered banks. We denote the currency-deposit ratio by cu and the reserve-deposit ratio as re. We can write the money supply multiplier as

$$\frac{M}{B} = \frac{cu + 1}{cu + re}$$

The smaller the reserve ratio, and the smaller the currency deposit ratio, the larger the money supply multiplier.

The currency-deposit ratio depends on the tastes and habits of the public. At one time, Canadian banks were required to hold a certain percentage of their deposits as cash reserves, where the percentage depended on the type of deposit. These requirements were completely removed as of July 1994. Since then, any cash reserves held by banks are for reasons analogous to the consumer's precautionary demand for money.

Banks are able to make credit available in the amount of their deposits minus reserves. When the base increases, banks are able to make more loans. These loans take the form of added deposits and more currency held by the public. The bank that receives the new deposits can then make more loans. This adjustment process describes the ***multiple expansion of bank deposits*** which, when added across all the banks in the economy, yields the money multiplier.

3. Short Run Control of the Money Supply

Cash reserve requirements were phased out beginning in November 1991, as they were deemed to be unnecessary for central bank control of the money supply.

The Bank of Canada implements monetary policy on a day-to-day basis through the ***overnight rate***, which is the interest rate at which banks borrow or lend to obtain their desired level of settlement balances. The Bank of Canada does this by lending and borrowing to keep the overnight rate within a target band of 0.5 percentage points. The ***bank rate*** is the equal to the upper end of this target band. The major role of the bank rate has been as a signal of the Bank of Canada's views concerning the appropriate level of interest rates and its intentions with regard to monetary tightness or ease.

Equilibrium in the money market is determined by setting money supply equal to money demand. The Bank of Canada can control either the money supply or the interest rate, but not the two independently. The reason is that the money demand curve gives us a fixed relation between interest and the money stock.

4. Targets and the Implementation of Monetary Policy

The issue of money supply targets arises when we introduce unpredictable shifts in the IS and LM curves. The problem is illustrated in Figure 18-1 (text Figure 18-1).

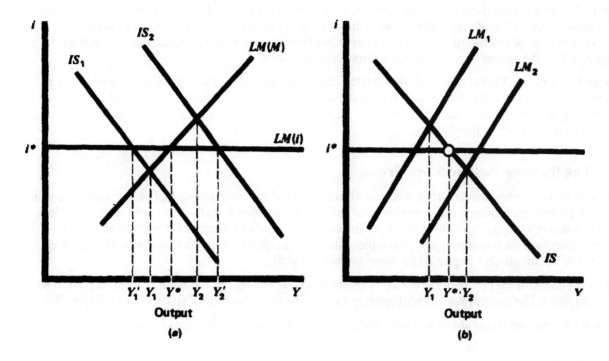

Figure 18-1

In part (a), we show a shifting IS curve. In this case the level of output stays closer to the target, Y*, if the money supply is fixed so that we move along the LM curve LM(M). In part (b), it is the LM curve that is shifting and output can be maintained at the target level by holding the interest rate constant.

During the period 1975–81, the Bank of Canada operated monetary policy using target rates of growth of the money supply. The above analysis suggests that this is appropriate if the money market is stable and the goods market is subject to substantial disturbances.

5. Financial Markets and Interest Rates

There is more than one interest rate in the economy; bonds of different maturities, in particular, have different interest rates. The relationship between the interest rates paid on bonds of differing maturity is called the **term structure of interest**.

Interest rates on long-term bonds are typically higher than interest rates on short-term bonds. Because holding one long-term bond is equivalent to holding a series of short-term bonds, *the interest rate on long-term bonds is equal to the average of the current interest rate on short-term bonds and expected future short-term interest rates, plus a **term premium** which compensates the holder for the risk associated with holding long- rather than short-term bonds.* Long-term bonds are typically perceived as riskier than short-term bonds because of their greater price volatility (variation in price).

The **expectations theory of the term structure** highlights the way that people's expectations of future short-term interest rates affect current long-term interest rates. The text observes that term premiums vary over time.

The *yield curve* shows the relationship between interest rates on assets of different maturities. Because long-term interest rates are typically higher than short-term interest rates, the yield curve is usually upward-sloping. A downward-sloping yield curve implies that people must expect short-term interest rates to fall in the future; this is sometimes a recessionary signal.

Boxes 18-2 and 18-3 in the text work through the details of calculating the *net present value* of assets whose payoff occurs in the future, and discuss the relationship between the net present value of a bond's *coupon payments* plus *face value* and its price. Increases in interest rates are shown to reduce bond prices —particularly *long-term* bond prices.

6. The Random Walk of Stock Prices

Because in an efficient market stock prices are based on all of the information that people have regarding a firm's profit opportunities, and, therefore, the value of the dividends that will be paid to stockholders, they should only change when new information becomes available. Changes in the price of a stock should, therefore, be completely unpredictable—stock prices should follow a *random walk*. (See the Review of Technique in Chapter 20 for more on random walks.)

While the stock market probably is not 100 percent efficient, changes in the stock market do tend to be unpredictable. The random walk model appears to describe the behaviour of stock prices fairly well.

Because stocks and bonds are substitutes, rising interest rates cause stock prices to fall.

7. Working with Data

The student is asked to retrieve from CANSIM and plot three interest rates: the bank rate, the prime rate, and the one-year conventional mortgage rate, and note how they closely follow each other.

KEY TERMS

cash reserves
settlement balances
clearing system
direct clearers
monetary base
open market operations
money multiplier
zero reserve requirements
drawdowns and redeposits

overnight rate
bank rate
intermediate and ultimate targets
maturity (or term) of a bond
term structure of interest
arbitrage
expectations theory of term structure
yield curve

FILL-IN QUESTIONS

1. Currency plus bank reserves form _____ , or
    _____.

2. The upper end of the Bank of Canada's band on the overnight rate is the _____.

3. The Bank of Canada lowers its holdings of bonds and decreases the money supply through a(n)
    _____.

4. The ratio of the money supply to the monetary base is the _____.

5. The effects of bank rate changes on expectations are called _____.

6. Public portfolio preferences affect the money supply through changing the _____.

7. The principal asset of the Bank of Canada is _____.

8. The relationship between the interest rates paid on bonds of differing maturity is called the _____.

9. Long-term bonds are typically perceived as _____ than short-term bonds because of their greater price volatility.

10. The _____ curve shows the relationship between interest rates on assets of different maturities.

11. Periodic payments made to bond-holders are called _____ payments.

12. The amount that a bond pays its holder upon expiration is called its _____.

13. Changes in the price of a stock should be completely _____.

14. The time remaining before a bond expires is referred to as the term, or _____ of the bond.

15. _____ involves the simultaneous sale and purchase of an asset at different prices, in different markets.

16. To formulate policy, _____ targets are used.

TRUE-FALSE QUESTIONS

T F 1. An increase in high-powered money increases the money supply.

T F 2. An increase in the public's preferences for currency vis-à-vis deposits increases the money supply.

T F 3. An increase in bank preferences for excess reserves increases the money supply.

T F 4. An increase in income increases the money supply.

T F 5. Transfer of Government of Canada deposits from the Bank of Canada to the chartered banks increases the money supply.

T F 6. Chartered bank demand for advances from the Bank of Canada has an important effect on the money supply.

T F 7. An increase in the monetary base works through money demand to lower the interest rate.

T F 8. An increase in chartered bank borrowing from the Bank of Canada increases the money supply.

T F 9. If output deviates from its equilibrium level mainly because the IS curve shifts about, then output is stabilized by keeping the money supply constant.

T F 10. If output deviates from its equilibrium level mainly because the demand for money shifts about, then the central bank should operate monetary policy by keeping the money supply constant.

T F 11. Term premiums appear to vary over time.

T F 12. When interest rates rise, so do bond prices.

T F   13. When interest rates rise, so do stock prices.

T F   14. Financial markets are interesting in and of themselves, but have little to do with macroeconomics.

T F   15. Asset prices should be easily predictable.

T F   16. Asset prices reflect people's expectations of future returns; only new information should make them change.

T F   17. It is sometimes, but not always, a recessionary signal when interest rates on long-term bonds are lower than interest rates on short-term bonds.

T F   18. People's expectations of future short-term interest rates affect current long-term interest rates.

MULTIPLE-CHOICE QUESTIONS

1. The money multiplier is

    a. negative
    b. between 0 and 1
    c. exactly 1
    d. greater than 1

2. An open market purchase increases

    a. the monetary base
    b. the money supply
    c. bank loans
    d. all of (a), (b), and (c)

3. Assets of the Bank of Canada include

    a. deposits of the government
    b. deposits of the chartered banks
    c. government securities
    d. all of (a), (b), and (c)

4. Liabilities of the chartered banks include

    a. government securities
    b. deposits at the Bank of Canada
    c. demand deposits
    d. all of (a), (b), and (c)

5. If the currency-deposit ratio is one-half and the reserve-deposit ratio is 10 percent, the money multiplier is

    a. −0.75
    b. 0.75
    c. 1
    d. 2.5

6. The money multiplier reaches a maximum when the currency-deposit ratio equals

    a. 0
    b. one-half
    c. 1
    d. infinity

7. The money multiplier reaches a maximum when the reserve-deposit ratio equals

    a. 0
    b. one-half
    c. 1
    d. infinity

8. Bank loans will increase following an increase in

    a. the reserve-deposit ratio
    b. the monetary base
    c. the bank rate
    d. all of (a), (b), and (c)

9. If output deviates from its equilibrium value mainly because of shifts in the IS curve

   a. then output is stabilized by keeping the money stock constant
   b. then output is stabilized by keeping the interest rate constant
   c. then neither policy can stabilize output
   d. then fiscal policy will stabilize output

10. Which of the following compensates bond-holders for the risk associated with holding long- rather than short-term bonds?

    a. yield curve
    b. coupon
    c. perpetuity
    d. term premium

11. The amount that a bond pays when it expires is called its

    a. coupon
    b. face value
    c. return
    d. (b) and (c)

12. The maturity of a bond is also called its

    a. term
    b. coupon
    c. face value
    d. return

13. A downward-sloping yield curve is _____ a recessionary signal.

    a. sometimes
    b. never
    c. always
    d. it's actually an expansionary signal

14. Stock prices should follow a

    a. distributed lag
    b. random walk
    c. predictable pattern
    d. cycle

15. Long-term bonds are riskier than short-term bonds because of their

    a. coupon variation
    b. unpredictable face value
    c. greater price volatility
    d. term premium

16. Which of the following prevents asset prices from diverging (prevents one asset from having many different prices)?

    a. monetary policy
    b. compound interest
    c. net present value
    d. arbitrage

CONCEPTUAL PROBLEMS

1. Why is a downward-sloping yield curve sometimes a recessionary signal?

2. Why isn't a downward-sloping yield curve *always* a recessionary signal?

3. Why shouldn't changes in asset prices be predictable?

APPLICATION QUESTIONS

1. Suppose that reserves are 10 percent of chequable deposits, and that people always hold 40 percent as much currency as they hold chequable deposits.

a) If the monetary base equals $100 billion, what is the level of M1?

b) If the monetary base is increased by $50 billion, by how much do chequable deposits increase?

2. The demand functions for currency and chequable deposits are given below. Reserves are 10 percent of chequable deposits. The monetary base equals $1150; GDP equals $2000. What is the interest rate?

$$CU = 0.5Y - 495i$$
$$D = Y - 50i$$

3. If the current rate of interest on three-month Treasury bills is 6 percent, and is expected to rise 1/2 of a percentage point each quarter (every three months), what should be the rate of interest on a one-year government bond? (Assume that the term premium is zero.)

4. If the current rate of interest on a one-year Treasury bond is 8 percent, and if the rate of interest on three-month Treasury bills is expected to remain at 6 percent, what must be the term premium for a one-year bond?

5. In this question you are asked to use balance sheets to illustrate the multiple expansion of deposits. We'll assume that there is only one bank and one person, Professor B. As the problem opens, Professor B has $200 on deposit. The bank is holding the $200 as reserves. The bank wishes to hold 10 percent of its deposits as reserves. The first set of balance sheets follows:

Table 18-1 First Balance Sheet

Professor B		Bank	
Assets	Liabilities	Assets	Liabilities
Deposit $200	None	Reserves $200	$200 Deposit
		(Desired 20)	
		(Excess 180)	
	$200 Net worth		
$200	$200	$200	$200

Professor B decides to borrow as much as possible from the bank, in order to finance advanced macroeconomic research. This being a worthy cause, the bank agrees to loan the entire $180 of reserves that they hold beyond the desired amount (which is $20 = 10% of the $200). Call this "excess reserves." Professor B signs the loan agreement, and the bank credits her account with the $180. Fill in the blanks in the second set of balance sheets.

Table 18-2   *Second Balance Sheet*

Professor B			Bank		
Assets	Liabilities		Assets		Liabilities
Deposit $____	$180	Loan	Reserves $200	$_____	Deposit
			(Desired _____)		
			(Excess _____)		
	$_____	Net worth	Loan	$ _____	

Advanced macroeconomic research being as expensive as it is, Professor B decides to go for another loan. The bank again agrees to loan all its excess reserves. The bank increases the size of Professor B's loan balance and credits Professor B's account. Fill out the details in the third set of balance sheets.

Table 18-3   *Third Balance Sheet*

Professor B			Bank		
Assets	Liabilities		Assets		Liabilities
Deposit $____	$_____	Loan	Reserves $_____	$_____	Deposit
			(Desired _____)		
			(Excess _____)		
	$_____	Net worth	Loan _____		
$____	$_____		$_____	$ _____	

Table 18-4   *Final Balance Sheet*

Professor B			Bank		
Assets	Liabilities		Assets		Liabilities
Deposit $____	$_____	Loan	Reserves $_____	$_____	Deposit
			(Desired _____)		
			(Excess 0)		
	$_____	Net worth	Loan _____		
$____	$_____		$_____	$ _____	

Clearly, this process could go on for a long time. Using what you've learned about the money multiplier, fill out a final set of balance sheets reflecting the final multiple expansion of deposits and zero excess reserves.

19 BIG EVENTS: THE ECONOMICS OF DEPRESSION, HYPERINFLATION, AND DEFICITS

FOCUS OF THE CHAPTER

The *Great Depression* of the 1930s left an indelible mark on economic history and led to the development of Keynesian economies. (The depression in Britain, where Keynes developed his theories, had begun in the 1920s.)

During the Great Depression, unemployment reached nearly one-fifth of the work force, prices fell by 20 percent, and the bottom dropped out of the stock market.

Very high inflation rates are due primarily to excessive money growth; the link between money and inflation is much weaker when inflation is low.

Large budget deficits, and the debts they create, are often the cause of hyperinflations; countries rarely print money to excess unless they feel they have no alternative.

Pervasive Canadian federal budget deficits have been a serious political and economic issue. Some people argue that they burden future generations; other argue that they do not.

Many countries have begun to worry about the way their social security systems are structured; pay-as-you-go social security systems have begun to appear unsustainable as population growth has slowed.

SECTION SUMMARIES

1. The Great Depression: The Facts

Along with most of the rest of the industrialized world, the economy of Canada collapsed between 1929 and 1933. GNP fell by 30 percent, unemployment rose by nearly 20 percent, prices fell 20 percent, and the value of stocks dropped almost 70 percent.

Monetary and fiscal policy responses were not helpful. The money supply fell sharply in the U.S. and in Canada. In the U.S. this reduction was largely due to a series of bank failures. While there was no central bank in Canada until 1935, our money stock fell too, because of a contraction in the operations of our chartered banks. Governments were concerned with balancing their budgets, and so did not undertake the expansionary measures that one might advocate based on a Keynesian model.

2. The Great Depression: The Issues and Ideas

It is now generally agreed that the Great Depression could have been avoided and that it is unlikely to happen again. Two camps of thought exist with respect to what caused the Depression. The Keynesian explanation rests on an autonomous decline in aggregate demand, in investment, and possibly in autonomous consumption. A monetarist explanation was advanced by Friedman and Schwartz, based on the reduction of the money supply.

3. Money and Inflation in Ordinary Business Cycles

It is accepted by many that in the long run, money growth affects the inflation rate but not output. In the shorter run, however, this is not the case. Changes in the velocity of money and economic growth can prevent a one-to-one relationship between money growth and inflation. This can be seen from the quantity theory equation:

$$MV = PY$$

which can be written in percentage change form and adjusted to take the form

$$B = m - y - v$$

where m is money growth, v is the percentage change in velocity, B is the inflation rate, and y is the growth rate of output.

In Canada and other countries, the relationship between money (M2) growth and inflation is somewhat close, but there are gaps due to output growth and velocity changes.

4. Hyperinflation

A working definition of hyperinflation is when an annual rate of inflation exceeds 1000 percent. Although high money supply growth is the direct cause of hyperinflation, this money growth itself is often caused by a large government budget deficit, which must be financed by printing new money. The high inflation makes the budget deficit problem worse, because it reduces the real value of the taxes collected.

High inflation also makes the measured deficit misleadingly high due to high interest on the debt, much of which is necessary simply to cover the inflation rate. Economists often look instead at the *inflation-adjusted deficit*, defined as:

$$inflation\text{-}adjusted\ deficit\ = total\ deficit - (inflation\ rate \times national\ debt)$$

This definition subtracts the component of the interest payments on the debt that are attributed directly to inflation.

A common method of stopping hyperinflation is the *heterodox approach to stabilization*. This approach combines monetary, fiscal, and exchange rate policies with incomes policies such as wage and price controls. It is more likely to succeed if measures are taken to correct the government deficit problem as well.

Since expectations play a large role in causing high inflation, a credible anti-inflationary policy can be very effective through lowering inflationary expectations and hence inflation itself. This can be difficult though. First, government credibility is not easily earned. Second, there may be inflationary inertia built into long-term contracts.

Given some estimate of the cumulative percentage loss of GDP as a result of policies to lower inflation, we define the *sacrifice ratio* as the ratio of this loss to the actual reduction in inflation. Based on the experience of the early 1980s, this ratio has been estimated to be 1.5, much lower than previous estimates.

5. Deficits, Money Growth, and the Inflation Tax

The government can finance its deficits in two ways: it can either sell bonds, or persuade the central bank to increase the monetary base. The Bank of Canada is said to *monetize* a deficit whenever it purchases some of the bonds that the government sells to finance that deficit. If it does not do this, the fiscal expansion behind the deficit will drive up interest rates; if it does, it runs the risk of causing inflation. It does not appear that the Bank of Canada monetizes the federal deficit.

Creating high-powered money serves as an alternative to taxation. The revenue collected through money creation is referred to as *seigniorage*. The total amount of seigniorage that can be collected is given by the formula

$$\textit{inflation tax revenue} = \textit{inflation rate} \times \textit{real money base}$$

As the growth rate of money becomes large, the real money stock falls to zero; the government cannot collect an arbitrarily large amount of tax revenue simply by printing money. The "inflation tax" appears to be quite low in industrialized countries, where the money base is small relative to the size of the economy. Countries with less developed financial sectors, where people hold large amounts of currency, appear able to generate more revenue by printing money.

6. Federal Government Finances

The Canadian federal government budget was in deficit every year from the mid-1970s until 1997. Two contributing factors were: a reduction in the growth rate of tax revenues in the 1970s, and rapid growth in government expenditure on interest on the debt in the 1980s.

Structural deficits measure the size that the budget deficit would be if output were at its full-employment level. *Cyclical deficits* are the difference between actual and structural deficits. The deficit is typically broken into two components: the *primary*, or *non-interest deficit*, and interest payments on the public debt. Canada's federal primary deficit has been in surplus since 1987.

The national debt of Canada, over $650 billion at the end of 1997, seems like a great burden. In per capita terms, however, that amounts to only $21,600 per person. The debt ratio, which is the ratio of debt to income, is less than one. We could pay back the entire debt using less than one year's output. Most of it does not need to be paid back, because we owe the bulk to ourselves. An increasingly large portion of the national debt, however, is owned by foreigners. That portion represents a tax burden that future Canadian taxpayers will have to carry. The debt also can lower investment and therefore decrease our potential for long-term growth.

Intergenerational accounting evaluates the costs and benefits of taxation and spending on various age groups. Kotlikoff found that U.S. fiscal policies of the 1980s helped those over 40 years of age and hurt those under 40, particularly young women.

7. The Canada Pension Plan

Canada currently uses a *pay-as-you-go* social security system, in which the taxes paid by those generations who are currently working are used to fund payments made to retirees. Due to declines in population growth, at some point in the near future we will either have to raise CPP payments or reduce the amount of benefits paid to each retiree. Canada does not face this problem alone. A vast number of countries will soon have to address the same problem.

8. Working with Data

The student is asked to compute M2 growth minus GDP growth, plot this difference against the inflation rate in a scatter plot, and look for a long-run relation.

THE LANGUAGE OF ECONOMICS

Key Terms

Great Depression	government budget constraint
Keynesian revolution	monetization
hyperinflation	seigniorage
heterodox approach to stabilization	inflation tax
credible policy	primary (or noninterest) deficit
credibility bonus	debt-income ratio
inflationary inertia	intergenerational accounting
sacrifice ratio	pay-as-you-go (social security) system

The Inflation Tax

How is inflation a tax? It is clear that it reduces the value of your money. If you leave a $20 bill in your coat pocket for a year or two, that $20 is likely to buy you fewer goods and services than it did before. How, though, does it provide revenue to the government?

When prices rise at a constant rate, the real money supply will fall at a constant rate unless the monetary base is expanded. Inflation, therefore, gives the federal government, through the Bank of Canada, the ability to print money without increasing the real money supply. Once it has printed that money, it can, of course, spend it.

REVIEW OF TECHNIQUE

Elasticity

The *elasticity* of x with respect to y is the percentage change in x that results from a 1 percent increase in y. It can be written in several ways:

$$\frac{\text{percentage change in } x}{\text{percentage change in } y} \quad \text{or} \quad \frac{\%\Delta x}{\%\Delta y} \quad \text{or} \quad \frac{\Delta x/x}{\Delta y/y} \quad \text{or} \quad \frac{\Delta x}{\Delta y} \quad \text{or} \quad \frac{y}{x}$$

The elasticity of any relation is independent of the units in which it is measured.

Certain formulas have the property that one variable has a *constant elasticity* with respect to another.

These are extremely convenient, as they generate a fixed relationship between the percentage change of one variable and the percentage change of another. Take the formula

$$x = ay^\alpha z^\beta$$

for example. If we take natural logarithms of both sides (see Review of Technique 17 if you need a brief review of natural logarithms), we find that

$$\ln x = \ln a + \alpha \ln y + \beta \ln z$$

or, looking at how this changes over time,

$$\Delta \ln x = \alpha\Delta \ln y + \beta\Delta \ln z$$

It is a property of natural logarithms that $\Delta \ln x = \%\Delta x$. We can write this yet another way to highlight the way in which the percentage change in x is related to the percentage changes in y and z:

$$\%\Delta x = \alpha\%\Delta y + \beta\%\Delta z.$$

If y increases by 1 percent, x will increase by $(\alpha \times 1)$ percent; if z increases by 1 percent, x will increase by $(\beta \times 1)$ percent. The elasticity of x with respect to y is just the coefficient α. The elasticity of x with respect to z is the coefficient β.

Note that the Cobb-Douglas production function is of this form; output will have a constant elasticity with respect to all factors of production. The Baumol-Tobin money demand function is, too, as it can be written as follows:

$$M/P = (bY)^{1/2} (2i)^{1/2}$$

The elasticities of money demand with respect to income and the interest rate are constant in this function.

FILL-IN QUESTIONS

1. Hyperinflations have, historically, tended to occur in the aftermath of _____.

2. _____ deficits tell us how big (or small) the budget deficit *would* be, if output were at its full-employment level.

3. The revenue collected through money creation is called _____.

4. The creation of high-powered money in order to generate revenues is referred to as an

   _____.

5. The Bank of Canada is said to _____ a deficit when it buys some or all of the bonds that the government sells to finance that deficit.

6. A _____ approach to stabilization consists of the simultaneous use of monetary, fiscal, exchange rate, and incomes policies.

7. The government can finance its budget deficits in two ways: it can either _____ or

   _____.

8. The non-interest deficit is also called the _____ deficit.

9. Countries with hyperinflation often have large, persistent _____.

10. Canada currently has a _____ social security system.

11. The component of the deficit that varies with the output gap is called the _____ deficit.

12. The ratio of debt to GDP is called the _____ ratio.

TRUE-FALSE QUESTIONS

T F 1. The Great Depression was specific to Canada; everyone else was just fine.

T F 2. Fault for the Great Depression has been attributed to both bad fiscal and bad monetary policy.

T F 3. Monetary policy was expansionary during the early years of the Great Depression.

T F 4. The Great Depression was accompanied by a sharp increase in prices.

T F 5. Very high inflation rates are primarily due to excessive money growth.

T F 6. The link between money and inflation is stronger in the short run than in the long run.

T F 7. Budget deficits are a problem in and out of themselves, but have little to do with hyperinflations.

T F 8. The velocity of money varies considerably in the short run, but not very much in the long run.

T F 9. Increasing the monetary base is an alternative to taxation.

T F 10. There is clear evidence that the Bank of Canada monetizes Canadian federal government budget deficits.

T F 11. Interest payments on the debt increase government spending and increase deficits.

T F 12. Pay-as-you-go social security systems are beginning to appear unstable as population growth slows.

T F 13. The national debt-to-income ratio in Canada reached the highest level it has ever been in the 1990s.

T F 14. Federal tax revenues as a fraction of GDP haven't changed very much over the last 30 years in Canada.

T F 15. In a pay-as-you-go government pension system, the benefit-contribution ratio can be much higher in a growing population than in a stable population.

T F 16. The portion of the national debt owned by domestic residents is a tax burden that either current or future Canadian taxpayers will have to pay.

T F 17. The portion of the national debt owned by foreigners is a tax burden that either current or future Canadian taxpayers will have to pay.

MULTIPLE-CHOICE QUESTIONS

1. The length and severity of the Great Depression was the fault of

    a. monetary policy   c. neither
    b. fiscal policy   d. both

2. The Depression of the 1930s was a _____ phenomenon.

    a. Canadian   c. western
    b. North American   d. global

---

3. The Great Depression began in Canada, in

   a. 1929   c. 1933
   b. 1931   d. 1935

4. If the nominal money supply is growing at 6 percent a year, real output is growing at 2 percent a year, and the velocity of money is constant, then the rate of inflation should be *(HINT: use the quantity equation.)*

   a. 3 percent   c. 8 percent
   b. 4 percent   d. 12 percent

5. If the nominal money supply is growing at 6 percent a year, and real output is growing at 2 percent a year, and the monetary base is fixed at $100 billion, how large will inflation tax revenues be?

   a. $400 billion   c. $4 billion
   b. $40 billion   d. 0

6. When the rate of inflation is higher than the rate of money growth, the real money supply

   a. rises   c. remains constant
   b. falls   d. could be any of the above

7. Hyperinflations are usually ended through

   a. currency reform   c. tight monetary policy
   b. reduced budget deficits   d. all of the above

8. There is a stronger link between the rate of money growth and the nominal rate of inflation in the

   a. long run   c. steady-state
   b. short run   d. not affected by time horizon

CONCEPTUAL PROBLEMS

1. What rate of money growth should Canada be able to maintain without causing inflation? Why?

2. Why should the monetary authority be concerned whether its inflation-reduction policy is credible? Explain.

3. What causes hyperinflations?

WORKING WITH DATA

Table 19-1 provides information on the monetary base and the CPI. On Chart 19-1 you can plot real inflation tax revenues over time.

To compute real inflation tax revenues, three calculations are required:

(i) compute the real monetary base (in $1992) by multiplying the (nominal) monetary base by the CPI and dividing by 100.
(ii) compute the inflation rate as the percentage increase in the CPI over the previous year.
(iii) compute the inflation tax (in constant $1992) as the inflation rate times the monetary base.

TABLE 19-1

Year	Monetary Base ($ billion)	CPI (1992=100)	Real Monetary Base (billions of $1992)	Inflation Rate (percent)	Real Inflation Tax Revenue (billions of $1992)
1980	16.0	52.4	30.6		
1981	17.2	58.9	29.2	12.4	3.6
1982	17.4	65.3			
1983	17.7	69.1			
1984	17.9	72.1			
1985	18.8	75.0			
1986	20.0	78.1			
1987	21.1	81.5			
1988	22.2	84.8			
1989	23.5	89.0			
1990	24.4	93.3			
1991	25.4	98.5			
1992	26.7	100.0			
1993	28.3	101.8			
1994	29.3	102.0			
1995	29.5	104.2			
1996	30.2	105.8			
1997	31.7	107.6			
1998	33.6	108.6			

Source: CANSIM web site

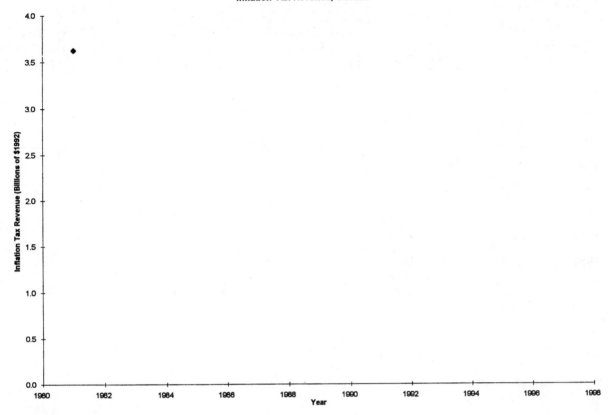

Chart 19-1

APPLICATION QUESTIONS

1. If the annual rate of inflation is 1000 percent, what must be the monthly rate of inflation?

2. If the annual rate of inflation is 2000 percent, what must be the daily rate of inflation?

3. How much inflation tax revenue would be generated in a country with a real money base of $1,000 and an inflation rate of 1000 percent?

4. How much inflation tax revenue would be generated in a country with a real money base of $500 and an inflation rate of 1000 percent?

5. What happens to the real money base, over time, when the growth rate of money becomes large and the nominal money supply is held constant? Given this, do you think that seigniorage is a good way to generate revenue?

20 ADVANCED TOPICS

FOCUS OF THE CHAPTER

This chapter presents an overview of four recent ideas and models that have revolutionized modern macroeconomics—rational expectations modelling, the random walk theory of GDP, real business cycle theory, and New Keynesian models of price stickiness. Not all of these ideas fit together—some, in fact, contradict each other.

Much of the technical material developed in this chapter is optional. Section 20-1 of the textbook provides a very readable overview of the ideas developed in later, optional sections, however. If you read nothing else, read that.

SECTION SUMMARIES

1. An Overview of the New Macroeconomics

This section provides an informal introduction to four subjects: rational expectations modelling, the random walk theory of GDP, real business cycle theory, and New Keynesian models of price stickiness. We discuss each briefly, noting how each is related to the traditional aggregate supply–aggregate demand model.

The rational expectations model outlined in this chapter (the Lucas model) tries to explain how output can deviate from potential output and unemployment from its natural rate without requiring that prices adjust sluggishly. In Lucas's model, people cannot directly observe the price level, and must therefore form *expectations* of it. When these expectations are wrong, people's estimates of the real wage are also wrong, which causes them to supply "too much" or "too little" labour—an amount greater or less than they would choose to supply if they knew what their real wage really was. The labour market does clear in this model; the main way in which the aggregate supply assumptions differ from the classical case of the AS-AD model is that the labour supply, in this case, depends on the expected real wage rather than the actual real wage.

The assumption that people's expectations are formed *rationally* (see The Language of Economics section of Chapter 7 for a review of the term "rational expectations") creates an even greater difference between this model and the standard AS-AD model. Only unanticipated AD shifts can affect output and unemployment in the short run. Instead of a price level which is slow to adjust to economic shocks (as is the case with the AS-AD model), we have here an expectation of the price level which fails, in the short run, to respond to changes in the economy when events occur without people's knowledge. (Eventually, as more information becomes available, such errors correct themselves.)

Unanticipated AD shifts do not affect people's expectations of the price level, so that nominal wage increases intended only to compensate workers for a higher price level look, to them, like increases in the real wage. This increased real wage they believe they are receiving makes them want to work more hours, raising output above its full-employment level for a time.

Anticipated AD shifts do affect people's expectations of the price level. They correctly guess, as a result, that the higher nominal raise that they are receiving as a result of the AD shift is merely compensating them for a higher price level, and choose to supply the same amount of labour.

Demand-side policies have little place in Lucas's model. Unless they come as a surprise to the public, they accomplish nothing. Announcements are the only tool that is needed to stabilize output. All that the government need do to combat a recession is to correct people's expectational errors.

Real business cycle (RBC) theory is a natural outgrowth of rational expectations models like this one. Having ruled out aggregate demand shocks as the source of business cycle fluctuations, the proponents of RBC theory turn to ***productivity shocks*** to explain why output can and does deviate from its full-employment (potential) level. They argue that small changes in productivity, which, because the labour market is assumed to remain in equilibrium, cause small changes in the real wage, can generate large fluctuations in employment (and therefore in output) because people can substitute leisure over time— work more hours when their wage temporarily rises, and take time off when their wage temporarily falls.

Both of these theories have a significant drawback: changes in the money supply, both anticipated and unanticipated, ***do*** appear to affect both output and unemployment in the short run in the real world. By testing the ***random walk theory of GDP***—the theory that economic shocks have permanent rather than temporary effects on output—economists have tried to determine whether AS or AD shifts dominate the business cycle. (Recall that only supply shocks have permanent effects on output; AD shocks affect output only in the short run.)

New Keynesian models of price stickiness try to justify, in microeconomic terms, the assumption made in the AS-AD model that prices do not adjust immediately to clear markets.

2. The Rational Expectations Revolution

This section develops a simplified rational expectations model, and compares it to a basic AS-AD model with exogenously specified expectations of the price level. Perfect foresight models—models in which people always correctly guess the price level, so that the difference between it and the expected price level is always zero—are introduced, and shown to be equivalent to rational expectations models when people have all the information they need to correctly ascertain the state of the economy (i.e., output never deviates from potential output in this model, because people's expectations are always exactly correct).

The result that anticipated changes in the money supply cannot affect output in rational expectations models is derived carefully and in great detail, as is the result that unanticipated changes in the money supply can.

The authors note that empirical evidence does not strongly support these results; anticipated changes in the money supply do appear to have real effects in the short run.

3. The Microeconomics of the Imperfect Information Aggregate Supply Curve (optional section)

This section develops Lucas's imperfect information model of the AS curve. While the model itself is interesting and worth working through for its own sake, the real benefit of this section is that it allows you to work with, instead of reading about, rational expectations. If you read nothing else, read Box 20-2, "A Visual Example of Forming an Expectation."

The main result of the Lucas imperfect information model is derived: The amount that unanticipated changes in aggregate demand affect output depends on the relative importance of aggregate shocks (shocks that hit the entire economy) and idiosyncratic shocks (shocks specific to one industry or region).

4. The Random Walk of GDP—Does Aggregate Demand Matter, or is it all Aggregate Supply?

This section introduces *trend and difference stationary* processes. A trend stationary process is one which is dominated by transitory shocks—shocks whose effect eventually dies away. A difference stationary process, on the other hand, is dominated by permanent shocks—shocks whose effects accumulate over time. The *random walk* is the classic example of such a process.

If GDP is trend rather than difference stationary, business cycles must be caused by short-lived aggregate demand shocks, as economists have traditionally believed. If it proves to be difference stationary, on the other hand, supply shocks must be driving output, as real business cycle theorists believe.

Statistically, it does look like output is dominated by permanent shocks—a controversial result, as it makes the sorts of fiscal and monetary policy that we have studied appear relatively unimportant. Luckily, there is a third possibility—one also supported by statistical evidence: GDP may instead be *trend stationary with breaks*, so that, while permanent shocks to productivity occur on rare occasions, aggregate demand shocks drive the business cycle within decades-long subperiods.

Statistical difficulties make it hard to determine with any certainty whether output is best characterized as difference stationary or as trend stationary with breaks. For this reason, the importance of AD shocks in the business cycle is likely to remain controversial for some time.

5. Real Business Cycle (RBC) Theory

This section develops a simple RBC model, in which temporary fluctuations in the productivity of labour cause people to work more in periods of high productivity, and less in periods of low productivity.

The degree to which people substitute leisure over time determines whether or not small shocks to people's productivity can generate fluctuations in output that are big enough to explain the business cycle. This is shown to depend on two *deep parameters,* which are parameters that are fundamental determinants of the microeconomic decisions people make (consumption, labour supply, etc.): β and y. These parameters determine the relative importance of consumption and leisure in a representative worker's utility. These appear too small to generate enough *intertemporal substitution* to explain the business cycle.

6. A New Keynesian Model of Sticky Nominal Prices

This section highlights several key aspects of New Keynesian models of price stickiness: their reliance on imperfect competition, so that individual firms have enough market power to set prices; the assumption that there is a small cost that firms incur when they choose to change their nominal prices; and the assumption that the private benefits of one firm changing its price are significantly smaller than the social benefits—i.e., there is an *externality* involved.

These elements, together, can be combined in such a way that an individual firm will not find it optimal to raise its price in response to a demand shock, despite the fact that it would be best for society if it (and all other firms) did so.

7. Working with Data

The student is asked to use an estimated equation of potential GDP, then use it to calculate potential GDP in each period and reproduce Figure 20-4 in the text.

THE LANGUAGE OF ECONOMICS

Key Terms

rational expectations equilibrium	imperfect competition
rational expectations	Lucas critique
policy irrelevance	perfect foresight
random walk	imperfect-information model
real business cycle (RBC) theory	trend (secular) component of GDP
propagation mechanisms	cyclical component of GDP
intertemporal substitution of leisure	trend stationary
productivity shock	difference stationary
New Keynesians	trend stationary with breaks
price stickiness	deep parameters
menu cost	

New Keynesians and New Classicists

Perhaps the biggest division in contemporary macroeconomics is between *New Keynesian* and *New Classical* economists. While both ground their theories in rational, maximizing behaviour, they disagree about one fundamental aspect of the economy—whether or not markets clear.

This is, of course, what the original Keynesians and Classicists disagreed about. The main difference today is that, instead of arguing generally about whether shifts in AD affect output, New Keynesians and New Classicists argue about whether *anticipated* changes in AD do so.

The rules of the argument have changed as well; while the original Keynesians were able to support their assumptions by arguing that prices in the real world simply did not appear to adjust quickly enough to keep markets in equilibrium, the New Keynesians face a more formidable task. They must show that these sticky prices can arise in a world full of rational, utility maximizing agents—that they are not inconsistent with fundamental microeconomic principles. Only then can they challenge the New Classicists on their own ground.

REVIEW OF TECHNIQUE

Taking a Random Walk

A *random walk* is the classic example of a difference stationary process—one whose level is permanently affected by shocks. This Review of Technique tells you how you might take a random walk.

Imagine yourself walking through a city. Every time you hit an intersection, you take the path of least resistance: you move in whatever direction the traffic signals suggest. You then continue moving in that direction until you hit another intersection that causes you to turn....

You can imagine that a person following this rule would not be able to predict where he or she would end up on any particular walk (this would be a bad strategy for, say, going to the zoo). Because all changes of direction have a permanent effect, his or her path is, in effect, random.

When a variable follows a random walk, it exhibits no tendency to return to its previous path after something makes it deviate from that path (the traffic signals, in our example above). Notice that this is true for y in the equation below:

$$y_t = y_{t-1} + u_t$$

The level of y does not change here unless y is hit by a shock (i.e., unless u_t is non-zero). When it does change, it changes permanently; it will not, except by coincidence, return to its previous level. This remains true when we add a "drift" term—a term which causes y to increase, or drift upwards, at a constant rate:

$$y_t = y_{t-1} + \beta + u_t$$

As before, shocks have a permanent effect on the level of y in this equation. Figure 20-1, which shows the path of a variable that follows this second process when it is interrupted only once by a shock $u_t = 1$,

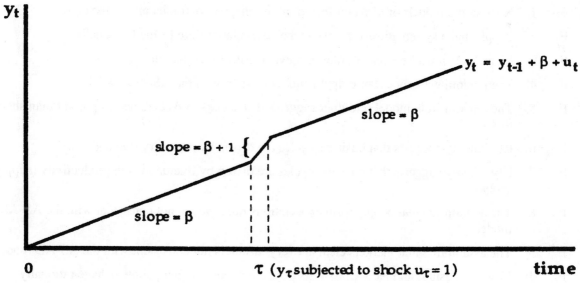

provides an example.

Figure 20-1

Advanced Topics

FILL-IN QUESTIONS

1. The _____ theory of output argues that most shifts in output are permanent, rather than transitory.

2. When expectations are formed _____, people use all (relevant) available information to make them.

3. There is no need for accommodating monetary or fiscal policy in a _____ _____. Deviations from full employment, and thus from potential output, result entirely from expectational errors.

4. If most shocks to output have permanent effects, changes in _____ are relatively unimportant.

5. In equilibrium real business cycle (RBC) theory, changes in output are primarily attributed to _____ shocks.

6. In RBC theory, transitory shocks can have permanent effects because people substitute _____ over time.

7. We call this *intertemporal substitution* a _____ mechanism.

8. New Keynesian models of price stickiness, which suggest that firms do not find it optimal to change their prices immediately in response to a shock, require firms to be able to set their prices, and thus assume that markets are _____ competitive.

9. The small cost associated with increasing one's prices is called a _____.

10. In Lucas's rational expectations equilibrium model, _____ changes in monetary policy have no effect on output.

TRUE-FALSE QUESTIONS

T   F   1. None of the models or ideas presented in this chapter contradict any of the others.

T   F   2. People make systematic errors, even when expectations are formed rationally.

T   F   3. Menu costs must be *huge* in order to prevent firms from changing their prices.

T   F   4. The random walk model of output is not consistent with the AS-AD model.

T   F   5. The random walk model of output suggests that shocks to AD are less important than shocks to AS.

T   F   6. RBC theory suggests that business cycles are driven by monetary fluctuations.

T   F   7. RBC theory suggests that business cycles are driven by fluctuations in productivity (supply shocks).

T   F   8. The assumption that people form expectations *rationally* is not consistent with the AS-AD model.

T   F   9. The assumption that markets clear at every instant is not consistent with the AS-AD model.

T   F   10. New Keynesians and New Classicists disagree about whether people behave rationally (*weigh the costs and benefits of their actions, and act accordingly*).

MULTIPLE-CHOICE QUESTIONS

1. Which of the following models/ideas does *not* go with the others?

   a. RBC theory
   b. random walk theory of output
   c. rational expectations equilibrium
   d. New Keynesian "sticky price" models

2. If output appears to fluctuate around a trend, changes in output are most likely driven by

   a. supply shocks
   b. demand shocks
   c. both
   d. neither

3. In the random walk model of output, changes in output are driven primarily by

   a. supply shocks
   b. demand shocks
   c. both
   d. neither

4. Supply shocks, in this chapter, are assumed to have _____ on the level of output.

   a. a temporary effect
   b. a permanent effect
   c. an unpredictable effect
   d. no effect

5. Demand shocks have _____ on the level of output.

   a. a temporary effect
   b. a permanent effect
   c. an unpredictable effect
   d. no effect

6. When expectations are formed rationally, errors

   a. do not exist
   b. can always be predicted
   c. can sometimes be predicted
   d. can never be predicted

7. In the New Keynesian model of price stickiness covered in this chapter, prices are sticky because

   a. there are long term contracts
   b. there are menu costs
   c. of the insider-outsider problem
   d. expectations are irrational

8. New Keynesians and New Classicists disagree about whether

   a. markets always clear
   b. output can diverge from potential output
   c. unanticipated changes in monetary policy affect output
   d. individuals behave rationally

9. In real business cycle theory, fluctuations in output are assumed to be caused by

   a. supply shocks
   b. demand shocks
   c. both
   d. neither

10. Which of the following is not an element of real business cycle theory?

   a. markets always clear
   b. anticipated changes in monetary policy affect output
   c. aggregate demand shocks are not important
   d. individuals behave rationally

CONCEPTUAL PROBLEMS

1. What are the New Keynesians trying to accomplish by building their models of price stickiness?

2. Why should anyone care whether or not prices are sticky?

3. Does the random walk model of GDP suggest that the AS-AD model is theoretically flawed? Explain.

4. What do real business cycle theorists believe causes output fluctuations?

APPLICATION QUESTIONS

1. Identify the "deep parameters" used in this chapter's RBC model. What values will cause strong intertemporal substitution? Justify your answer, appealing to a relevant equation.

2. Does empirical evidence suggest that the parameter values that you identified in Question 1 are realistic? (i.e., does there appear to be a strong intertemporal substitution of leisure in our world?)

3. When, in Lucas's Imperfect Information Model, will unexpected changes in AD have the biggest effect on output? Why?

4. Do AD or AS supply shocks appear to drive the business cycle, according to the empirical evidence presented in Section 20-4? Explain.

5. Table 20-1 provides equations that describe trend stationary and a difference stationary processes which are subjected to the same shocks for six periods. Graph the trend stationary process on Chart 20-1 and the difference stationary process on Chart 20-2, and compare them. Without knowing

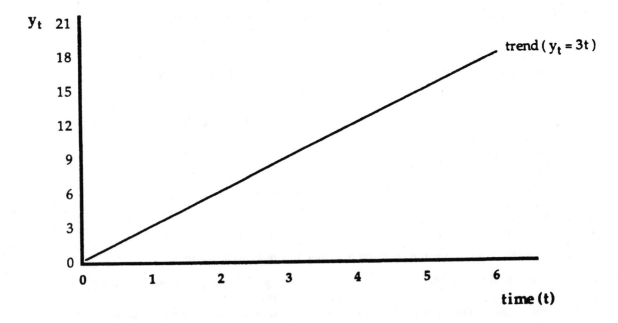

beforehand, would you be able to guess which was which?

Chart 20-1

TREND STATIONARY PROCESS

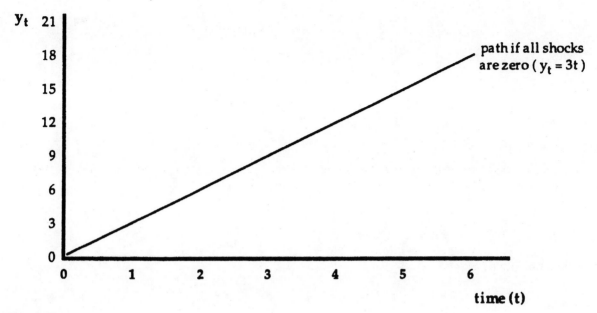

Chart 20-2

DIFFERENCE STATIONARY PROCESS (RANDOM WALK)

TABLE 20-1

Period (t)	Shock (u_t)	Trend Stationary Process ($y_t = 3t + u_t$)	Difference Stationary Process ($y_t = y_{t-1} + 3 + u_t$)
0	0	0*	0*
1	1	4	4
2	2	8	9
3	1	10	13
4	0	12	16
5	−1	14	18
6	0	18	21

* We are assuming, for simplicity, that $y_0 = 0$ for both processes.

ANSWERS TO QUESTIONS AND PROBLEMS

Chapter 1

Fill-In Questions

1. growth theory
2. aggregate supply/demand
3. aggregate supply
4. aggregate demand

5. aggregate demand
6. Phillips
7. business cycle
8. consumer price index
9. balance of trade

True-False Questions

1. True.
2. False—output in the long run is determined entirely by the *aggregate supply* curve.
3. True.
4. False—*nearly everything* you will learn can be fit into this framework!

Working with Data (See next pages for Chart 1-1 and Table 1-1.)

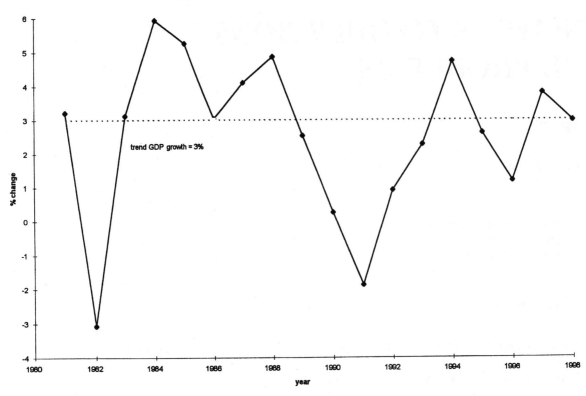

Percentage Change in GDP

trend GDP growth = 3%

Chart 1-1

Answers to Questions and Problems

TABLE 1-1

Year	Canadian GDP	Percent change from previous year
1980	431.8	
1981	445.7	3.2
1982	432.0	−3.1
1983	445.5	3.1
1984	471.9	5.9
1985	496.7	5.3
1986	511.8	3.0
1987	532.8	4.1
1988	558.7	4.9
1989	572.9	2.5
1990	574.4	0.3
1991	563.6	−1.9
1992	568.8	0.9
1993	581.8	2.3
1994	609.3	4.7
1995	625.3	2.6
1996	632.8	1.2
1997	656.9	3.8
1998	676.5	3.0

Chapter 2

Fill-In Questions

1. GDP
2. depreciation
3. factors of production; factor payments
4. transfer payments
5. gross private domestic investment
6. exports; imports
7. government budget deficit
8. value added
9. adjusted GNP
10. GDP deflator
11. double counting
12. nominal interest rate; inflation rate

True-False Questions

1. False—roughly 3/4 of all factor payments are paid to *labour*.
2. True.
3. True.
4. True.
5. False.
6. True.
7. False—the text discusses several reasons GDP (and GNP) are imperfect measures of welfare.

8. False—the GDP deflator does not include import prices.
9. True.
10. True.
11. False. See Figure 2-1 in the text. It was negative in 1975.

Multiple-Choice Questions

1. c   2. b   3. b   4. d   5. d   6. d   7. d   8. a   9. d   10. d   11. d

Conceptual Problems

1. GDP would increase. This would not necessarily reflect a change in the physical output of the economy.

2. Personal computers are an example.

3. The trade deficit ($-NX$) must equal the budget deficit ($G + TR - T$)

4. The government could decrease its spending, reduce the amount of money it gives out in the form of transfer payments, or increase taxes. A decrease in saving without a corresponding decrease in investment could also achieve this, as could an increase in exports without a corresponding increase in imports. Keep in mind, however, that it isn't always easy to change just one of these things.

Working with Data

TABLE 2-1

Year	GDP deflator	Percent change from previous year
1980	72.3	—
1981	80.2	10.9
1982	87.1	8.6
1983	91.8	5.4
1984	94.8	3.3
1985	97.2	2.5
1986	100.0	2.9
1987	104.7	4.7
1988	109.4	4.5
1989	114.5	4.7
1990	117.9	3.0
1991	121.1	2.7
1992	122.7	1.3
1993	124.5	1.5
1994	125.9	1.1
1995	129.0	2.5
1996	130.9	1.5
1997	131.8	0.7
1998	131.3	−0.4

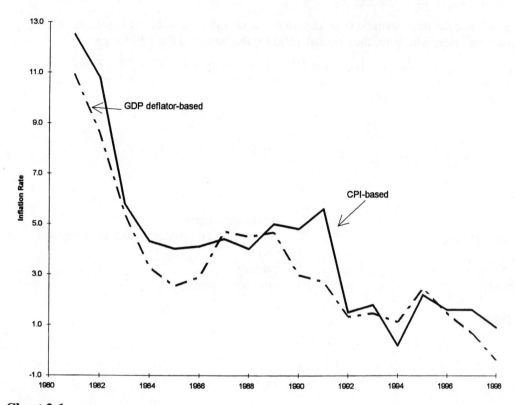

CPI- and GDP deflator-based Inflation

Chart 2-1

CPI- AND GDP-DEFLATOR-BASED INFLATION

Application Questions

1. $GDP = C + I + G = \$1,000 + \$100 + \$300 = \$1,400$

   Because the government's budget is balanced and net exports are zero, saving equals investment: $S = I = \$100$.

2. We know that $(S - I) = (G + TR - T) + NX$. If we solve this equation for I, we find that investment is equal to saving minus the budget deficit + the trade deficit, or that investment equals $160: $I = S - (G + TR - T) + (-NX) = \$200 - \$50 + \$10 = \$160$.

3. Disposable Income = Total Income + Transfers – Taxes = Total Output + Transfers – Taxes. Total output (GDP) is given to us in the problem; the difference between taxes and transfers $(TR - T)$ is not. We do know enough about the government's budget deficit, however, to figure it out: $(G + TR - T) = (\$250 + TR - T) = \$40$, so $TR - T = \$40 - \$250 = -\$210$.

   Disposable Income = $GDP + TR - T = \$1,000 - \$210 = \$790$.

4. We know that $GDP = C + I + G + NX$. This tells us that $NX = GDP - C - I - G$. GDP, C, and I are given to us; G is not. Luckily we can figure it out from the information that we have been given about the budget deficit (BD), and about the difference between transfers and taxes: $BD = G + TR - T$, so $G = BD - (TR - T) = \$120 - \$20 = \$100$.

   $NX = GDP - C - I - G = \$500 - \$350 - \$150 - \$100 = -\$100$.

5. Inflation (π) is just the *rate of change* of the price level:
    $\pi = (2 - 1.75)/1.75 = .143$, or 14.3 percent.

6. Value added is $20. Take the total revenue from the final sale of $550 and subtract the value of the intermediate good purchases, which are the original $500 for the bird, and the $30 for gas.

7. Using $I = S - (G + TR - T) + (-NX)$, we know that NX did not change while $G + TR - T$ has increased (since T decreased). Therefore $(I - S)$ has decreased. We cannot say anything about the direction of change of I or S individually.

Chapter 3

Fill-In Questions

1. Cobb-Douglas
2. marginal product of labour
3. real wage
4. leisure
5. full employment
6. aggregate supply
7. rate of time preference; real rate of interest
8. saving
9. quantity
10. velocity of money

True-False Questions

1. True.
2. False.
3. True.
4. False.
5. True.
6. True.
7. False—the simplifying assumptions of this model imply that everyone who wishes to work at the equilibrium wage can do so.
8. True—this is another way of saying that the Classical aggregate supply curve is vertical.
9. False—it is given by the real rate of interest.
10. False—investment equals the sum of government and private saving.

Multiple-Choice Questions

1. d   2. d   3. c   4. b   5. b

Conceptual Problems

1. The Fisher effect says that the real interest rate is not affected by changes in the inflation rate. In other words, any change in the inflation rate should be matched by changes in the nominal interest rate. The demand and supply of loans should be determined by the expected real rate of return. If the inflation rate increased (more precisely, the expected future inflation rate) both demanders and suppliers of loans should be content with a similar-sized increase in the nominal interest rate. One of the reasons this may not hold as well in the actual data is that actual inflation may turn out to be different than expected.

2. Money supply growth in the long run is thought to be a primary determinant of the inflation rate. By announcing a credible target growth rate in a time of high inflation, central bankers also hoped to convince citizens that the inflation would be lower in the near future. This expectation itself would help to lower inflation through a reduction in wage demands for example.

Answers to Questions and Problems

Application Questions

1. $MPN = dY/dN = 4K^{.5}(dN^{.5}/dN) = 4K^{.5}(.5N^{-.5N}) = 2K^{.5}N^{-.5}$.

2. $W/P = MPN = 2K^{.5}N^{-.5}$. So $20/10 = 2(9)^{.5}N^{-.5}$, and $2 = 6N^{-.5}$, and $N^{.5} = 6/2 = 3$, and $N = 9$. From the production function, real output is $2(9)^{.5}(9)^{.5} = 18$.

3. We have the same labour demand function $W/P = 2K^{.5}N^{-.5} = 6N^{-.5}$ when $K = 9$. But instead of being given the values W and P, we are given the labour supply function $W/P = 1.5N^{.5}$. Solve for N by equating the right hand sides of the labour demand and supply equations: $6N^{-.5} = 1.5N^{.5}$, so that $6/1.5 = N$ or $4 = N$. Therefore real output is $Y = 4(9)^{.5}(4)^{.5} = 4(3)(2) = 24$. The real wage is $W/P = 6(4)^{.5} = 6(2) = 12$. (Note that the real wage is lower than in Question 2 due to different labour supply conditions, resulting in higher labour demand, higher labour input, and higher real output.)

4. Private saving can be determined from the equation: $S = S^P + S^G = I$. The government budget deficit counts as negative government saving, so $S^G = -20$. Since $I = 25$, then $S^P = 20 + 25 = 45$.

Chapter 4

Fill-In Questions

1. marginal product of labour; decreases
2. total factor productivity
3. physical
4. human
5. converge
6. returns to scale
7. exogenous
8. saving (or investment)
9. absolute; conditional
10. conditionally

True-False Questions

1. False—it will change the rate at which *total* potential output grows at the steady-state.
2. True.
3. True.
4. False—the saving rate does not affect the growth rate of output at the steady-state.
5. False—they must also have the same saving rate.
6. False—not as long as there are external benefits associated with private investment (i.e., as long as individual producers are unable to capture all of the benefits associated with their investment).
7. False—they must also have the same rate of saving and the same marginal product of capital.
8. True.
9. False—changes in the saving rate permanently raise the growth rate of output in endogenous growth models.
10. False.

Multiple-Choice Questions

1. d   2. d   3. a   4. d   5. b   6. a   7. a   8. c   9. a   10. d

Conceptual Questions

1. All factors of production have diminishing marginal returns; productivity growth (technological improvement) is exogenous.

2. (a) is a stock variable; (b) and (c) are flow variables (depreciation is a flow out of the capital stock; investment is a flow into it).

3. Capital has a constant marginal product in endogenous growth theory, whereas it has a diminishing marginal product in neo-classical theory. The production function, as a result, has increasing rather than constant returns to scale.

4. Yes—the exponents add to one.
    No—the exponents do not add to one. (Because they add to a number greater than one, this second production function has increasing returns.)

5. An increase in the rate of saving will increase the growth rate of output in an endogenous growth model.

6. An increase in the rate of saving will have no effect on the growth rate of output in the neo-classical model, as it is assumed not to affect the rate of technological improvement.

7. Endogenous growth theory, insofar as it is able to explain what determines the growth rate of technology, can explain what causes countries on the cutting edge of technology to grow. It *can't* explain differences in growth rates across countries.

Working with Data

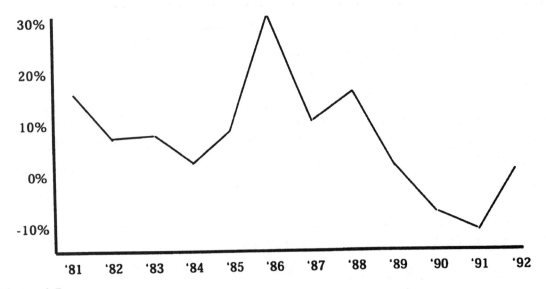

Figure 4-5

Answers to Questions and Problems

GROWTH RATE OF PER CAPITA GDP, BULGARIA

Year	Per capita GDP	Percent change from previous year
1980	3139	—
1981	3623	15.4
1982	3888	7.3
1983	4221	8.6
1984	4366	3.4
1985	4773	9.3
1986	6284	31.7
1987	6918	10.1
1988	8030	16.1
1989	8135	1.3
1990	7529	−7.4
1991	6715	−10.8
1992	6774	0.9

Source: Penn World Tables

Bulgaria's revolution occurred in 1989. As was (and is) the case with many transition economies, its output fell for several years following the adoption of basic market reforms.

Application Questions

1. a) Capital's share of income = 1/4. It is always the power to which K is raised in a constant returns to scale, Cobb-Douglas production function.

   In general, capital's share of income is given by the equation:
   $(i \times K)/Y = (MPK \times K)/Y.$

   b) We know from (a) that $MPK \times K/Y = 1/4$. All we need to do is rearrange this equation: $(Y/K) = MPK / (1/4) = 4 \times MPK = $ *capital's share of income* $\times MPK.$

   c) Labour's share of income = 3/4. It is always the power to which L is raised in a constant returns to scale, Cobb-Douglas production function.

   In general, capital's share of income is given by the equation: $(w \times N)/Y = (MPN \times N)/Y.$

   d) We know from (c) that $MPN \times N/Y = 3/4$. Rearrange this equation, we find: $(Y/N) = MPN/(3/4) = (4/3) \times MPN = $ *labour's share of income* $\times MPN.$

e) This function does have constant returns to scale: $(1/4) + (3/4) = 1$. To show this more rigorously, try doubling both the amount of capital and labour used in production. The level of output should double as well: if $Y_0 = K_0^{1/4} N_0^{3/4}$, the $Y_1 = (2K_0)^{1/4}(2N_0)^{3/4}$ can be written as:

$$Y_1 = (2K_0)^{1/4}(2N_0)^{3/4} = (2)^{1/4}(K_0)^{1/4}(2)^{1/4}(N_0)^{3/4} = (2)^{1/4+3/4} K_0^{1/4} N_0^{3/4} = 2(K_0^{1/4} N_0^{3/4}) = 2Y_0$$

Doubling K and N doubles Y.

f) $\dfrac{Y}{N} = \dfrac{K^{1/4} N^{3/4}}{N} = \left(\dfrac{K^{1/4}}{N^{1/4}}\right)\left(\dfrac{N^{3/4}}{N^{3/4}}\right) = \left(\dfrac{K}{N}\right)^{1/4}$, or $y = k^{1/4}$

2. a) It will increase. (Total output increases because the number of workers increases; the investment function ($sf(k)$) shifts upward. The population, however, has NOT increased; there's more output for everyone to share.)

b) Nothing.

c) Labour's share of income can't have changed. It's still the power (θ) to which N is raised in the Cobb-Douglas production function.

d) Labour's productivity ($Y/N = (1/\theta) \times MPN$) will fall. The increase in the labour supply will drive down the marginal product of labour.

3. a) Nothing.

b) Nothing.

c) Nothing.

d) This will still fall, for the same reason as before.

4. The investment function ($sf(k)$) will shift upward. Per-capita output will increase, quickly at first, and then more slowly, gradually moving toward its new steady-state level. See Figure 4-6.

5. Potential output will grow by: $\Delta Y/Y = [(1 - \theta \times \Delta N/N] + [\theta \times \Delta K/K] + \Delta A/A = [(1 - .25) \times (.5)] + [(1 - .75) \times (.5)] + 0 = .5$ (or 50%.)

The capital-labour ratio will not change, as capital and labour are both increasing by the same amount.

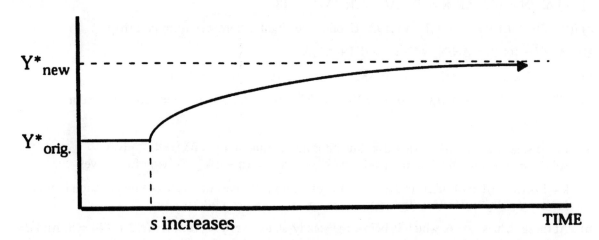

Figure 4-6

6. a) $\dfrac{Y}{N} = \dfrac{K^{1/2}N^{1/2}}{N} = \dfrac{K^{1/2}}{N^{1/2}} = \left(\dfrac{K}{N}\right)^{1/2} = k^{1/2}$ or $y = \sqrt{k}$

b) We require $MPK(k^*)$, where $MPK(k) = dy/dk = \dfrac{1}{2\sqrt{k}}$. The golden rule

is $MPK(k^*) = n + d$. So:

$$\dfrac{1}{2\sqrt{k^*}} = n + d = 0.25$$

$$\sqrt{k^*} = \dfrac{1}{2 \times 0.25} = \dfrac{1}{0.5} = 2$$

$$k^* = (2)^2 = 4$$

7. We know that y grows at the rate $sa - (n + d)$, where $a = y/k$. All that we have to do is plug in the values of a ($a = y/k = f(k)/k = k/k = 1$), n, d, and s given in the problem: $\Delta y/y = sa - (n + d) = (0.3 \times 1) - (0.05 + 0.20) = 0.3 - 0.25 = 0.05$ or 5%.

8. a) i) Y=114.87   ii) Y = 119.33   iii) Y = 119.96   iv) Y = 126.337   v) Y = 137.09

b) ii) $\Delta N/N = 0$; $\Delta K/K = .1$; $\Delta A/A = 0$; $\Delta Y/Y = .04$

iii) $\Delta N/N = .075$; $\Delta K/K = 0$; $\Delta A/A = 0$; $\Delta Y/Y = .045$

iv) $\Delta N/N = 0$; $\Delta K/K = .2$; $\Delta A/A = .1$; $\Delta Y/Y = .1$

v) $\Delta N/N = .075$; $\Delta K/K = .1$; $\Delta A/A = .1$; $\Delta Y/Y = .185$

c) ii) .039   iii) .044   iv) .1   v) .193   (Notice the slight differences from part (b).)

9. Use $\Delta Y/Y = [(1-2) \times \Delta N/N] + [2 \times \Delta K/K] + \Delta A/A$

  a) $.23 = .7 \times .2 + .3 \times \Delta K/K + 0$ so $\Delta K/K = (.23 - .14)/.3 = .09/.3 = .3$ or 30 percent

  b) $.23 = .7 \times .2 + .3 \times \Delta K/K + .06$ so $\Delta K/K = (.23 - .14 - .06)/.3 = .03/.3 = .1$ or 10 percent

10. a) In the steady-state, $sf(k) = (n + d)k$. Substituting the function $y = f(k) = 4k^{1/2}$ gives
    $s(4k^{1/2}) = (n + d)k$. Dividing both sides by $k^{1/2}$ gives $4s = (n + d)k^{1/2}$. Solving for k gives

    $k = [4s/(n + d)]^2$ and substituting this value of k into f(k) gives the steady-state per capita output
    level: $y = 4k^{1/2} = 16s/(n + d)$

  b) At these values, $y = 6$, which is below the steady-state level $y = (16 \times .1)/(.12 + .08) = 8$. And $k = (y/4)^2 = 2.25$ which is below its steady-state value $[(4 \times .1)/(.12 + .08)]^2 = 4$. At the output level $y = 6$, then, per capita savings ($s \times y = .1 \times 6 = .6$) exceeds the per capita capital replacement requirement $((n + d)k = (.12 + .08)2.25 = .45)$. The model predicts an increase in the per capita capital stock and output levels, k and y.

11. a) Use $sy = (n + d)k$. So $.2 \times (10k^4) = (.02 + .08)k$, or $2k^4 = .1k$, or $20k^4 = k$, or $20 = k^6$.

    Solving for k gives $k = 20^{1/6} = 20^{1.67} = 147.4$. And $y = 10k^4 = 10 \times 147.4^4 = 73.69$.

  b) i) Since $y = ak$, there is a constant marginal product of capital, and we are looking at an endogenous growth model. There is no steady state solution. However, we could find the value for a for which the per capita saving and per capita capital requirement functions are the same. In such a case, the model does not imply endogenous growth, although output is not determined without adding more information to the model. Total per capita saving is $sy = s(ak) = (.2a)k$. The per capita capital requirement is $(n + d)k = .1k$. The two functions overlap when $.2a = .1$, or $a = .5$.

     ii) If $a > .5$, from (i) we can see that per capita saving will exceed the capital requirement at any value of k and y, and the condition for endogenous growth is met.

Chapter 5

Fill-In Questions

1. exchange rate
2. current account
3. capital account
4. balance of payments
5. fixed exchange rate regime

6. floating exchange rate regime
7. dirty or managed floating exchange rate regime
8. depreciation
9. devaluation
10. real exchange rate

Answers to Questions and Problems

True-False Questions

1. False—purchases of foreign assets go in the capital and financial account, but the returns on those investments go in the current account.
2. False.
3. True.
4. True.
5. True.
6. False—net foreign investment must equal the trade balance.
7. False.
8. False—it has been a managed floating system.
9. True.

Multiple-Choice Questions

1. b   2. d   3. c   4. b   5. c   6. b   7. b   8. a

Application Questions

1. Initially, there are four droolers to the dollar. A 50 percent devaluation leaves two droolers to the dollar. Another 20 percent leaves 1.6 droolers per dollar. One drooler is now worth 62.5 cents.

2. Apply the relationship derived in the review of technique section. (a) The Canadian dollar depreciates by 3 percent per year. (b) The Canadian inflation rate is 2 percent. (c) The U.S. inflation rate is 1 percent.

3. The country would have a trade surplus, or positive net exports. Their net foreign investment (lending) must also be positive. This corresponds to Figure 5-1 in the text.

Chapter 6

Fill-In Questions

1. business cycle
2. output gap
3. decrease
4. aggregate demand
5. vertical; potential output
6. horizontal
7. nominal money stock
8. classical; long run
9. right; aggregate demand; right; (classical) aggregate supply

True-False Questions

1. False—Classical assumptions are most appropriate in the long run.
2. True.
3. True.
4. True.
5. False.
6. False—they show how *output* changes.
7. True.
8. False—government spending has no effect on real output when the AS curve is vertical.
9. True.
10. False—demand management policies are useful only for short term results.

Multiple-Choice Questions

1. b   2. c   3. b   4. c   5. d   6. a   7. a   8. b   9. c

Conceptual Problems

1. The aggregate demand curve slopes downward because as the price level falls, real money balances increase and cause the real interest rate to fall. This decrease in the real interest rate raises investment demand, which, in turn, increases aggregate demand.

2. It seems senseless to assume that we can increase output an infinite amount; there has to be some limit.

3. They raise the productivity of one or more factors of production (labour, capital, etc.).

4. a, b, and d are expansionary; c and e are contractionary.

Application Questions

1. Taxes, government transfers, government spending, and the money supply are all held constant along the AD curve.

2. a) output will increase; the price level may also increase.

    b) in the long run, output will return to potential output (i.e., will fall if it exceeds potential output in the short run, and will rise if it is below potential output). The price level will adjust in whatever way makes this happen (i.e., will rise if output exceeds potential output in the short run, and will fall if output is below potential output in the short run).

    c) In order to answer parts (a) and (b), we must first assume a starting point for AD. Do we begin with output below potential output, equal to potential output, or above potential output? If we begin at a point where output lies below potential output, we must make an assumption about the AD shift: at the new short-run equilibrium, does output equal potential output, exceed potential output, or still lie below it? These assumptions will change the way we think output will behave in the transition from the short to the long run.

3. a) A reduction in the money supply raises real interest rates.

    b) This increase in real interest rates makes investment more costly (imagine that the firm has to borrow the money to invest). Investment demand falls and, as a result, so does aggregate demand.

Chapter 7

Fill-In Questions

1. natural rate of unemployment
2. fall
3. sticky
4. labour; unemployment
5. rise
6. Phillips
7. aggregate supply
8. expectations-augmented
9. Okun's law
10. systematic errors

True-False Questions

1. False—the economy is only at full employment when output equals potential output.
2. False—the economy returns to full employment in the long run.
3. True.
4. False—in the long run, unemployment is at its natural rate, and inflation equals expected inflation.
5. False—changes in policy can affect people's inflationary expectations, shifting the Phillips curve and making this inflation/unemployment tradeoff much more difficult to exploit.
6. True.
7. True.
8. False.
9. False
10. False.

Multiple-Choice Questions

1. b   2. b   3. a   4. c   5. c   6. d   7. a   8. c   9. d

Conceptual Problems

1. Output and unemployment are connected through the production function; when unemployment rises, firms use less labour and, therefore, produce less output.

2. It tells you how quickly prices adjust; higher values of λ mean that prices will adjust more quickly to return the economy to its long-run equilibrium. Both our recessions and our booms would become shorter if λ increased, making it less important for the government to intervene.

Working with Data

The expected rate of inflation during the 1961–1969 period appears to have been about 2 percent. If the

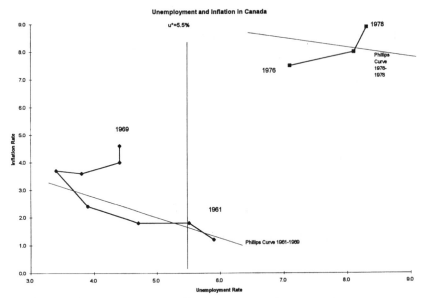

natural rate of unemployment was actually 5.5 percent, then the mid- and late-1960s appears to have been a period of high aggregate demand, with unemployment below the natural rate, resulting in an increase in inflation, and probably in the expected rate of inflation as well, by 1969.

If the natural rate of unemployment was still 5.5 percent in the 1976–1978 period, then a Phillips curve passing near these points, with a slope of about -0.33, would suggest an expected rate of inflation in the 9 percent to 10 percent range. Another possibility is that by this period the natural rate of unemployment had risen to the 7 percent to 8 percent range, which would imply an expected rate of inflation closer to the rate actually experienced during this period of around 8 percent.

Application Questions

1. a) $B^e_1 = .12$, so $B_1 = .12 - .5(.07-.07) = .12$

    $B^e_2 = B_1 = .12$, so $B_2 = .12 - .5(.07-.07) = .12$

    $B^e_3 = B_2 = .12$, so $B_3 = .12 - .5(.07-.07) = .12$

    b) $B^e_1 = .12$, so $B_1 = .12 - .5(.09-.07) = .11$

    $B^e_2 = B_1 = .11$, so $B_2 = .11 - .5(.09-.07) = .10$

    $B^e_3 = B_2 = .10$, so $B_3 = .10 - .5(.09-.07) = .09$

    c) $B^e_1 = .12$, so $B_1 = .12 - .5(.05-.07) = .13$

    $B^e_2 = B_1 = .13$, so $B_2 = .13 - .5(.05-.07) = .14$

    $B^e_3 = B_2 = .14$, so $B_3 = .14 - .5(.05-.07) = .15$

Answers to Questions and Problems

2. a) $B^e_1 = (.12 + .12)/2 = .12$, so $B_1 = .12 - .5(.07-.07) = .12$

$B^e_2 = (B_1 + B_0)/2 = (.12 + .12)/2 = .12$, so $B_2 = .12 - .5(.07-.07) = .12$

$B^e_3 = (B_2 + B_1)/2 = (.12 + .12)/2 = .12$, so $B_3 = .12 - .5(.07-.07) = .12$

b) $B^e_1 = (.12 + .12)/2 = .12$, so $B_1 = .12 - .5(.09-.07) = .11$

$B^e_2 = (B_1 + B_0)/2 = (.11 + .12)/2 = .115$, so $B_2 = .115 - .5(.09-.07) = .105$

$B^e_3 = (B_2 + B_1)/2 = (.105+ .11)/2 = .1075$, so $B_3 = .1075 - .5(.09-.07) = .0975$

c) $B^e_1 = (.12 + .12)/2 = .12$, so $B_1 = .12 - .5(.05-.07) = .13$

$B^e_2 = (B_1 + B_0)/2 = (.13 + .12)/2 = .125$, so $B_2 = .125 - .5(.05-.07) = .135$

$B^e_3 = (B_2 + B_1)/2 = (.135+ .13)/2 = .1325$, so $B_3 = .1325 - .5(.05-.07) = .1425$

Chapter 8

Fill-In Questions

1. borrowers or debtors; creditors or lenders
2. cash
3. sacrifice ratio
4. Okun's law
5. labour force
6. redistributional
7. hysteresis

True-False Questions

1. False—although we call it a "rate," it is actually a stock variable.
2. False—a person must also be actively seeking work.
3. True.
4. False.
5. True.
6. True.
7. True.
8. False—there would be no frictional employment.
9. False—unemployment benefits can change it.

Multiple-Choice Questions

1. b   2. a   3. d   4. b   5. a

Conceptual Problems

1. Lost output for society, lost income, and lower standard of living for unemployed.

2. If the longer period of job search helps individuals to find jobs at which they are happier and more productive, this effect of unemployment insurance may be entirely a good thing. If it simply allows people to stay home and watch more television, it may not.

3. It is hard to imagine a society with no frictional unemployment, where nobody ever spends time between jobs. We could, of course, pass a law that prevents people from quitting their job unless they have another one lined up, but would that really be a good thing?

4. There are extremely small costs associated with low (i.e., single digit) levels of inflation, especially when this inflation is perfectly anticipated. We also will find, later in the text, that it can be quite costly, in the short run, to reduce inflation. These two ideas suggest that it may not be worthwhile for us to completely eliminate inflation—the costs may well outweigh the benefits.

Working with Data

We might expect to find that unemployment is below its natural rate when output growth is above its trend. But we don't. Perhaps the trend assumed in Chart 1-1 is incorrect, or has "breaks"—points at which the trend changes.

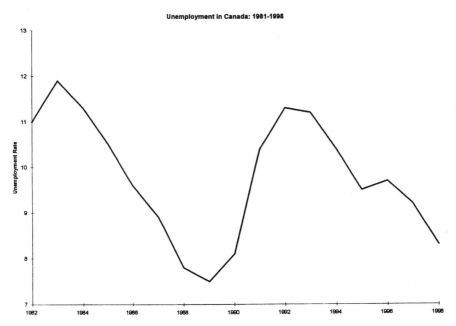

Chart 8-1

UNEMPLOYMENT IN CANADA: 1981–1998

Application Questions

1. When teenagers make up 40 percent of the labour force, the aggregate rate of unemployment is [(.4) × (.10)] + [(.6) × (.05)] + .075 or 7.5 percent.

   When teenagers make up 60 percent of the labour force, the aggregate rate of unemployment is [(.6) × (.10)] + [(.4) × (.05)] = .080 or 8.0 percent.

2. a) In any given month, there will be two people who are unemployed just for that month, three people who are at different points in their three-month spells of unemployment, and 12 people who are each at a different point in their 12-month spell of unemployment. Adding these together, we find that 17 out of every 100 people are in the unemployment pool in the typical month, or that the rate of unemployment in this typical month is 17/100 = .17 or 17 percent.

Answers to Questions and Problems

b) The average duration of unemployment among the flow of workers into unemployment is

$(1 + 1 + 3 + 12)/4 = 17/4 = 4.25$ months.

c) Among the stock of unemployed workers, as noted in part (a) there are two who are unemployed for one month, three for three months, and 12 for 12 months. Taking the weighted average gives: $[(2 \times 1) + (3 \times 3) + (12 \times 12)]/17 = 9.12$ months. Notice that it makes a big difference whether we are taking the average duration of the stock or the flow.

Chapter 9

Fill-In Questions

1. real exchange rate, or terms of trade
2. classical
3. Bretton Woods system
4. purchasing power parity
5. J-curve
6. switching
7. reducing
8. reduction in the real exchange rate

True-False Questions

1. False.
2. True.
3. False.
4. True.
5. False.
6. True.
7. False—devaluation is an expenditure reducing policy.

Multiple-Choice Questions

1. c   2. b   3. b   4. d   5. a   6. c

Application Questions

1. a) The spending cut causes a reduction in aggregate demand, which will lower income and interest rates. The lower interest rates will cause the currency to depreciate. After some time this will help to increase income by increasing export demand and reducing imports. In addition, prices adjust downward due to output being below potential, which also increases income. In the new long run equilibrium, interest rates and income are back to their original levels. Since government spending is lower, something must have increased to keep income the same. That thing is net exports. Unlike the response to monetary policy, with a permanent fiscal policy change such as this, the real exchange rate will not return to its original level. Domestic goods and services still will be less expensive in foreign currencies at the new long run equilibrium.

b) The decrease in the money supply causes an increase in interest rates and a decrease in income. The interest rate increase causes the currency to appreciate. After some time this decreases income even more by causing domestic goods and services to be more expensive to foreigners. In the long run, however, the negative output gap causes prices to fall. The resulting increase in real balances M/P causes a reduction in the interest rate. Eventually both interest rates and income return to their original long run equilibrium values. Prices are lower, and PPP implies that the nominal exchange rate e must end up lower than its original value (that is, the value of the domestic currency is higher than originally).

Chapter 10

Fill-In Questions

1. inside
2. outside
3. lags; expectations; uncertainty
4. decision
5. automatic stabilizers
6. inside
7. outside
8. Lucas critique
9. targets
10. instruments

True-False Questions

1. False.
2. False.
3. True.
4. False.
5. False—They make output less sensitive to those changes.
6. True.
7. False—we should mix them.
8. True.

Multiple-Choice Questions

1. c   2. d   3. b   4. b   5. b   6. a

Conceptual Problems

1. This is an introspective question. You must find your own answer.

2. This is another one of those introspective questions. Many people worry about the effect of policy lags on such fine-tuning; there is some question about whether policy effects can be timed precisely enough to successfully fine-tune.

Answers to Questions and Problems

Working with Data

TABLE 10-1

Year	Unemployment	M1	CPI	Real Money Balances
1990	8.1	40.9	93.3	0.438
1991	10.4	42.4	98.5	0.430
1992	11.3	47.5	100.0	0.475
1993	11.2	53.7	101.8	0.528
1994	10.4	56.7	102.0	0.556
1995	9.5	61.5	104.2	0.590
1996	9.7	70.1	105.9	0.662
1997	9.2	80.0	107.6	0.743
1998	8.3	86.1	108.6	0.793

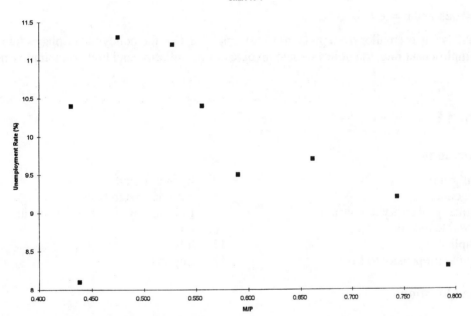

Chart 10-1

Chart 10-1

With the exception of the first two observations, a downward-sloping pattern is evident. However, for many other time periods and countries, this is not the case.

Application Questions

1. The loss function is $L = .5(Y - 10)^2 = .5(\beta M - 10)^2$. The marginal loss function is the derivative of this loss function with respect to M, which we can obtain using the chain rule for differentiation: $dL/dM = [dL/d(\beta M)]times[d(\beta M)/dM] = (\beta M - 10)\beta$. For each part, we set the probability-weighted-average of this function equal to zero, then solve for M.

   a) $\beta = 2$, so solve for M in $2(2M - 10) = 0$, giving M = 5.

   b) Solve for M in $.5[1.5(1.5M - 10)] + .5[2.5(2.5M - 10)] = 0$. This becomes:

   $1.125M - 7.5 + 3.125M - 12.5 = 0$, giving $4.25M = 20$, or M = 4.71.

   c) Solve for M in $(2/3)[1(M - 10)] + (1/3)[4(4M - 10)] = 0$. This becomes:

   $(2/3)M - (20/3) + (16/3)M - (40/3) = 0$, giving $(18/3)M = 20$, or M = 3.33.

2. We need to substitute out the $(u - u^*)$ term from the loss function using the Phillips curve relation, then minimize the loss function with respect to B, then solve for u. From the Phillips curve, $u - u^* = u - .08 = -(B - .06)/2$. Substituting this into the loss function gives $L = -(a/2)(B - .06) + B^2$. The derivative with respect to B is $(dL/dB) = -(a/2) + 2B$. Setting this equal to zero gives the loss-minimizing inflation rate $B = a/4$. With this value of B, we can solve for u from the Phillips curve: $u = .08 - (B - .06)/2$. For the particular values of a given in the question, these policy choices turn out to be:

   a) B = .10 and u = .06

   b) B = .05 and u = .085

   c) B = .025 and u = .0975

Note that as a gets smaller from parts (a) to (c), implying that the policymaker places less weight on the unemployment rate, the policy choice involves lower inflation and higher unemployment.

Chapter 11

Fill-In Questions

1.	equilibrium	7.	budget deficit
2.	endogenous	8.	automatic stabilizer
3.	marginal propensity to consume	9.	full-employment budget surplus
4.	disposable income	10.	one
5.	multiplier	11.	lower
6.	marginal propensity to save	12.	imports

True-False Questions

1. False.
2. False.
3. True.
4. False.
5. False.
6. True.

7. False.
8. False.
9. False.
10. True.

Multiple-Choice Questions

1. a   2. b   3. a   4. b   5. b   6. a   7. c   8. a   9. b   10. b   11. a   12. c

Conceptual Problems

1. $1 million increase in government spending; the multiplier for government spending is greater than the multiplier for government transfers. (Some of the increase in transfers is saved, not spent.)

2. a, b, c, and d are endogenous; e and f are exogenous.

3. Tax revenues change with the business cycle. As a result, so does the budget deficit.

4. The effect of business cycle fluctuations on the budget deficit is eliminated.

Application Questions

1. $S = Y - C = Y - \bar{C} - cY = -\bar{C} + (1 - c)Y$

2. a) $\alpha_G = 1/(1 - 0.9) = 1/0.1 = 10$

   b) $100 \times \alpha_G = 100 \times 10 = 1000$

   c) $100 \times (\alpha_G \times mpc) = 100 \times 10 \times 0.9 = 900$

3. a) $\alpha_G = 1/(1 - 0.9(2/3)) = 1/(1 - 0.6) = 1/0.4 = 2.5$

   b) $100 \times \alpha_G = 100 \times 2.5 = 250$

   c) The increase in government spending will increase the deficit by $100; tax revenues, however will also rise... in this case, by $250 \times 1/3 \cong \$83.33$. The budget deficit, as a result, will rise (or the surplus fall) by $100 - \$83.33 = \$16.67$.

4. a) $\alpha_G = 1/(1 - .9(2/3) + .1) = 1/(1 - .6 + .1) = 1/0.5 = 2$.

   b) $\$100 \times \alpha_G = \$200$.

   c) The increase in government spending will increase the deficit by $100. Tax revenues, however, will also rise, in this case by $200 \times (1/3) = \$66.67$. As a result, the budget deficit will rise (or the surplus fall) by $100 - \$66.67 = \$33.33$.

5. exogenous: I, G, TR, NX. endogenous: AD, C, TA, BS. In addition, the IU = Y – AD = 0 equation makes IU exogenous and Y endogenous.

6. $Y = [10 + .8(Y + TR - .25Y)] + 20 + G + 0$

   $= [10 + .8TR + 20 + G] + [.8Y - .8(.25)Y]$

   $= [30 + .8TR + G] + .6Y$

   $Y - .6Y = .4Y = 30 + .8TR + G$

Answers to Questions and Problems

$Y = 75 + 2TR + 2.5G$

Given that G = 30 and TR = 20, then Y = 190. Therefore AD = 190, C = 162, TA = 47.5, and BS = -2.5.

7. From the answer to Question 6, the multiplier is dY/dG = 2.5. Alternatively, it equals

$1/(1-c(1 - t) + m)$. Here, $c = .8$, $t = .25$ and $m = 0$, so the multiplier is $1/(1 - .8(1 - .25)) = 1/.4 = 2.5$.

8. From the answer to Question 6, we see that increasing G by 2 will increase Y by 5, to Y = 195. Increasing TR by 2 will increase Y by 4, to 194.

9. Proceed by substituting out Y in the budget equation, to get it purely as a function of the exogenous variables G and TR.

$BS = TA - G - TR = tY - G - TR = .25(75 + 2TR + 2.5G) - G - TR = 18.75 - .375G - .5TR$

When TR = 20, then BS = 8.75 - .375G. Therefore BS = 0 when G = 23.333.

10. a) A quick way to get the value of NX is to note that NX enters the aggregate demand equation the same way that G does, so the effect on Y of a one-unit change in X will be the same as the effect of a one-unit change in G, which is 2.5. When NX = 0, we saw from Question 6 that Y = 190. For Y = Y* = 202, an increase of 12, NX must have increased by 12/2.5 = 4.8. Therefore NX = 4.8.

b) $BS = tY - G - TR = .25(202) - 30 - 20 = 0.5$

Chapter 12

Fill-In Questions

1. goods
2. investment
3. flatter
4. money
5. cash

6. steep
7. flat
8. fiscal; monetary
9. equilibrium conditions
10. AD

True-False Questions

1. False.
2. True.
3. True.
4. True.
5. False—decreasing the money supply raises interest rates, which lowers investment.
6. True—there will be different equilibria for different combinations of taxes, transfers, and government spending.
7. True—there will be different equilibria when real money balances differ.
8. True.
9. False—it depends on the tax rate.
10. False—the increase in government purchases shifts it further.

Multiple-Choice Questions

1. b   2. c   3. b   4. b   5. d   6. b   7. b   8. b   9. c   10. b

Conceptual Problems

1. Output, income, disposable income, the price level, the real interest rate, investment, and consumption.

2. Changes in the IS-LM equilibrium represent shifts in/movements along the aggregate demand curve.

3. The marginal propensity to consume, the tax rate (when proportional income taxes are used), and the sensitivity of investment demand to changes in the interest rate.

   The presence of a proportional income tax makes the IS curve steeper.

4. The sensitivity of money demand to changes in income and the interest rate.

Application Questions

1. a) The equation for the IS curve can be found as follows:

   $$Y = C + I + G + NX = (100 + .8(Y - 500)) + (200 - 1000i) + 550 + 0$$
   $$(1 - .8)Y = 450 - 1000i$$

   $$Y = \frac{1}{0.2}(450 - 1000i), \text{ or } Y = 2250 - 5000i$$

   b) The equation for the LM curve can be found by setting the supply of real money balances equal to the demand for them:

   $$900 = \frac{1}{2}Y - 7000i, \text{ or } Y = 1800 + 14000i$$

   c) We find the equilibrium real interest rate by locating the intersection of these two curves (i.e., setting output along the IS curve equal to output along the LM curve and solving for i):

   $$2250 - 5000i = 1800 + 14000i$$
   $$19000i = 450$$
   $$i = 450/19000 \cong 0.024, \text{ or } 2.4 \text{ percent}$$

   We then plug the equilibrium value of i back into the equation for the IS or the LM curve (we choose the IS curve here):

   $$Y = 2250 - (5000 \times (450/19000)) \cong \$2131.58$$

   Having found Y, we can now find $(Y - \overline{T})$ and solve for C:

   $$C = 100 + .8(Y - \overline{T}) \cong 100 + .8(2131.58 - 500) = \$1405.26$$

   And, knowing i, we can solve for I:

   $$I = 200 - 1000i = 200 - (1000 \times (450/19000)) \cong 176.32$$

2. a) The equation for the IS curve can be found in the following way:

   $$Y = C + I + G + NX = (100 + .8(1 - t)Y) + (200 - 1000i) + 700 + 0$$
   $$(1 - (0.8 \times 0.66))Y = 1000 - 1000i$$
   $$(1 - 0.528Y) = 1000 - 1000i$$

$Y = \dfrac{1}{0.472}$ (1000 – 1000i), or Y $\cong$ 2118.64 – 2118.64i

b) The equation for the LM curve can be found by setting the supply of real money balances equal to the demand for them:

$900 = \dfrac{1}{2} Y - 7000i$, or $Y = 1800 + 14000i$

c) In order to answer this question, we must first find the equilibrium of Y—the level of output for which both goods and money markets are in equilibrium. We could solve for i first, as we did in the last problem. We could also, however, write the equations for the IS and LM curves as functions of i rather than Y:

IS: $1000i = 1000 - 0.472Y$, or $i = (1000 - 0.472Y)/1000$

LM: $14000i = Y - 1800$, or $i = (Y - 1800)/14000$

and set the real interest rates along each curve equal to each other:

$$\dfrac{1000 - .472Y}{1000} = \dfrac{Y - 1800}{14000}$$

$(1000 - 0.472Y) \times 14000 = (Y - 1800) \times 1000$
$7608Y = 15800000$, or Y $\cong$ \$2076.76

We can now find the initial value of the budget deficit $(\overline{G} - tY)$:

$\overline{G} - tY \cong 700 - (0.33 \times \$2076.76) = \$14.67$

d) First, figure out how much income needs to be increased, if tax revenues are to exactly offset government spending $(\overline{G} - tY)$:

$Y = \overline{G}/t = 700/0.33 \cong \$2121.21$

Having found this, we can find the level of real money balances required to generate it.

First, find the interest rate from IS that is necessary for equilibrium in the goods market at this level of Y. (Graphically, we are locating the necessary point on the IS curve.) Then plug the values of Y and i in the LM curve and solve for real money balances (M/P). (Graphically, we are finding the value of M/P necessary to make the LM curve shift so that it crosses the IS curve at the necessary point.)

Solving for i from IS:

$i = (1000 - .472Y)/1000 = (1000 - .472(2121.21))/1000 = -.00121$

Note that this is unrealistically small, but let's continue, and find the value of M/P from LM that would make this happen in the model:

$(M/P) = Y/2 - 7000i = 2121.21/2 - 7000 (- .00121) = 1061.45$

Real money balances must be increased by \$1061.45 – \$900 = \$161.45 in order to balance the budget.

e) In the short run, we have not had to worry about potential output. In part (d), we used monetary policy to push output to \$2076.76. If this is above potential output, it cannot be sustained in the long run without ever-increasing inflation.

3.

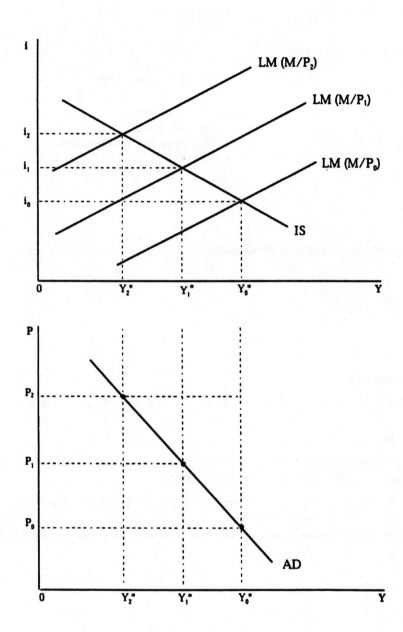

Chart 12-1

Answers to Questions and Problems

Chapter 13

Fill-In Questions

1. liquidity trap
2. classical case
3. relatively steep
4. relatively flat
5. crowding out
6. accommodating
7. nominal interest rate; rate of inflation
8. interest rate
9. decreases
10. open market operations

True-False Questions

1. True.
2. True.
3. False
4. False—it also depends on the slope of the IS curve.
5. False.
6. True.
7. True.
8. False.
9. False.
10. True.

Multiple-Choice Questions

1. b   2. a   3. c   4. b   5. b   6. a   7. d   8. a   9. c   10. a

Conceptual Problems

1. When proportional income taxes are present, the multiplier α_G becomes smaller. This makes the IS curve steeper, reducing the effectiveness of monetary policy.

2. The smaller multiplier associated with proportional income taxes makes fiscal policy less effective as well. Although the IS curve is steeper with these taxes, the IS curve will not shift as much in response to a change in government spending. The overall effect of the income taxes is to reduce the expansionary effect.

Answers to Questions and Problems

TABLE 13-1

Year	Unemployment	M1	CPI	Real Money Balances
1990	8.1	40.9	93.3	0.438
1991	10.4	42.4	98.5	0.430
1992	11.3	47.5	100.0	0.475
1993	11.2	53.7	101.8	0.528
1994	10.4	56.7	102.0	0.556
1995	9.5	61.5	104.2	0.590
1996	9.7	70.1	105.9	0.662
1997	9.2	80.0	107.6	0.743
1998	8.3	86.1	108.6	0.793

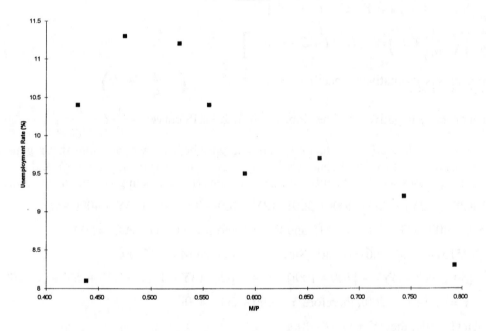

Chart 10-1

Chart 13-1

With the exception of the first two observations, a downward-sloping pattern is evident. However, for many other time periods and countries, this is not the case.

Answers to Questions and Problems

Application Questions

1. The IS curve will shift outward by an amount $\$100 \times \alpha_G$.

2. The AD curve will shift outward, but, if the LM curve is upward sloping, by an amount that is smaller than that of the IS shift, due to crowding out.

3. Holding i constant, we see that Y increases (the LM curve shifts outward) by an amount $\$100/k$.

   Recall that k tells us how sensitive people's demand for money is to changes in their income. A large K means that their money demand is relatively sensitive to changes in their income; a small k means that it is relatively insensitive to such changes.

4. The AD curve will shift outward, but, with a downward-sloping IS curve, by an amount that is smaller than that of the LM shift.

5. When the AS curve is flat—the price level is fixed.

6. When the AS curve is vertical—the level of output is fixed.

7. To answer this, we must see how the equation for the IS curve is affected. Let's begin by writing the equation for the goods market equilibrium: $Y = C + I + G$.

   $$Y = \overline{C} + c(1 - t)Y + \overline{I} - bi + \overline{G} + d(Yp - Y)$$

   Having done this, to get IS we must solve for i (write i as a function of Y):

   $$i = -\frac{1}{b}\left[(1 - c(1 - t) + d)Y - \overline{C} - \overline{I} - \overline{G}dYp\right]$$

   $$= -\frac{1}{b}\left[\left(\frac{1}{\alpha_G} + d\right)Y - \overline{C} - \overline{I} - \overline{G} - dYp\right]$$

   The slope of this alternatively-specified IS curve is: $-\frac{1}{b}\left(\frac{1}{\alpha_G} + d\right)$

   It is steeper (more negative) that the slope of our regular IS curve: $-\frac{1}{b}\left(\frac{1}{\alpha_G}\right)$

   Monetary policy is less effective than it would otherwise be, as any expansions that it generates will be automatically offset by fiscal contractions (decreases in government spending), and any contractions it causes will be offset by fiscal expansions (increases in government spending).

8. $Y = 30 + .9(Y - .2Y) + 200 - 200i + 300 - .12Y - 200i + G = 530 + .6Y - 400i + G$

   $.4Y = 530 - 400i + G$. Set $Y = 2515$ and $R = .06$ and solve for G, get $G = 500$.

   $M/P = 2(2515) - 10000(.06) = 4430$. Since $P = 110$, then $M = 487300$.

9. a) $Y = [50 + .9(Y - .3Y)] + [100 - 100i] + G + [200 - .13Y - 100i] = 350 + .5Y + G - 200i$

   so $.5Y = 350 + G - 200i$, therefore $Y = 700 + 2G - 400i$.

   When $G = 500$, then $Y = 1700 - 400i$.

   b) $M/P = Y - 1600i$, so $154,000/100 = Y - 1600i$, or $1540 = Y - 1600i$. Substitute in the IS curve and solve for i: $1540 = (1700 - 400i) - 1600i = 1700 - 2000i$.

   $2000i = 160$, so $i = .08$. Therefore $Y = 1700 - (.08)400 = 1700 - 32 = 1668$.

c) LM is still $1540 = Y - 1600i$. If $Y = 1684$, then $1540 = 1684 - 1600i$, so $1600i = 144$ and $i = .09$. Then from IS: $Y = 700 + 2G - 400i$,

$$1684 = 700 + 2G - 400(.09),$$

$$2G = 1684 - 700 + 36 = 1020. \quad \text{So } G = 510.$$

Chapter 14

Fill-In Questions

1. net exports
2. perfect capital mobility
3. beggar-thy-neighbour
4. depreciation

5. depreciation
6. repercussion; spillover
7. into; increasing; increase
8. decrease; increase

True-False Questions

1. False.
2   False.
3. True.
4. False—it is the *BP* curve that is horizontal.
5. True.
6. False—there is an appreciation and complete crowding out.
7. False—net exports decrease.
8. False—this is true under a fixed exchange rate and perfect capital mobility.
9. True.
10. True.

Multiple-Choice Questions

1. b   2. a   3. a   4. c   5. d   6. a   7. a   8. a   9. c   10. d

Conceptual Problems

1. An increase in the money stock lowers the interest rate. The domestic currency depreciates, increasing the demand for exports, raising GDP.

2. Domestic GDP, consumption, and disposable income all will increase. The increase in the money stock will prevent any crowding-out of the effect of the government spending increase.

Working with Data

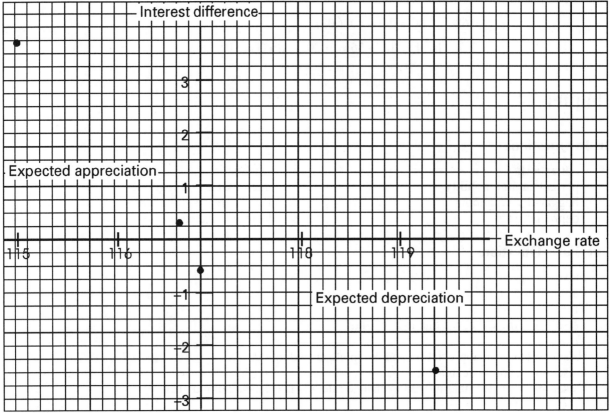

Chart 14-1

Application Questions

1. An investor could invest one Canadian dollar in Canada and end up with $1.06 C. Alternatively, she could use the Canadian dollar to purchase 60 U.S. cents and end up with 60(1.04) = 62.4 U.S. cents. These two outcomes must be expected to have equal value a year from now. For the 62.4 U.S. cents to equal $1.06 C, the value of a Canadian dollar at the end of the year must be expected to equal 62.4/1.06 = 58.87 U.S. cents. Note that this is about 2 percent less than 60 cents U.S., constituting a 2 percent expected depreciation in the Canadian dollar, reflecting the two percentage point difference in the interest rates.

2. exogenous: I, G, TR, X.   endogenous: AD, C, Q, NX, TA, BS. In addition, the IU = Y – AD = 0 equation makes IU exogenous and Y endogenous. Compared to Chapter 11, the new treatment of net exports has made net exports endogenous, since it now depends on income through the imports variable Q, which must also be endogenous. Exports X now appear in the model, and are exogenous.

3. $Y = [10 + .8(Y + TR - .25Y)] + 20 + G + [30 - (10 + .1Y)]$

    $= [10 + .8TR + 20 + G + 30 - 10] + [.8Y - .8(.25Y) - .1Y]$

    $= [50 + .8TR + G] + .5Y$

Y - .5Y = .5Y = 50 + .8TR + G

Y = 100 + 1.6TR + 2G

Given that G = 30 and TR = 20, then Y = 192. Therefore AD = 192, C = 163.6, Q = 29.2, NX = 0.8, TA = 48, and BS = -2.

4. From the answer to Question 2, the multiplier is dY/dG = 2. Alternatively, it equals

$1/(1-c(1-t)+m)$. Here, $c = .8$, $t = .25$ and $m = .1$, so the multiplier is $1/(1 - .8(1 - .25) + .1) = 1/.5 = 2$. Note that this is smaller than the multiplier in Chapter 11, because now some of the new spending is made on imports.

5. From the answer to Question 2, we see that increasing G by 2 will increase Y by 4, to Y = 196. Increasing TR by 2 will increase Y by 3.2, to 195.2. Note again that the increases are smaller than they were in Chapter 11.

6. Proceed by substituting out Y in the budget equation, to get it purely as a function of the exogenous variables G and TR.

BS = TA – G – TR = tY – G – TR = .25(100 + 1.6TR + 2G) – G – TR = 25 - .5G - .6TR

When TR = 20, then BS = 13 - .5G. Therefore BS = 0 when G = 26.

7. Proceed as in Question 6, but this time with the net exports equation.

NX = X – Q = 30 – (10 + .1Y) = 20 - .1(100 + 1.6TR + 2G) = 20 – 10 - .16TR - .2G. When TR = 20, then NX = 10 - .16(20) - .2G = 6.8 - .2G. Therefore NX = 0 when .2G = 6.8, or G = 34.

8. a) A quick way to get the value of X is to note that X enters the aggregate demand equation the same way that G does, so the effect on Y of a one-unit change in X will be the same as the effect of a one-unit change in G, which is 2. When X = 30, we saw from Question 6 that Y = 192. For Y = Y* = 202, an increase of 10, X must have increased by 10/2 = 5. Therefore X = 35.

   b) BS = tY – G – TR = .25(202) – 30 – 20 = 0.5. Note that this is the same as in Chapter 11. We are at the same income level, with the same equations describing government spending and taxing behaviour, so the full employment government budget surplus is the same.

Chapter 15

Fill-In Questions

1. life-cycle/permanent income
2. save
3. greater
4. greater
5. random walk
6. working; in retirement
7. life-cycle
8. durable goods
9. booms; recessions
10. Ricardian equivalence

True-False Questions

1. True.
2. False—they draw very similar conclusions.
3. True.
4. True.
5. False—it changes too little.
6. False—they should see savings fall.

7. True.
8. True.
9. False.
10. True

Multiple-Choice Questions

1. c   2. b   3. c   4. a   5. a   6. c   7. a   8. d

Conceptual Problems

1. People use all available information to estimate their permanent income; only *new information* (inherently unpredictable) will cause them to change those estimates. Because people try to consume roughly the same amount of goods and services each period, only a change in those estimates will cause them to consume a different amount in one period than another.

2. If people live longer and continue to retire at the same age, the fraction of their lives spent working will fall. They will have to save more during their working years to provide for their longer retirements.

3. An increase in the interest rate should reduce the present value of people's future income; permanent income should fall.

4. This question requires a bit of introspection. If you are young and short on collateral, however, you probably are at least somewhat liquidity constrained.

Application Questions

1. We want to spread the financial gain that we get from this tax cut evenly over the rest of our lives.

   A permanent tax cut will raise our lifetime income by $30 \times \$100$, or $3,000—our labour income by $100 each year. We want to spread that gain over the next 40 years. This means that we can increase our consumption by $3,000/40, or $75 each year. A temporary tax cut will raise our permanent income by much less; a tax cut that lasted only one year, once we spread its benefit over our lifetimes, would allow us each to increase consumption by only $100/40, or $2.50 each year.

2. Expansionary fiscal policy will be more effective when people are liquidity constrained. They will spend more of the money they receive (their marginal propensities to consume are higher). The multiplier will be larger.

3.

TABLE 15-1

Permanent Income (YP)	Total Income (Y)	Consumption* (C = cYP)
$500	$400	$400
$500	$500	$400
$500	$600	$400
$1,000	$900	$800
$1,000	$1,000	$800
$1,000	$1,100	$800

* We assume that c, the marginal propensity to consume, is 0.8.

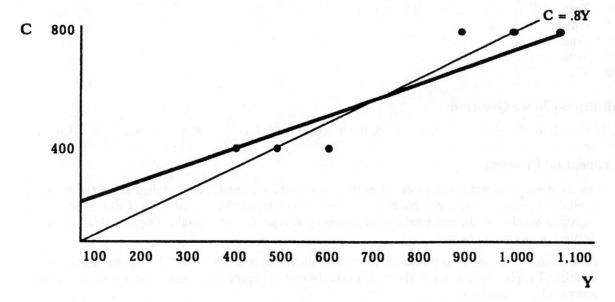

Chart 15-1

People having bad years look like they're consuming too much; people having good years look like they're consuming too much. The mpc appears to be smaller than 0.8 and the consumption function looks like it has a positive intercept. We'd really like to graph consumption against permanent income.

Chapter 16

Fill-In Questions

1. business fixed investment; residential investment; inventory investment
2. business fixed investment
3. depreciation
4. user
5. flexible accelerator
6. just-in-time
7. investment tax credits
8. q
9. inventories
10. potential output

True-False Questions

1. True
2. False—rising interest rates decrease investment.
3. True.
4. False—investment is a flow variable.
5. True.
6. True.
7. False.
8. True.
9. True.
10. True.

Multiple-Choice Questions

1. b   2. a   3. d   4. a   5. b   6. a   7. b   8. a   9. a   10. a

Conceptual Problems

1. An increase in the real interest rate raises the rental costs of capital. The marginal benefit of using capital to produce goods and services is unaffected. As a result, the capital stock at which the marginal benefit and the marginal cost of acquiring another unit of capital are equal (which is the desired capital stock) falls.

2. An increase in the rate of depreciation also raises the rental cost of capital. The argument made in Problem 1 applies here as well. The increase in the rate of depreciation makes any given capital stock more costly to maintain.

3. The price of whatever product the firm is making will rise with the price level; the firm's profits will therefore also rise (in nominal terms) with the price level. The firm will be able to costlessly repay the component of the nominal interest rate that reflects that increasing price level out of its higher nominal profits.

Working with Data

TABLE 16-1

Year	Real GDP	Gross Investment	Annual Change in Real GDP	Annual Change in Investment
1985	496.7	85.5		
1986	511.8	91.6	15.1	6.1
1987	532.8	102.9	21.0	11.3
1988	558.7	113.2	25.9	10.3
1989	572.9	120.9	14.2	7.7
1990	574.4	109.7	1.5	−11.2
1991	563.6	104.6	−10.8	−5.1
1992	568.8	101.4	5.2	−3.2
1993	581.8	106.8	13.0	5.4
1994	609.3	115.6	27.5	8.8
1995	625.3	116.8	16.0	1.2

Source: Bank of Canada Review.

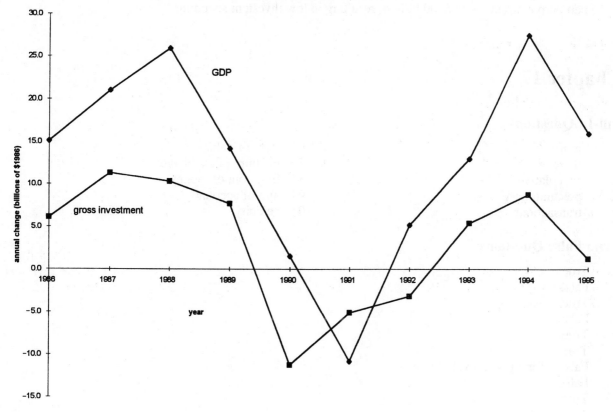

Chart 16-1

Answers to Questions and Problems

Application Questions

1. Next period's net investment will be $\frac{1}{2}(20000 - 12000) = \frac{1}{2}(8000) = 4000$.

   Next period's capital stock will therefore be $12000 + 4000 = 16000$, making the subsequent period's net investment equal to $\frac{1}{2}(20000 - 16000) = \frac{1}{2}(4000) = 2000$.

2. a) $K^* = (0.25 \times 16000)/((0.12 - 0.06) + 0.10) = 4000/0.16 = 25000$

   b) $K^* = (0.25 \times 32000)/((0.12 - 0.06) + 0.10) = 8000/0.16 = 50000$

   c) $K^* = 4000/(2 \times 0.16) = 12500$

3. Year 1: $K = 200 + .6(240 - 200) = 200 + .6(40) = 224$.

   net investment is $224 - 200 = 24$. gross investment is $24 + .1(200) = 24 + 20 = 44$

   Year 2: $K = 224 + .6(240 - 224) = 233.6$

   net investment is $233.6 - 224 = 9.6$. gross investment is $9.6 + .1(224) = 32.0$

4. It should be highest in case (i), with the highest upward change in GDP. When GDP rises, more capital stock is required than before. In case (ii), GDP has already been at $600 billion and so the desired capital stock is more likely to be already close to the desired level. And in case (iii) GDP had been even greater than $600 billion, so in that case many firms may have more capital than they need when output has fallen to $600 billion, resulting in low investent spending.

Chapter 17

Fill-In Questions

1. more
2. more
3. speculative
4. precautionary
5. transactions
6. store of value
7. medium of exchange
8. flight out of money
9. unit of account
10. velocity

True-False Questions

1. True.
2. False.
3. True.
4. False.
5. True.
6. True.
7. False—for a given level of wealth.
8. False.
9. True.
10. True.

Multiple-Choice Questions

1. d   2. c   3. a   4. c   5. b   6. d   7. a   8. c   9. c   10. d

Conceptual Problems

1. E.g., transactions motive: to pay bills and buy coffee in the morning.

2. The ones that immediately spring to mind are gold, silver, gems, beads, and giant stone slabs—the last on the Isle of Yap in the Pacific.

Application Questions

1. $V = \dfrac{1000000}{500000} = 2$

2. The Baumol-Tobin equation says that the amount of money you will wish to hold is given by the equation

$$M^* = \sqrt{\frac{tcY}{2i}}$$

Plugging in the values for tc, Y and i that are given in the problem, we find that

$$M^* = \sqrt{\frac{\$1.50 \times 100000}{2 \times 0.06}} = \sqrt{1250000} \cong \$1118.03$$

3. The velocity of money is the same whether defined in terms of dollars or of cents. It is the ratio of nominal output to the nominal money supply. Both of these quantities are measured in the same units, whether dollars or cents. A switch in units from one to the other would change the numerator and denominator by the same proportion. The effects would cancel, leaving the numerical value of the velocity unchanged.

Chapter 18

Fill-In Questions

1. high-powered money, the monetary base
2. bank rate
3. open market sale
4. money multiplier
5. announcement effects
6. currency-deposit ratio
7. government bonds
8. term structure of interest
9. riskier
10. yield
11. coupon
12. face value
13. unpredictable
14. maturity
15. arbitrage
16. intermediate

True-False Questions

1. True.
2. False—a higher currency-deposit ratio means a lower money multiplier and so a lower money supply.
3. False—this also lowers re and thus the money multiplier.
4. False—income has nothing to do with the money supply.
5. True.
6. False.
7. True.
8. True.
9. True.
10. False.
11. True.
12. False—when interest rates rise, bond prices fall.
13. False.
14. False—they are the vehicle through which monetary policy affects the economy.
15. False—they should be *unpredictable*.
16. True.
17. True.
18. True.

Multiple-Choice Questions

1. d	2. d	3. c	4. c	5. d	6. a	7. a	8. b	9. a	10. a
11. b	12. a	13. a	14. b	15. c	16. d				

Conceptual Problems

1. It may signal tight monetary policy causing high short-term interest rates, which can be recessionary.

2. Interest rates rise for all sorts of other reasons. High short-term interest rates could be the result of expansionary fiscal policy.

3. It all goes back to the *rational expectations hypothesis*. Because people use all of the information to which they have access to form expectations of asset returns, any changes in the price of an asset must occur because new information has become available. We can't predict the content of this new information; hence, we should not be able to predict the changes in asset prices that result from it.

Application Questions

1. $CU = 0.4D$
   $M1 = CU + D = 0.4D + D = 1.4D$
   $B = CU + 0.1D = 0.4D + 0.1D = 0.5D$
   a) $M1/B = (1.4D)/(0.5D)$
   $M1 = 2.8B = 2.8(100) = 280$ billion
   b) $B = 0.5D$; $\Delta D = 2\Delta B = 2(50) = 100$ billion

2. $B = CU + 0.1D = (0.5Y - 495i) + 0.1(Y - 50i) = 0.6Y - 500i$
   $i = (0.6Y - H)/500 = (0.6(2000) - (1150))/500 = 50/500 = 10$ percent

3. It should be the average of the short-term rates for that year:
   $(0.06 + 0.065 + 0.07 + 0.075)/4$, or 6.75 percent.

Answers to Questions and Problems

4. 8% − 6% = 2%

5.

First Balance Sheet

Professor B		Bank	
Assets	**Liabilities**	**Assets**	**Liabilities**
Deposit $200	None	Reserves $200	$200 Deposit
		(Desired 20)	
		(Excess 180)	
	$200 Net worth		
$200	$200	$180	$180

Second Balance Sheet

Professor B		Bank	
Assets	**Liabilities**	**Assets**	**Liabilities**
Deposit $380	$180 Loan	Reserves $200	$380 Deposit
		(Desired 38)	
		(Excess 162)	
	$200 Net worth	Loan 180	
$380	$380	$380	$380

Third Balance Sheet

Professor B		Bank	
Assets	**Liabilities**	**Assets**	**Liabilities**
Deposit $542	$342 Loan	Reserves $200	$542 Deposit
		(Desired 54.2)	
		(Excess 145.8)	
	$200 Net worth	Loan 342	
$542	$542	$542	$542

Professor B		Bank	
Assets	**Liabilities**	**Assets**	**Liabilities**
Deposit $2000	$1800 Loan	Reserves $200	$2000 Deposit
		(Desired 200)	
		(Excess 0)	
	$200 Net worth	Loan 1800	
$2000	$2000	$2000	$2000

Chapter 19

Fill-In Questions

1. wars
2. structural (or full-employment)
3. seigniorage
4. inflation tax
5. monetize
6. heterodox
7. issue debt; increase the money base
8. primary
9. government budget deficits
10. pay-as-you-go
11. cyclical
12. debt-income

True-False Questions

1. False.
2. True.
3. False.
4. False.
5. True.
6. False—it is stronger in the long run than in the short run.
7. False—they are often at the root of them.
8. True.
9. True.
10. False.
11. True.
12. True.
13. False.
14. True.
15. True.
16. False—we merely owe it to ourselves.
17. True.

Multiple-Choice Questions

1. d   2. d   3. a   4. b   5. c   6. b   7. d   8. a

Conceptual Problems

1. The money supply should be able to grow at the average rate of real output growth without generating any long-term inflation. 3 percent? 4 percent? There isn't a consensus.

2. If its policy is not credible, people's expectations will not change and *the Phillips curve will not shift downward*. The output-inflation tradeoff will be much more severe.

3. Most countries that have experienced hyperinflation also have had enormous deficits and economies without well-developed financial institutions. These circumstances lead to high rates of money growth.

Working with Data

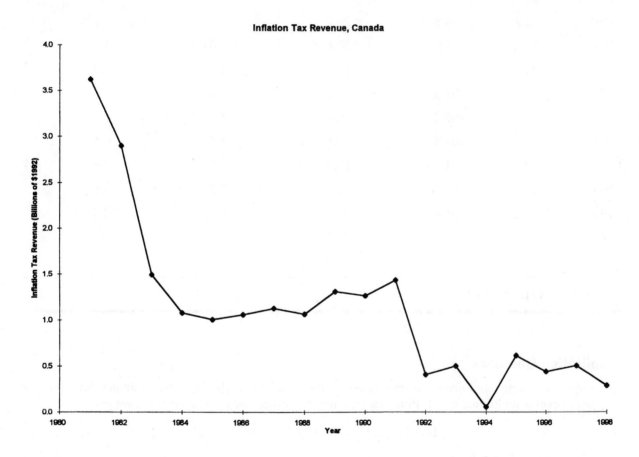

Inflation Tax Revenue, Canada

Chart 19-1

There was much more variation in the inflation rate than in the real monetary base during this period, so the plot of inflation tax revenues is similar in shape to a plot of the inflation rate.

TABLE 19-1

Year	Monetary Base ($ billion)	CPI (1992=100)	Real Monetary Base (billions of $1992)	Inflation Rate (percent)	Real Inflation Tax Revenue (billions of $1992)
1980	16.0	52.4	30.6	—	—
1981	17.2	58.9	29.2	12.4	3.6
1982	17.4	65.3	26.7	10.9	2.9
1983	17.7	69.1	25.7	5.8	1.5
1984	17.9	72.1	24.9	4.3	1.1
1985	18.8	75.0	25.0	4.0	1.0
1986	20.0	78.1	25.6	4.1	1.1
1987	21.1	81.5	25.9	4.4	1.1
1988	22.2	84.8	26.2	4.0	1.1
1989	23.5	89.0	26.4	5.0	1.3
1990	24.4	93.3	26.2	4.8	1.3
1991	25.4	98.5	25.7	5.6	1.4
1992	26.7	100.0	26.7	1.5	0.4
1993	28.3	101.8	27.8	1.8	0.5
1994	29.3	102.0	28.7	0.2	0.1
1995	29.5	104.2	28.3	2.2	0.6
1996	30.2	105.8	28.5	1.5	0.4
1997	31.7	107.6	29.5	1.7	0.5
1998	33.6	108.6	30.9	0.9	0.3

Source: CANSIM web site

Application Questions

1. We use the compound interest formula to solve this problem. With 1000 percent annual inflation, the price level is multiplied by 11. Plugging this into the compound interest formula, we get:

$$11 = (1 + r)^{12}, \text{ or } (1 + r) = 11^{1/12} = 1.221$$

or r = 22 percent per month.

2. Again, we apply the compound interest formula:

$$21 = (1 + r)^{365}, \text{ or } (1 + r) = 21^{1/365} \cong 0.0084 \text{ or } 0.84 \text{ percent}$$

Answers to Questions and Problems

3. Inflation tax revenues are equal to the real money base × the rate of inflation: $1,000 × 10 = $10,000

4. Inflation tax revenues fall when the real money base shrinks: $500 × 10 = $5,000.

5. The real money base falls to zero as the rate of inflation becomes large. Inflation revenues fall as a result. In the long run, this is a destructive way to attempt to create revenue.

Chapter 20

Fill-In Questions

1. random walk
2. rationally
3. rational expectations equilibrium model
4. aggregate demand
5. productivity (or supply, technology)

6. labour (or leisure)
7. transmission
8. imperfectly
9. menu cost
10. anticipated (or expected)

True-False Questions

1. False.
2. False.
3. False.
4. False—it merely suggests that supply rather than demand shocks drive the business cycle.
5. True.
6. False.
7. True.
8. False.
9. True.
10. False.

Multiple-Choice Questions

1. d   2. b   3. a   4. b   5. a   6. d   7. b   8. a   9. a   10. b

Conceptual Problems

1. New Keynesian models of price stickiness try to justify, on microeconomic foundations, the assumption that prices do not adjust quickly enough in the short run to clear markets, so that output need not equal potential output. In doing this, they build an environment in which anticipated changes in fiscal and monetary policy can affect output.

2. If prices are not sticky (i.e., if they are able to adjust to keep markets in equilibrium), fiscal and monetary policies have little, if any, role in stabilizing output. Anticipated changes in AD will not affect output.

3. No. The random walk model of GDP merely suggests that supply shocks are more prevalent than demand shocks.

4. Real business cycle theorists argue that changes in the productivity of labour (we could call these supply or technology shocks) drive output fluctuations (the business cycle).

Application Questions

1. β and γ. The line above equation 34 in Chapter 20 suggests that there will be strong intertemporal substitution of leisure when $\beta + \gamma$ is close to 1:

$$\%\Delta L = 3 \times [^{(1-\gamma)} /_{(1-\gamma-\beta)}] \times \%\Delta a$$

   The denominator in the above equation approaches zero in that case, making the value of $\%\Delta L$ very large.

2. No. There seems to be very little intertemporal substitution of leisure.

3. Unexpected changes in AD will have the greatest effect on output when they occur very rarely (i.e., when most changes in the price of a firm's good turn out to be changes in its relative price). "*You can't fool all of the people all of the time.*"

4. They jury's still out on this one. We cannot reject the hypothesis that supply shocks have played an important role in driving output fluctuations. We are not sure however, how often they occur; if they occur very rarely, demand shocks may play an important role in the business cycle.

5.

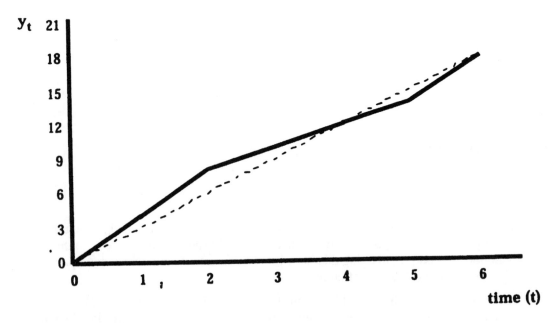

Chart 20-1

TREND STATIONARY PROCESS

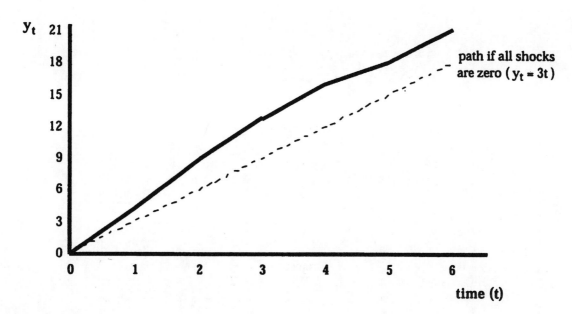

Chart 20-2

DIFFERENCE STATIONARY PROCESS (RANDOM WALK)

It's not always easy to tell the difference between these processes, especially when the trend (or "drift" in the case of the difference stationary process) and shocks are not known.